GOD, EVIL AND THE LIMITS
OF THEOLOGY

GOD, EVIL AND THE LIMITS OF THEOLOGY

Karen Kilby

t&tclark
LONDON • NEW YORK • OXFORD • NEW DELHI • SYDNEY

T&T CLARK

Bloomsbury Publishing Plc

50 Bedford Square, London, WC1B 3DP, UK
1385 Broadway, New York, NY 10018, USA
29 Earlsfort Terrace, Dublin 2, Ireland

BLOOMSBURY, T&T CLARK and the T&T Clark logo are trademarks of
Bloomsbury Publishing Plc

First published in Great Britain 2020
This paperback edition published in 2021

Copyright © Karen Kilby, 2020

Karen Kilby has asserted her right under the Copyright, Designs and
Patents Act, 1988, to be identified as Author of this work.

Cover image: Mimadeo / Alamy Stock Photo

For legal purposes the Introduction on p. 1–3 constitutes an extension
of this copyright page.

All rights reserved. No part of this publication may be reproduced or transmitted
in any form or by any means, electronic or mechanical, including photocopying,
recording, or any information storage or retrieval system, without prior
permission in writing from the publishers.

Bloomsbury Publishing Plc does not have any control over, or responsibility for,
any third-party websites referred to or in this book. All internet addresses given in
this book were correct at the time of going to press. The author and publisher regret
any inconvenience caused if addresses have changed or sites have ceased to
exist, but can accept no responsibility for any such changes.

A catalogue record for this book is available from the British Library.

A catalog record for this book is available from the Library of Congress.

ISBN: HB: 978-0-5676-8457-8
PB: 978-0-5676-9820-9
ePDF: 978-0-5676-8458-5
eBook: 978-0-5676-8459-2

Typeset by Deanta Global Publishing Services, Chennai, India

To find out more about our authors and books visit www.bloomsbury.com
and sign up for our newsletters.

CONTENTS

INTRODUCTION ... 1

Chapter 1
PERICHORESIS AND PROJECTION: PROBLEMS WITH SOCIAL
 DOCTRINES OF THE TRINITY ... 5

Chapter 2
AQUINAS, THE TRINITY AND THE LIMITS OF UNDERSTANDING ... 17

Chapter 3
IS AN APOPHATIC TRINITARIANISM POSSIBLE? ... 31

Chapter 4
THE TRINITY AND POLITICS: AN APOPHATIC APPROACH ... 45

Chapter 5
THE STATUS OF THE CONCEPT: A REFLECTION ON JOHN ZIZIOULAS'
 BEING AS COMMUNION ... 61

Chapter 6
EVIL AND THE LIMITS OF THEOLOGY ... 67

Chapter 7
SIN, EVIL AND THE PROBLEM OF INTELLIGIBILITY ... 85

Chapter 8
GRACE AND PARADOX ... 99

Chapter 9
CHRISTIAN THEOLOGY, ANTI-LIBERALISM AND MODERN JEWISH
 THOUGHT ... 111

Chapter 10
JULIAN OF NORWICH, HANS URS VON BALTHASAR AND THE STATUS
 OF SUFFERING IN CHRISTIAN THEOLOGY ... 121

Chapter 11
BEAUTY AND MYSTERY IN MATHEMATICS AND THEOLOGY ... 139

Bibliography ... 155
Index ... 161

INTRODUCTION

'If you understand it, it is not God.'[1] Most Christian theologians in one way or another subscribe to the principle articulated by Augustine of Hippo. It gives theology, considered as an intellectual discipline, some of its most distinctive and puzzling qualities. How does one engage in a mode of enquiry – an enquiry which includes argument, disagreement and debate – if one presumes in advance that the 'thing' under discussion is and must remain mysterious, beyond understanding? This is a question which makes itself felt, it seems to me, across all of theology: it is not an issue which can simply be delegated to those who examine a specifically 'apophatic tradition', to specialists on Denys the Areopagite and Meister Eckhardt and John of the Cross, nor is it something which can be put out of mind after some preliminary reflection on analogy, metaphor and the nature of religious language.

    I cannot claim that the chapters which follow provide a comprehensive treatment of this question. However, each chapter does engage with it in some way, wrestling with one aspect or another of the problem of how to think about mystery. They can be read as a single whole, a cumulative case for an overall theological perspective, the elements of which are drawn together in the final chapter under the – perhaps unlikely – auspices of a reflection on the nature of pure mathematics. They can also, however, be read individually – each chapter, an essay in its own right, on the Trinity, sin, suffering, grace and so on, and each at the same time also an exploration of the place of mystery in theology. It is important to me that the chapters retain this capacity for independent existence both for pragmatic reasons – I hope this will allow what is contained in this volume a wider use – and for reasons of principle. Theology as an intellectual discipline is difficult, complex and elusive, beyond the capacity of any one of us to come to terms with fully. There is something about the diffidence of the essay genre which provides a way of acknowledging the impossibility of the tasks of theology, even if one may nevertheless wish to make bold claims within an essay.

    Each of these chapters had its origins in one or more invited lecture or conference paper. I was not thinking, as I responded to these invitations, to be producing the chapters of this book. It was only in retrospect that I realized that whatever I was asked to speak on, I seemed to return to a common set of concerns. I am very grateful therefore to all the lecture and conference organizers who, through their

---

1. Augustine, Sermon 117, *Patrologia latina* 38, 663: '*Si enim comprehendis, non est deus*'.

varied invitations, distracted me from what I felt at the time I really ought to be doing, and gradually dragged this book out of me. The first chapter began in a pair of lectures I gave to fulfil my duties as a Gifford postdoctoral research fellowship in St Andrews in 1996, and others had their origins in invitations to speak at the Catholic Theological Association (2002), 'The Future of the Past: Conference on the Nouvelle Théologie' in Cambridge (2004), the Christian Systematic Theology and Eastern Orthodox Studies Units of the American Academy of Religion (2005 and 2015), a joint Colloquium of the Philosophy and Theology Departments at Villanova University (2005), the Society for the Study of Theology (2009), 'Traces of Judaism in Contemporary Thought' conference in Krakow (2010), 'The Presences of Christ Colloquium in honour of Nicholas Lash' in Durham (2011), the Society for the Study of Christian Ethics (2014), the Los Angeles Theology Conference (2014) and the Leuven Encounters in Systematic Theology Conference (2017). I have benefitted greatly from comments and questions from those who attended these and subsequent papers and lectures.

A number of colleagues have read and advised on portions of this material at one stage or another. Among them have been Isobel Wollaston, Philip Goodchild, Henri-Jérôme Gagey, Chris Insole, Simon Oliver, Paul Murray, Susannah Ticciati and Simeon Zahl. It is no fault of theirs that I have not always been able to absorb all their advice. I am also grateful to a whole host of friends and colleagues for the conversations which have over the years formed the backdrop of my thought, including Gene Rogers, Nick Healy, Anna Williams, Denys Turner, Mary Cunningham, the late Ed Ball, Agata Bielik-Robson, Anna Rowlands and Linn Tonstad. Some colleagues have been especially encouraging and helpful in moving me towards the actual publication of this volume, including Mike Higton and Lewis Ayres. I have benefitted in a range of ways from the students I have come into contact with over the years, and I am particularly grateful for the thoughts and help of Myka Lahaie and Edward Epsen and for the wisdom and calm efficiency of Joshua Mobley as he helped prepare this volume for publication. On the other side, I owe a considerable debt to George Lindbeck and Kathryn Tanner – my first teachers of theology – who shaped my thought and those of my fellow students without ever seeking to create disciples: the continuing influence of Tanner will be particularly clear in the chapters of this volume. Finally, Anna Turton's patience with and enthusiasm for this project has meant a great deal to me.

Versions of many – though not all – of these essays have appeared previously in print. Where I have the sense that an essay is already widely read, I have kept any alteration to a minimum. This is particularly so with Chapters 1, 2, 3 and 6. In other cases, I have allowed myself more freedom to alter and to expand.

I am grateful for the permissions granted to use a version of or materials from the following:

'Perichoresis and Projection: Problems with Social Doctrines of the Trinity', *New Blackfriars* 81 (2000): 432–45. © 2000 Dominican Council. Used by permission of John Wiley and Sons.

'Aquinas, the Trinity and the Limits of Understanding', *International Journal of Systematic Theology* 7 (2005): 414–27. © 2005 John Wiley and Sons. Used by permission of John Wiley and Sons.

'Is an Apophatic Trinitarianism Possible?', *International Journal of Systematic Theology* 12 (2010): 65–77. © 2010 John Wiley and Sons. Used by permission of John Wiley and Sons.

'Trinity and Politics: An Apophatic Approach', taken from *Advancing Trinitarian Theology: Explorations in Constructive Dogmatics*, edited by Oliver D. Crisp and Fred Sanders, 75–93. Copyright © 2014 Oliver D. Crisp, Fred Sanders and contributors. Used by permission of Zondervan. www.zondervan.com

'Evil and the limits of theology', *New Blackfriars* 84 (2003): 13–29. Dominican Council. Used by permission of John Wiley and Sons.

'Julian of Norwich, Hans Urs von Baltthasar, and the Status of Suffering in Christian Theology', *New Blackfriars* 99 (2018): 298–311. © 2018 Provincial Council of the English Province of the Order of Preachers. Used by permission of John Wiley and Sons.

'Christian Theology, Anti-Liberalism and Modern Jewish Thought', in Agata Bielik-Robson, and Adam Lipszyc (eds), *Judaism in Contemporary Thought: Traces and Influence* (Abingdon: Routledge, 2014), 155–64. © 2014 Agata Bielik-Robson, Adam Lipszyc and contributors. Reproduced by permission of Taylor & Francis Group.

'Beauty and Mystery in Mathematics and Theology', *Imaginatio et Ratio* 2 (2013): 3–14. Used by permission of Wipf and Stock Publishers. www.wipfandstock.com.

A version of Chapter 8, 'Grace and Paradox', is forthcoming as 'Catholicism, Protestantism and the Theological Location of Paradox: Nature, Grace, Sin', in Peter de Mey and Wim Francois (eds), *Ecclesia Semper Reformanda: Renewal and Reform Beyond Polemics* (Leuven: Peeters, 2020).

Chapter 1

PERICHORESIS AND PROJECTION

PROBLEMS WITH SOCIAL DOCTRINES OF THE TRINITY

Over the last three decades there has been a great outpouring of writings from both Catholic and Protestant theologians on the doctrine of the Trinity, almost all of which, ironically, have lamented the neglect of the doctrine.[1] Again and again one reads that although the Trinity is central and crucially important to Christianity and Christian theology, it has not been given adequate treatment. It is unacceptable, theologians protest, that the Trinity has come to be regarded as an obscure and complex theological technicality, a piece of celestial mathematics impossible to understand and with little relevance to the life of the ordinary Christian. Karl Rahner remarked that modern Christians were 'almost mere "monotheists"', paying lip service to the Trinity but in practice ignoring it. If it were announced that the dogma had been a mistake and was to be erased from official Christianity, nobody, he thought, would be too bothered, neither the ordinary believing Christians nor the authors of theological textbooks.[2] Rahner's diagnosis has been widely accepted and widely regretted. The consensus is that the Trinity is at the heart of Christianity, and both theology and piety have gone astray if it is regarded as belonging to the specialists. A retrieval (it is believed) is needed: the Trinity must be understood once again (one reads) as a positive and central element in the Christian faith rather than an embarrassing obscurity, and as profoundly *relevant* to the life of individual Christians, to the life of the church, and perhaps beyond.

If there is a consensus about the problem, there is also something increasingly approaching consensus as regards the nature of the solution: the chief strategy used to revivify the doctrine and establish its relevance has come to be the advocacy of a *social* understanding of the Trinity. This line of thought has been gaining momentum especially since the publication of Jürgen Moltmann's *The Trinity and*

---

1. This was originally published in *New Blackfriars* 81, no. 957 (November 2000): 432–45. The flow of writings on the Trinity since then has not diminished, though the lament over the neglect of the doctrine has mostly disappeared.

2. Karl Rahner, *The Trinity*, trans. Joseph Donceel (New York: Crossroad, 1997), 10–11.

the Kingdom of God,³ and by now has achieved, in many quarters, dominance – it has become the new orthodoxy. Increasingly, indeed, one finds references to it in popular Christian literature and hears its influence in Trinity Sunday sermons.⁴

In what follows I want to raise some doubts about the new orthodoxy. My argument will not be directed against social analogies to the Trinity as such: in themselves these analogies are perhaps no worse than any others. The way in which they are very often used, however, and the claims which are made for them are, I shall argue, deeply problematic.

II

The first step is to offer a brief characterization of contemporary social theories of the Trinity. Most basically social theorists propose that Christians should not imagine God on the model of some individual person or thing which has three sides, aspects, dimensions or modes of being; God is instead to be thought of as a collective, a group, or a society, bound together by the mutual love, accord and self-giving of its members. Many social theories of the Trinity share considerably more than this minimal basis, however. In particular I want to draw attention to three frequently recurring features: first, a certain understanding of the meaning of the word '*person*' in the classical Trinitarian formula; secondly, a particular picture of the *history* of the doctrine of the Trinity; and thirdly a tendency to wax enthusiastic when it comes to explaining how the three in the Trinity can also be one.

First of all, then, the term 'person'. All Christian theologians who want to consider themselves orthodox are committed to the proposition that God is three 'persons'. And all modern theologians seem to agree that the meaning of person in the context of the Trinity is not simply identical with our current understanding of the word. But as to just *how* different the meaning is, and in what way, there is not such unanimity. Those twentieth century theologians who do not espouse social theories tend to emphasize what a highly technical term 'person' is in the Trinitarian formula, how it has almost *nothing* to do with our modern notion.

---

3. Jürgen Moltmann, *The Trinity and the Kingdom of God* (New York: Harper and Row, 1981), originally published in German in 1980.

4. In the two decades since this was published, the situation has changed to some degree. Social trinitarianism remains strong at a popular level, but it has fewer enthusiastic adherents among academic theologians. This is I presume the result of a number of criticisms directed against it, of which this essay was one. In addition to work by patristic scholars such as Michel Barnes, cited below, and Lewis Ayres, see Kathryn Tanner's 'Trinity', in William T. Cavanaugh and Peter Manley Scott (eds), *The Wiley Blackwell Companion to Political Theology*, 2nd ed. (Oxford: Wiley Blackwell, 2019), 363–75; and Stephen R. Holmes, *The Quest for the Trinity: The Doctrine of God in Scripture, History and Modernity* (Downers Grove: Intervarsity Press, 2012).

1. Perichoresis and Projection

Both Barth and Rahner, for instance, suggest that the term is in fact so misleading to the untrained that in most contexts theology would do better to abandon it altogether, to substitute a different terminology. They suggest such alternatives as 'mode of subsistence' or 'mode of being'. The problem, they think, is that because of the evolution of the word's meaning, when we hear 'three persons' we inevitably think of three separate 'I''s, three centres of consciousness, three distinct wills and so on, and this, they insist, must be rejected as outright tritheism. So in all but the most technical contexts it is counterproductive to continue to use the word.

Social theorists, on the other hand, acknowledge that the meaning of the word person has changed, but not quite so radically as these others think – not so much that the word itself needs to be abandoned. What is needed is not a new word but only that in using the word 'person' Trinitarian theology put up a resistance to *some* features of the modern secular understanding of this notion. Our contemporary society's basic understanding of the word, of what it means to be a person, in other words, needs to be reformed by a return to the true Trinitarian understanding. The problem with our usual notion of personhood lies in its connotations of individualism, in the assumption that ultimately each person is an isolated being over against all others. A proper understanding of the Trinity and of the Trinitarian perichoresis (to which I shall return shortly) counteracts this, in their view, and enables one to understand persons as by their very nature interactive, interdependent, in communion with one another.[5]

So the first point that unites the social theorists is that they are, comparatively speaking, quite happy to carry on using the term person in a Trinitarian context. The second, as I mentioned, is a certain reading of the history of doctrine. Social theorists very often distinguish sharply between the way the doctrine of the Trinity was worked out in the East, and how it developed in the West.[6] In particular, it is often claimed that the Cappadocians in the East took as their starting point the three persons of the Trinity and *then* asked about unity whereas Augustine in the West began with the oneness of God, with an abstract notion of the divine substance, and then puzzled over how to give an account of the threeness of the persons. And it is in this Augustinian precedence of oneness over threeness that the whole Western tradition went wrong, according to the social theorists' typical account. They see as one of the consequences of Augustine's approach, for instance, the fact that from the thirteenth century onwards theological textbooks begin with a treatise on the one God *de Deo Uno*, and only then move on to God's threeness, *de Deo Trino*, and they see this in turn as linked to the contemporary problem of irrelevance: if one has already been introduced to God, learned the basic facts as it were, before ever the question of the Trinity is raised, then it is no surprise that

---

5. One can find examples of this fundamentally positive approach to 'persons' in writings of Moltmann, Gunton and Boff, to name but a few. Cf. Chapter 1 of John D. Zizioulas, *Being as Communion* (New York: St. Vladimir's Seminary Press, 1985) for a similar line of thinking in a somewhat different context.

6. Gunton and Moltmann once again provide examples of this.

the latter will come to seem simply an intellectual difficulty, a secondary bit of information to be reconciled with a prior, less problematic understanding of God.

The third common characteristic of contemporary social doctrines of the Trinity is the enthusiasm their proponents exhibit when it comes to accounting for how the three persons in God are one. This can be made clear by way of a contrast. One might say that, if one follows Augustine (or at least Augustine as he is understood by the social theorists) and begins from God's oneness, then the problem of the Trinity is to find a way of accommodating God's threeness, whereas if one begins with the social theorists from the three persons then the problem is to find a way of making sense of the claim that God is one. But in fact social theorists do *not* speak of a problem. Instead they tend to see the question of how the three are one as the point where the doctrine comes into its own.

Often social theorists at this point invoke the patristic concept of perichoresis. It is the divine perichoresis which makes the three one, and it is perichoresis which makes the Trinity a wonderful doctrine. There is among the three divine persons, it is said, a kind of mutual interpenetration which is not to be found among human persons, and it is because of this perfect interpenetration that the three persons are one God. 'The doctrine of the perichoresis', writes Jürgen Moltmann, 'links together in a brilliant way the threeness and the unity, without reducing the threeness to the unity, or dissolving the unity in the threeness'.[7] Moltmann characterizes this perichoresis as a process whereby each person, by virtue of their eternal love, lives *in* the other two and 'communicates eternal life' to the other two; as a circulation of the eternal divine life; as a fellowship; and as a 'process of most perfect and intense empathy'.

The social theorists' enthusiasm for perichoresis comes out in two ways. First, God is presented as having a wonderful and wonderfully attractive inner life. I already mentioned Moltmann's notion of 'the most perfect and intense empathy' existing between the persons. Another proponent of the social doctrine, Cornelius Plantinga, in what is in general a very carefully constructed and restrained presentation, writes of the Trinity as 'a zestful, wondrous community of divine light, love, joy, mutuality and verve', where there is 'no isolation, no insulation, no secretiveness, no fear of being transparent to another'.[8] So the interrelatedness of the Trinity, the divine perichoresis, makes God intrinsically attractive.

Secondly, and more significantly for our purposes, God's inner life is presented as having positive implications for that which is not God. It is worth looking at some examples. Patricia Wilson-Kastner, in the final chapter of *Faith, Feminism and the Christ*, commends the doctrine of the Trinity, conceived according to the social analogy, on the grounds that it is supportive of feminist values. The most commonly heard feminist assessment of the Trinity is, of course, rather different,

---

7. Moltmann, *The Trinity and the Kingdom of God* (London: SCM, 1981), 175.

8. Cornelius Plantinga, Jr, 'Social Trinity and Tritheism', in Ronald J. Feenstra and Cornelius Plantinga, Jr (eds), *Trinity, Incarnation and Atonement* (Notre Dame: University of Notre Dame Press, 1989).

and rather more negative. Usually the attention is on the problematic nature of the language of Father and Son. Whereas abstract philosophical theism may be able to assert that God has no gender, Christian Trinitarianism is tied to speaking of God in these all male terms – or, at best, in language that is two thirds male and one third neuter. But Wilson-Kastner argues that feminists should in fact prefer a Trinitarian understanding of God to what she terms strict monotheism. Imaging God as three persons, she writes, 'encourages one to focus on interrelationship as the core of divine reality, rather than a single personal reality', and a single personal reality is almost always, she suggests, whatever the theory may be, 'imaged as male'.⁹ When in the history of Christian thought the emphasis has been on the *one* God, this has been God the Father in heaven, ruler of all, the dominant one, the 'only and unquestioned deity' who 'modelled on a cosmic scale the male dominant behaviour expected of all men, living in splendid and absolute isolation'. The Trinity, on the other hand, understood according to the social theory, supports the sort of vision and values favoured by feminists:

> Because feminism identifies interrelatedness and mutuality – equal, respectful and nurturing relationships – as the basis of the world as it really is and as it ought to be, we can find no better understanding and image of the divine than that of the perfect and open relationships of love.¹⁰

Wilson-Kastner's account is influenced by, though not identical to, that of Jürgen Moltmann. He too sets up a contrast between the positive implications of the socially conceived Trinity and the undesirable corollaries of the alternative, which he calls Christian monotheism, and by which he means Christian trinitarianism as it has traditionally been understood in the West. Moltmann argues that Christian monotheism corresponds to, and has been used to legitimate, certain forms of government. In early Christianity it was the Roman empire: corresponding to the *one* God there is the *one* empire which brings peace to the warring nations, and the one emperor, who is '*the visible image* of the invisible God', whose will is law, who makes and changes laws but is not himself bound by them.¹¹ Later, seventeenth-century notions of the absolute right of kings owed something to this same monotheism: the king is 'above the community of men because he occupie[s] the place of God on earth'; the king's sovereignty must be absolute because it is a 'portrait' of the majesty of God.¹²

In a similar way Moltmann suggests connections between Christian monotheism and a certain kind of ecclesiology. The justification for the role of the pope in the Roman Catholic church – the role of guaranteeing the unity of the

---

9. Patricia Wilson-Kastner, *Faith, Feminism and the Christ* (Philadelphia: Fortress Press, 1983), 122–3.
10. Ibid., 127.
11. Moltmann, *The Trinity and the Kingdom*, 195.
12. Ibid., 196.

church – goes along the lines, Moltmann suggests, of 'one church – one pope – one Peter – one Christ – one God'.[13] Moltmann argues that the 'theological justification of papal authority and the unity of the church it guarantees is visibly dominated by the monotheistic way of thinking'.[14]

The only way Christian theology can *avoid* providing a legitimization for absolutism of various kinds is if it adopts a *properly* Trinitarian understanding of God, which is to say a social doctrine of the Trinity. It will then be seen, Moltmann tells us, that 'it is not the monarchy of a ruler that corresponds to the triune God; it is the community of men and women, without privileges and without subjugation'.[15] Because the persons of the Trinity have everything in common, Moltmann writes, 'except for their personal characteristics, ... the Trinity corresponds to a community in which people are defined through their relations with one another and in their significance for one another, not in opposition to one another, in terms of power and possession'.[16] Something similar holds in ecclesiology: just as a merely monotheistic doctrine of God 'justifies the church as hierarchy', so, he writes, 'The doctrine of the Trinity constitutes the church as "a community free of dominion." ... Authority and obedience are replaced by dialogue, consensus and harmony'. Therefore a 'presbyterial and synodal church order and the leadership based on brotherly advice are the forms of organization that best correspond to the doctrine of the social Trinity'.[17]

Finally, let me mention the work of Colin Gunton.[18] Some of his concerns are similar to Moltmann's – they share the belief, for instance, that the social trinity has a role in helping us to find a way beyond the unappealing modern political alternatives of individualism and collectivism. But primarily Gunton takes up the question of the doctrine of the Trinity and its broader significance on the level not of politics but of *metaphysics*. If God created the world, one would expect to find some marks of the creator on the creation, one would expect that something about the nature of *being* in our world should reflect the nature of God. And so if God is the Trinity, one might hope to find some trace of this in the world. Gunton rejects, however, the traditional search for the *vestigia Trinitatis*, traces of threeness, or three-in-oneness, here and there in the creation – this would be, he suggests, too *mathematical* an understanding of the whole matter. It is not on the precise *number* of the persons that we should focus, but instead, he proposes, on their *perichoresis*. Perichoresis can be understood, according to Gunton, as a

---

13. Ibid., 201.
14. Ibid.
15. Ibid., 198.
16. Ibid.
17. Ibid.
18. In what follows I shall be drawing primarily on *The One, The Three and the Many* (Cambridge: Cambridge University Press, 1993), but see also his 'Trinity, Ontology and Anthropology', in Christoph Schwöbel and Colin E. Gunton (eds), *Persons: Divine and Human* (Edinburgh: T&T Clark, 1991).

transcendental, as a concept which captures something universal about all being and which is also suggestive and fruitful for further reflection. The notion of perichoresis, of the 'interrelation and interanimation' of the persons in God, of the 'unity deriving from the dynamic plurality of [the] persons', can provide a useful and suggestive way of thinking about created being on all levels.[19] Gunton explores this in connection with three strata of being – personal being, non-personal being (i.e. the material world) and the world of culture and art – and then in turn he applies the notion of perichoresis to the relations *between* these layers of being. To give just one example, in the realm of the personal the concept of perichoresis helps us think about close relationships – indeed relationships which are constitutive of persons – without abandoning notions of particularity and difference, without a loss of the self. So Gunton writes that 'our particularity in community is the fruit of our mutual constitutiveness: of a perichoretic being bound up with each other in the bundle of life'.[20]

In the hands of these thinkers, then, the claim that God though three is yet one becomes a source of metaphysical insight and a resource for combating individualism, patriarchy and oppressive forms of political and ecclesiastical organization. No wonder the enthusiasm: the very thing which in the past has been viewed as the embarrassment has become the chief point upon which to commend the Christian doctrine of God: not an intellectual difficulty but a source of insight, not a philosophical stumbling block but something with which to transform the world.

III

It is possible to put questions to social theorists on a number of levels. One could ask whether the history of theology really presents as simple a picture as they suggest.[21] Or again, one could ask whether the implications of a doctrine of God for political arrangements are quite so clear as they assume. Could not very different conclusions be drawn from one and the same understanding of God? An emphasis on the unity of God, on the oneness of a God who stands apart from, over-against the world, could arguably be used to *undermine* as well as to legitimate hierarchical and absolutist forms of government. Before the one God who transcends the world, it might be said, for instance, all human beings are levelled: all alike are creatures, absolutely different from their creator, and any

---

19. Gunton, *Many*, 152.
20. Ibid., 170.
21. This has indeed been questioned by historical theologians. Cf. for instance the arguments of Michel René Barnes in 'The Use of Augustine in Contemporary Trinitarian Theology', *Theological Studies* 56 (1995) and 'Rereading Augustine on the Trinity', in Stephen T. Davis, et al., *The Trinity* (Oxford: Oxford University Press, 1999).

attempt by some to lord it over the others can be seen as a sinful attempt to usurp the place of God.[22]

In what follows I want however to develop a different kind of objection, one centring on the issue of projection. I will argue, first, that there is a high level of projection in the theories that I have been discussing, and secondly, that this is not accidental, but built into the nature of the social theorists' approach. It might be said that this is true of all theology: I will therefore aim to show, thirdly, that even if projection always has a role to play in theology, it is here playing a distinctive, and a distinctly problematic, one.

Some of the language already quoted raises the first suspicions of projection: social theorists speak of intense empathy, of verve and zest. Where exactly, one might wonder, did they acquire such a vivid feeling for the inner life of the deity?

Another suspicion of projection arises if one probes a bit further into Patricia Wilson-Kastner's feminist commendation of the social Trinity. One might have thought her emphasis on the mutuality of the Trinity would run into trouble with the strand in feminist thought which holds that what women need is not to be urged towards mutuality and interrelatedness, but to learn to reclaim their own autonomy, to become aware of their own distinct desires and needs, to become aware of themselves as something *other* than wife, mother, sister – one might have thought, in other words, that it would be problematic to hold up for women an image of God as persons who are so *utterly* bound up in and defined by relationships that they lose even their numerical distinctness. But Wilson-Kastner is in fact well aware of this difficulty, well aware that it is not *just* mutuality and inter-relatedness that need to be promoted. 'The human person', she writes, has '*two* essential dimensions': in addition to 'the self-transcending, other-directed, outward oriented' dimension there is 'the self-focused, the centred, the self-conscious' dimension.[23] When things work properly these two sides of a person nourish each other, so that relationship is not at the expense of autonomy: 'the more one reaches out to other and is accepting of connections [she writes], the more one comes to consciousness of and possession of the self.'[24] And in the Trinity, she suggests, *both* sides, both these dimensions, are superlatively represented: the Trinity

> is a unity of three centers of awareness and centeredenss [this is the one side – the persons of the Trinity are each centered in themselves] who are also perfectly open and interdependent on each other [this is the other side]. The 'persons' of the Trinity are three centers of divine identity, self-aware [the one side]

---

22. Cf. Kathryn Tanner, *The Politics of God* (Minneapolis: Augsburg Fortress, 1992) for an extended discussion of the different ways in which a belief in God's transcendence can function politically.
23. Wilson-Kastner, *Feminism*, 126.
24. Ibid.

and self-giving in love [the other side], self-possessed [the one-side] yet freely transcending the self in eternal trinitarian interconnectedness [the other side].[25]

So although Wilson-Kastner's emphasis is on the support the doctrine of the Trinity lends to an ethic of mutuality, she is careful to make it clear that this is a mutuality of persons who have, one might say, a very health sense of self.[26]

There are two things to note about Wilson-Kastner's account. First of all, she seems to be willing to say some very precise things about the Trinity. Not only are there three centres of consciousness, but these centres are themselves centred, self-aware and self-possessed. Secondly, the account diverges in an interesting way from that of Moltmann. Moltmann insists that the Trinitarian persons do not first exist and then enter into relationship, but are constituted and defined by their relationships; Wilson-Kastner, on the other hand, writes of the persons as self-possessed yet freely transcending the self – in other words, in some sense they do not have to, but choose to go out of themselves in relationships. Why, one might ask, do they take opposite positions here, and how would one go about adjudicating between them? The most likely account of the difference, it seems to me, is that while Wilson-Kastner has her eyes on the danger to women of lacking a sense of self and so emphasizes that each of the persons is 'self-possessed', Moltmann is focused on the excessive individualism of the modern West and so maintains that the persons are constituted by their relationships. To adjudicate the difference, then, one would need to decide whether, all things considered, it is better for us to think of ourselves as self-possessed and going out into relationships, or as entirely constituted by our relationships. Once that question has been settled, the Christian theologian can then say, that is how God is too.

From an examination of particular examples of social theories of the Trinity, then, one can form the impression that much of the detail is derived from either the individual author's or the larger society's latest ideals of how human beings should live in community. I want to go one step further, however, and suggest that this is no accident: it is not just that as it happens social theories of the Trinity often project our ideals onto God. Rather it is built into the kind of project that most social theorists are involved in that they *have to be* projectionist.

Why is this? Let me start again from the beginning. For the social theorists, to put the matter crudely, God is more appropriately modelled on three human beings than on one. But social theorists do not want to be tritheists, so they must say that although three human persons make three human beings, three divine persons, even if they are separate centres of will and self-consciousness and so on, make only one God. What is it, then, that makes the three into one? I do not

---

25. Ibid.

26. Denis Edwards, in a similar vein, suggests that the Christian ideal of love, as represented by the Trinity, 'concerns self-possession as well as self-giving, love of self as well as love of other'. *The God of Evolution: A Trinitarian Theology* (New York: Paulist Press, 1999), 16.

think one can pretend to find, outside of a few proof texts in the Gospel of John, any very clear help in the New Testament in understanding this. And whatever it is, it must be something beyond our experience, since in our experience three persons are, quite simply, three people. This whatever it is, this thing which is beyond our experience which binds the three into a one, however, is given a label – it is called the divine perichoresis. And in order to describe the perichoresis, the social theorist points to those things which do to some degree bind human persons together, into couples or families or communities – interrelatedness, love, empathy, mutual accord, mutual giving and so on. What binds God into one is then said to be like all the best that we know, only of course, unimaginably more so. It has to be more so, since it has to make the three persons into one God and not just into one family of Gods.

Now of course any language that is used about God is drawn from human experience in some way or other, and so it is arguable that in talk about God it is always a matter of saying that God is just like such-and-such that we know, only unimaginably more so. What is particularly distinctive about the social theorists' strategy, however, is that what is at its heart a suggestion to overcome a difficulty is presented as a key source of inspiration and insight. So the social theorist does not just say, perhaps the divine perichoresis, which we can understand as being akin to our best relationships, only better, makes the three Persons into one God; she goes on to say, should we not model our relationships on this wonderful thing, the divine perichoresis?

In short, then, I am suggesting we have here something like a three stage process. First, a concept, perichoresis, is used to name what is not understood, to name whatever it is that makes the three Persons one. Secondly, the concept is filled out rather suggestively with notions borrowed from our own experience of relationships and relatedness. And then, finally, it is presented as an exciting resource Christian theology has to offer the wider world in its reflections upon relationships and relatedness.

To bring out what is distinctive and problematic about the role of projection in these theories, it will be helpful to consider an analogy. Anselm, in formulating his doctrine of atonement, famously drew on feudal concepts of honour and justice. So one can say, to some degree at least he projected contemporary concepts and ideals onto God. And, one might want to argue, in so doing his theology may have served to legitimate and reinforce those very ideas and the corresponding social structures. But suppose Anselm had gone on to say that the main relevance of the doctrine of the atonement, the new and important thing that it teaches us, is that at the very heart of God is the notion of *honour*: it teaches us that God is all about honour and what is due to one's honour, and that we too must in various ways make these concepts central to our lives. If Anselm had, in other words, trumpeted as the most important thing about the doctrine those very concepts which he himself had imported to solve the intellectual difficulty posed by it, if he had said, these concepts are the heart of the doctrine, they are what we must learn about God and ourselves from the doctrine of the atonement, then I think, he would have been doing a very different, and a much more worrying, kind of theology.

Projection, then, is particularly problematic in at least some social theories of the Trinity because what is projected onto God is immediately reflected back onto the world, and this reverse projection is said to be what is in fact *important* about the doctrine.

I began by noting a concern in recent theology to re-establish the vitality and relevance of the doctrine of the Trinity, and in fact I think it is here that the whole thing actually starts to go wrong. Does the Trinity need to be relevant? What *kind* of relevance does it need to have? The doctrine of the Trinity arose in order to affirm certain things about the divinity of Christ, and, secondarily, of the Spirit, and it arose against a background assumption that God is one. So one could say that as long as Christians continue to believe in the divinity of Christ and the Spirit, and as long as they continue to believe that God is one, then the doctrine is alive and well; it continues to inform the way they read the Scriptures and the overall shape of their faith. But clearly many theologians are wanting something in addition to this, something beyond this, some one particular insight into God that this particular doctrine is the bearer of. It is when one gets to thinking about three being one, and how this might be possible, that most Christians grow puzzled, silent, perhaps even uninterested, and this is what so many theologians are troubled by. It is therefore (though few would quite admit it directly) the abstraction, the conceptual formula, the three-in-oneness, that many theologians want to revivify, and if one is going to make an abstraction, a conceptual formula relevant, vibrant, exciting, it is natural that one is going to have to project onto it, to fill it out again so that it becomes something the imagination can latch onto.

IV

If not the social doctrine, what then? The beginnings of an alternative are present already in what was said above. I suggested that problems arise when one looks for a particular insight into God of which the doctrine of the Trinity is the bearer. My own proposal, then, is not that one should move from the social back to, say, a psychological approach to the Trinity – this would simply be to look for a *different* insight – but rather that one should renounce the very idea that the point of the doctrine is to give insight into God.

The doctrine of the Trinity, I want to suggest, does not need to be seen as a descriptive, first order teaching – there is no need to assume that its main function must be to provide a picture of the divine, a deep understanding of the way God really is.[27] It can instead be taken as grammatical, as a second order proposition,

---

27. Some years after this essay was first published, Simon Oliver drew my attention to the fact that the language of this sentence, and particularly the denial of a 'descriptive' role to the doctrine, might be read as a rejection of the reality of the immanent Trinity, as some form of modalism. I would have done better, and expressed my position more clearly, perhaps, if I had written instead 'even *though* it must be understood as descriptive, there is

a rule, or perhaps a set of rules, for how to read the Biblical stories, how to speak about some of the characters we come across in these stories, how to think and talk about the experience of prayer, how to deploy the 'vocabulary' of Christianity in an appropriate way.[28] The doctrine on this account can still be seen as vitally important, but important as a kind of structuring principle of Christianity rather than as its central focus: if the doctrine is fundamental to Christianity, this is not because it gives a picture of what God is like *in se* from which all else emanates, but rather because it specifies how various aspects of the Christian faith hang together.

But surely, one might respond, if I am told that God must be spoken of as three persons and one substance, I will inevitably try to make sense of this. If God must be spoken of in this way, what does that mean about how God really is? The question, perhaps, is inevitable, and the history of theology is littered with (conflicting) attempts to answer it. What I am suggesting, however, is that it is nevertheless a secondary question – affirming a doctrine of the Trinity does not depend on being able to answer it, nor does establishing the relevance of the doctrine depend on finding the 'right' answer to it.

Theologians are of course free to speculate about social or any other kind of analogies to the Trinity. But they should not, on the view I am proposing, claim for their speculations the authority that the doctrine carries within the Christian tradition, nor should they use the doctrine as a pretext for claiming such an insight into the inner nature of God that they can put it to work to promote social, political or ecclesiastical regimes.

---

no need to assume that its main function must be to provide a picture of the divine ...'. As a result of his comments and those of other interlocutors, I was able to formulate my position a little more clearly in 'Is an apophatic Trinitiarianism possible?', which is Chapter 3 of this volume. See particularly the second section of that essay.

28. Readers of George Lindbeck's *The Nature of Doctrine* (Philadelphia: Westminster, 1984) will immediately recognize his influence here. It is worth noting, however, that one need not commit oneself to a grammatical interpretation of doctrine in general in order to consider whether the Trinity in particular is best thought of in this light.

Chapter 2

AQUINAS, THE TRINITY AND THE LIMITS OF UNDERSTANDING

In this paper I will offer a reading of certain aspects of the thought of Thomas Aquinas on the doctrine of the Trinity – in particular, a reading of some of the more technical elements of Thomas's treatment, of things he has to say about processions, relations, and about the persons of the Trinity in relation to the divine essence. I will propose that at least some of what Thomas lays out here is best understood (or at the very least that it *can* be understood) in terms of theology reaching its limits, in terms, to put it very bluntly, of the dead ends of theology. At various stages Thomas proposes things, I shall argue, that we cannot possibly grasp or make sense of, and if we suppose Thomas to be someone from whom we can learn, we should perhaps neither skip lightly past these elements in his thought, nor try to persuade ourselves that if we strain and squint hard enough we can *just about* see what he means. We should at least consider the possibility that one of the things to learn from Thomas can be learned precisely from the way in which he is content to present us, at times, with proposals which neither he nor we can grasp. My aim, then, is to look to Thomas to explore something about the limits of theology, and about the way we ought to conduct ourselves in the presence of that which we cannot grasp.[1]

To begin with, however, a little about the context in which this reading of Thomas takes place. Much has been written in the last few years on the Trinity in Aquinas, and much of this has been written with the aim of rehabilitating Thomas and so rediscovering the value of his Trinitarian thought. The need for this rehabilitation stems from the fact that, in the broader revival of Trinitarian theology over the last 40 years or so, Aquinas has often been presented as a classic example of thinking about the Trinity gone wrong, Trinitarian theology done in such a way as to make the doctrine seem sterile, confusing and irrelevant. To provide a context for my

---

1. The usual way to approach such a question would of course be to turn to such texts as *Summa Theologiae*, I, Q12 and 13. Here I am deliberately beginning *not* from Thomas's general statements about the limits of knowledge of and language about God, but rather with particular examples of Thomas' theological practice. I will say a little below about how I think the two are related.

own proposal, then, I need first to lay out what have become common criticisms of Aquinas, and then to say a little about the various renewed readings of Thomas which have called these criticisms into question.

One of the most influential articulations of the view that Thomas represents Trinitarian theology gone wrong comes from the pen of Karl Rahner.[2] The problem begins, according to Rahner, with the fact that Aquinas divides what he has to say about God in the *Summa Theologiae* into two parts, the first of which discusses the one God, and the second the question of the three persons and their interrelations. The impression this leaves, according to Rahner and many who have taken up his complaint, is that one can first say a great deal about God – about God's simplicity, perfection and eternity, about God's love, justice and mercy, about God's providence and power – before ever one comes to reflect on God as Trinity. The Trinity becomes a kind of afterthought, which one struggles valiantly but not very successfully to make sense of in the context of an already drawn picture of God.

A closely related objection takes issues with Thomas' focus on the so-called immanent Trinity, on the Trinity *in se*, God in God's self, as distinct from what is usually called the economic Trinity, the Trinity as it is known to us through the incarnation and the sending of the Holy Spirit. Aquinas is not infrequently reproached for discussing the Trinity in a way that is abstract and irrelevant, detached from salvation history or from anything that could matter to us.

Thomas is rarely censured in isolation: most often the context is a criticism of the whole Western tradition of Trinitarian reflection. The pattern was set by Augustine, and it is his influence, and the influence of what is a little clumsily referred to as his psychological analogy, that is the root of the problem, a problem which, according to many, is seen today in the fact that the doctrine of the Trinity so easily appears to be an intellectual puzzle with no relevance to the faith of most Christians.

If the criticism of Aquinas is typically to be found within a sweeping rejection of a Western approach to the Trinity, this in turn is often, though not always, linked to a broader condemnation of a too philosophical conception of God. When one begins, as Augustine and all who follow him are said to, with God's substance, with a God conceived as one, one is beginning with something that is, or may seem to be, open to general philosophical reflection in a way that the three persons of God are not – or perhaps one begins in this way because one is already captured by a philosophical pre-conception of what God is like. This is a criticism which does not always remain at a merely abstract and methodological level: often the same theologians who reject the Augustinian approach to the Trinity want to jettison central elements of the classical patristic and medieval conception of the divine nature – elements which are seen as merely the product of philosophical influence, such as, for instance, simplicity, aseity, eternity, immutability and impassibility.[3] 'The Christian God', a genuinely trinitarian God, is presented in partial or complete

---

2. Rahner, *The Trinity*, esp. 15–21.

3. Here one should think not of Rahner, but of Jürgen Moltmann and those who have followed him.

contrast with the too philosophical God which had a grip over so much of the Christian tradition.

It has, then, in large parts of contemporary theology, become common, first, to be dismissive of Thomas on the Trinity; secondly, to see the whole Western tradition of reflection on the Trinity as inadequate; and thirdly, to seek to arrive at a more authentically Christian and Trinitarian conception of God by rejecting some of the tradition's supposedly philosophical ideas about God. It is against such a background that the rehabilitation and retrieval of Thomas' Trinitarian thought is currently taking place. A particularly systematic and sustained retrieval is to be found in a stream of work coming from French Dominicans such as Gilles Emery[4] and Jean-Pierre Torrell,[5] and in English speaking writers, such as Matthew Levering,[6] who have taken up their thought.[7] But the protest against a maligned Thomas is not limited to these circles. A. N. Williams, in the course of a discussion of deification in Thomas, lays out a very elegant and persuasive account of Aquinas on God, which, at least in passing, seriously undermines many aspects of the popular reading of him,[8] and Rowan Williams in his 2001 Aquinas lecture takes up the defense of Thomas against Catherine Mowry LaCugna.[9]

The Thomas who emerges from these various retrievals bears only a slight resemblance to the Thomas so frequently dismissed in contemporary Trinitarian theology. True, he discusses God as one before he comes to the three persons, and true, he is influenced by Augustine's analogy, but beyond this, there is little in what one might call the standard portrait and the standard critique of Aquinas, as set out by the likes of Rahner and Moltmann, that turns out to have any purchase on the actual Thomas.

Thus, for instance, recent commentators have been at pains to insist that Thomas' trinitarian theology is in fact thoroughly Scriptural: it is from Scripture, it is in the service of Scripture, it aims to deepen and protect our understanding of Scripture. Gilles Emery writes of the 'deep Biblical and Patristic foundations of [Thomas's] trinitarian doctrine'; its aim is 'to manifest the deep sense of the Gospel'; it 'starts

---

4. Cf. especially Gilles Emery, *Trinity in Aquinas* (Ypsilanti: Sapientia Press, 2003).

5. Cf. *Saint Thomas Aquinas: Volume 2 Spiritual Master* (Washington, DC: Catholic University of America Press, 2003).

6. Cf. Levering's use of Emery and Torrell in *Scripture and Metaphysics: Aquinas and the Renewal of Trinitarian Theology* (Oxford: Blackwell, 2004).

7. Nicholas Healy's marvelously lucid treatment of Aquinas as theologian in *Thomas Aquinas: Theologian of the Christian Life* (Aldershot: Ashgate, 2003) also pays tribute to the work of Emery and especially Torrell, though Healy clearly modifies and goes beyond their approach in important ways.

8. A. N. Williams, *The Ground of Union: Deification in Aquinas and Palamas* (Oxford: Oxford University Press, 1999), 34–64.

9. 'What Does Love Know? St. Thomas on the Trinity', *New Blackfriars* 82 (2001): 260–72.

from Scripture in order to return to Scripture'.[10] Matthew Levering takes up these themes with particular emphasis in his *Scripture and Metaphysics*.

A number of these works of retrieval are particularly persuasive in pointing to a thorough integration of Thomas' treatment of God as one and God as three.[11] The *De Deo Uno* in subtle ways anticipates and prepares for the subsequent treatment of God as three – not least in the discussion of God's knowing and willing; the treatise on the Trinity (as it is often called) draws repeatedly on the understanding of theological language, and on the notion of divine simplicity, which were pivots of the first part of his treatment of God. Thomas does not, then, present the Trinity as a datum of revelation which is awkwardly appended to a philosophical presentation of God, but deliberately and progressively develops a single treatment of God, albeit a treatment in which a distinction between different ways of talking about God must be maintained; throughout the whole of the treatment of God, furthermore, Thomas is using metaphysics in service of what is, throughout, a treatment drawing on and oriented towards the reading of Scripture.

Finally, the accusation that Thomas's treatment, beginning as it does with the so-called immanent Trinity, is dry, abstract, and technical, and that it inevitably seems irrelevant, has elicited responses on at least two levels. First, though it is certainly true that Thomas starts with the immanent Trinity, he does so in order to move on to questions of God's relation to the world. Just as the second, Trinitarian part of his treatment of God is prepared for and subtly anticipated in the first 26 questions of the *Summa Theologiae*, so too the treatment of God's relations *ad extra* are prepared and anticipated in the discussion of the internal relations of God.[12] The more one can appreciate the larger movement of the *Summa*, in other words, and understand the way the treatment of the Trinity fits into and contributes to this plan, the less one will see it as isolated, abstract and cut-off from what might be really significant. A first line of defense, then, is to better situate Thomas's treatment of the Trinity in its context. But it is also sometimes suggested that it is a mistake to look for Trinitarian theology to have too practical a payoff, socio-politically or otherwise: it is wrong to insist that the doctrine of the Trinity must be justified in some sort of *functional* way. If our end, our salvation is, as Thomas supposes, to know God's essence in the beatific vision, then it is in the very nature of faith to wish for and to strive after, even in this life, whatever dim anticipation of this vision we can achieve. And so it is in the very nature of theology to be contemplative, to strive after 'insight into the inner nature of God'.[13]

---

10. Torrell, *Trinity in Aquinas*, 319, 317.

11. This is done in a particularly elegant and effective manner by Anna Williams in the second chapter of her *The Ground of Union*.

12. This is a point that, once again, Anna Williams brings out particularly effectively.

13. This is a phrase which Levering quotes from my own earlier article, which appears as the Chapter 1 of this volume. He uses the phrase to affirm what I had there denied.

And so it is quite right that a discussion of the immanent Trinity should take pride of place in a theology oriented towards contemplation.

There is, then, something of a *ressourcement* going on in connection with Thomas on the Trinity. On the whole this is a much needed and valuable rereading of Aquinas, and one which ought to make the kind of broad and rapid dismissal of Thomas together with the whole Augustinian tradition, which *has* come so easily to many contemporary theologians, considerably more difficult. But there may also be a certain danger to such retrievals, or to some of them. The instinct of some of Thomas's defenders is so strongly to say that his writing on the Trinity *is* after all genuinely meaningful, that it is not dry and empty but rather rich and theologically important, that it coheres and contributes to a contemplative theology, that they may run the risk of wanting to make sense of more than Thomas thought he could make sense of, of glossing over and giving scant attention to those elements in his thought that resist any real explanation – and therefore, as I have suggested, they may fail to learn from him something that should be learned.

My aim in suggesting that there are theological dead ends to be found in Aquinas' treatment of the Trinity, then, is not to revert to a stereotypical dismissal of Thomas, but rather to attempt to read him positively but differently, to retrieve something from Aquinas which is at some points different, at least in emphasis, from that which others have been finding.

In what follows I shall look at three points in the development of Thomas's treatment of the Trinity in the *Summa Theologiae* – his introduction of the idea of processions in God, his presentation of the persons of God as subsisting relations, and his discussion of these relations in relation to the divine essence – and argue that at each of these points Thomas serenely presents us with something that we can make nothing of, and that he does not expect us to – or at least that this is a way of reading what he is doing which ought to be considered.

There is a difficulty to the kind of case I am attempting, the difficulty of showing that something does *not* make sense, that it can*not* be grasped or imagined or understood, especially in the absence of any general theory of meaning or understanding. I know of no neat way to sidestep this problem, but I shall make my case as best I can on two levels. The first will be from the text of Aquinas, trying to show the radical if understated way in which he alters the functioning of words we think we know in using them in a Trinitarian context, and how unconcerned he seems to be about offering explanations for things which appear to cry out for explanation. The second level on which I will argue is a more general one: I want to show that the principle of charity in interpretation need *not* require us to suppose that Thomas was himself able to make sense of everything he said about the Trinity, because it might in fact be a virtue rather than a weakness of Trinitarian theology to leave certain things radically, and very clearly, unexplained.

In the *Summa Theologiae* Thomas starts his treatment of the three persons of God with a discussion of the notion of *procession* in God. This is the overarching category which will include both the generation of the Son from the Father and the way in which the Holy Spirit comes forth from both Father and Son. And in the very first article where he treats this,[14] Thomas already puts procession beyond what we can imagine or make sense of – or this is one way of reading what he does.[15]

Thomas distinguishes between a material procession, a procession which is in some way bodily, and an intelligible procession. His examples of material processions are local movement (as when one processes up an aisle, for instance) and a procession from cause to effect, as, for instance, the procession of heat 'from the agent to the thing made hot' – so I put the poker into the fire and the heat from the fire processes into the poker. Intellectual procession is different in that the procession is not external to the agent: when I understand an object, I form a conception of it, and this, Thomas says, is a procession in me – the concept processes from my understanding – but it remains within me. If I speak of the object, the word that I use signifies the conception, and this word is something external to me. But even if I do not give voice to it, there is still the conception I have formed, called the 'word of the heart', which proceeds from but remains internal to me.

Now, I think we already struggle a bit to make sense of conceiving in terms of intellectual emanation or procession. But if we can think of a word going out from us, then perhaps we can also think of the conception to which the word points as going forth in some way from us, though remaining within us. Or, to put it a little differently, perhaps we can see that it makes sense to distinguish the conception the mind forms from the mind itself, and so to see the former as something which proceeds from the latter.

Thomas is clear that it is to our understanding of intelligible procession rather than bodily procession that we should look to think about processions in God. The problem is that the very thing which just about allows us to make sense of the idea of a procession in the intellect must now be taken away. Thomas tells us that 'the more perfectly [something] proceeds, the more closely it is one with the source whence it proceeds', and so in the case of God, 'the divine Word is of necessity perfectly one with the source whence He proceeds, without any kind of diversity'.[16] If I am right to think that we had to begin with only a very tenuous grasp on the idea of intellectual procession, but that, by thinking of a conception as distinct from the mind which does the conceiving, we could just about see the meaning of speaking of an emanation or procession, then here Thomas has cut the ground from under us. In God we precisely *cannot* think of difference between that which

---

14. *ST* 1.27.1.

15. For an alternative and interesting construal of the significance of Thomas' treatment of processions (and indeed of subsistent relation), cf. Rowan Williams' 'What does love know?' Whether Williams' reading, which on the face of it seems to present Thomas's discussion as insight-bearing at these points, is decisively at odds with mine, is an interesting question, especially in light of his references to conceptual Möbius strips (263) and the risk of the collapse of the discourse on itself (266).

16. *ST* 1.27, 1 ad 2.

proceeds and that from which it proceeds: divine simplicity requires the denial of this. Thomas is presenting us with a procession that is so perfect that we in fact have no idea why it could not also be called 'not a procession'.

This is not intended as a criticism. Thomas is committed to the language of procession for Scriptural reasons. He offers a neat diagnosis of the common flaw uniting the apparently opposite heresies of Arianism and Sabellianism – they both take this Biblical language of procession to mean an outward act. So we must, because of Scripture, speak of procession in God, and we must, to avoid heresy, think of this as an inward procession. For a combination of Scriptural reasons, traditional precedent, and considerations deriving from Thomas's own theological system, the primary created model for thinking of inward processions he chooses is the procession of the word, or the conception, in the human intellect. What I am suggesting, however, is that by the time the language deriving from this model has been suitably reshaped to make it appropriate for speaking of God – reshaped, in particular, to bring it into conformity with the principle of divine simplicity – it cannot serve as a carrier of any *insight* into God. We do not, from the created analogue, get a glimpse into the nature of God: rather, we so modify the language drawn from this analogue that when we arrive at a language to talk about God, it is a language we quite clearly *cannot* understand. What is a procession which does not occur in time, nor involve change, nor allow of any diversity between the one who processes and the one from whom the procession takes place? I have no reason to affirm that there is no such thing, but also no way of grasping or imagining what it might be. Every element in the idea of intellectual procession that I might, imaginatively, get a grasp of, has had to be denied.

The second point to consider is Thomas's treatment of the persons of the Trinity as subsisting relations. Thomas follows Augustine, who in turn follows Gregory of Nazianzus, in suggesting that the persons of the Trinity be thought of as relations – not as *having* relations, but as *being* relations. This, it should be noted, is a considerably more radical proposal than that made by some contemporary proponents of a social theory of the Trinity, who suggest that the three persons of God are so intensely related in love and mutual self-giving that they are one. It is not that first there are three somethings, who then are very closely related to each other – the persons simply *are* relations.

A first, and as we will see too simple, way to express what is odd and difficult here is this: how can one have relations without the things which are to be related, relations without *relata*? We tend to think of relations as existing between two somethings – there are two objects, or two people, and the relation between them. Can we understand what it means to speak of a relation without, to put it very crudely, the endpoints which are joined by it?

The reason this is too simple an approach is that Aquinas does not think of relations in quite the way we usually do. For him a relation is normally an accident of some substance – it inheres in something, but is distinctive in that it is always 'towards another', towards something outside the substance. So if Robert and Andrew are friends, then the relation of being Andrew's friend is an accident which inheres in Robert, but which has to do with Robert's being referred to something beyond himself, namely to Andrew. Similarly, of course, there would be a relation of being Robert's friend which inheres in Andrew, but which refers to another, namely to Robert.

This basic pattern has to undergo a number of modifications in order for speaking about relations in God to be possible. First of all, because of, once again, the doctrine of divine simplicity, in God there are no accidents. So a relation *in* God is not an accidental modification of God, but it is God himself. Of the two kinds of things that can be said of a relation, then – that it is *in* something, and that it is towards another – we have radically modified the first: it is not *in* something, it simply *is* the thing. But what about the second element, the 'towards another'? The persons of the Trinity clearly do not exist by being related to something outside God. The 'towards another' which is central to the notion of relation must mean another in God – it is another whose otherness, then, is not immediately easy to grasp. But it is perfectly clear, one might respond – the other is of course another divine person. If we remember once again, however, that what a person is is a subsisting relation, then it is not necessarily so clear – we have a subsisting relation, a relation in God which is God, which is a relation to what is itself a subsisting relation. What has happened here is not so much that the idea of relation has been used to clarify the way we must think of God, but rather the exigencies of what must be said of God have been used to confuse what is meant by relation.

At this point some might suppose that Aquinas is doing something ontologically very important – he is pointing us towards a radically non-substantialist metaphysics where primacy is accorded to relationship. Even if a general ontology along these lines would be a good thing to be able to develop, however, I think there is little evidence of Aquinas aiming to do this. We do not find Aquinas championing a wholesale revolution along these lines in Aristotelian metaphysics, nor do we find him pointing to the conceptuality of divine relations as something which, considered abstractly, will illuminate or transform our conceptions of relationship or being in general. God is precisely *contrasted* with us on this point, since we have relations accidentally.[17] What Thomas does is simply to begin with the category of relation as he takes it to be normally understood, and then introduce as many modifications as are necessary to make use of it in speaking of something internal to God – without taking any particular pains to explain how we are to try to grasp or picture this stretched and strained notion of relation – without taking any pains, that is to say, to explain what it *means*.

The final example of St Thomas calmly presenting us with statements about God which he does not expect us to understand is in my opinion the clearest. The persons of God, we have said, are subsistent relations. How are the persons related to God's essence? We have seen that simplicity requires us to say that the subsistent relation is identical to the essence. Relation and essence in God do not differ really, Aquinas tells us, but only in their 'mode of intelligibility'. We understand

---

17. Fergus Kerr makes this point in *After Aquinas: Versions of Thomism* (Oxford: Blackwell, 2002), 198.

something different by these two things, but the difference we must affirm to be *only* in our way of understanding, not in God himself.[18] Precisely the opposite, however, must be affirmed about the relations in relation to *each other*. Thomas is at great pains to insist that relations in God are *real* relations. He does also have a conception of merely notional relations, but to speak this way of relations in God would be to fall into Sabellianism. And if relations in God are real, they are also really distinct. Thomas insists on this point in article 3 of question 28: relations in God are distinguished not only in our understanding, but really in God. So to recap, we have one kind of distinction – between a subsisting relation and the essence – which exists only in 'the mode of intelligibility', not really in God – and another kind of distinction – between one subsisting relation and another – which Thomas insists exists not only in our understanding but in reality, in God. The subsisting relations are each really identical to the essence, and only differ from it in our understanding, but they *really*, and not only in our understanding, differ from each other. The interesting thing here is the serenity with which Thomas seems to pass the question this raises by.[19] He has laid things out in such a way as to make a problem more or less leap off the page at us – how can two things be absolutely identical with a third, and yet not identical with each other? – but he seems hardly to think it worth commenting on.

There is of course nothing really distinctive in Thomas's laying alongside of each other statements whose relationship eludes us, at this point in particular. What has just been described is nothing but a technical version of the Trinitarian pattern of speech that the Father is God, and the Son is God, but the Father is not the Son. This fundamentally puzzling element of Trinitarian orthodoxy – two things identical to a third not being identical to each other – is something that is faithfully repeated in Thomas's technical discussions of subsisting relations and essence. The thing to notice here is that Aquinas's technical language does not serve to resolve this difficulty – it does not get rid of or explain or make clear to us how it could be possible that $a = b$ and $a = c$ but b does not equal c. And there is no indication that Thomas is trying to do this. His technical treatment seems designed to very clearly delineate what we cannot know, rather than to overcome our not knowing.

As was suggested earlier, it is in the nature of the case that what is being argued here – that at some points at least Thomas is not trying to give us insight, that his proposals are instead a way of clearly articulating a lack of insight – can never be definitively established. It cannot be ruled out that another will look at the examples given and say no, I can just about grasp what Thomas is pointing to here,

---

18. *ST* 1. 28, 2.

19. Timothy Smith, in *Thomas Aquinas' Trinitarian Theology: A Study in Theological Method* (Washington, DC: Catholic University of America Press, 2003) writes that 'Thomas shies away from an answer as to exactly how the divine essence can be truly one and the Persons identical to it but distinct among themselves' (150). More broadly, his very detailed treatment seems to be pointing in the same direction as my much more cursory one: Smith writes, for instance, that 'Thomas is not so much probing the mystery as protecting it' (157).

even though it is very difficult. Part of what is at stake in deciding which route to go down – is whether we should suppose Thomas is straining to offer us glimmers of understanding, trying to help us in '[squint] in the infinite light',[20] or whether he is carefully presenting us with intellectual dead-ends – is whether we can see the latter course as something that would be in any way respectable, a worthwhile thing for theology to be doing. Can one say that at various points Aquinas offers us not the least bit of understanding, without thereby maligning Thomas? If in fact he does not manage to make his account intelligible at certain points, would we not do better to pass these by quietly, given that we live in a time when theologians have already too many quick and easy reasons to dismiss Aquinas?

Much here depends on one's underlying conception of the doctrine of the Trinity and its purpose. If one presumes that the point of the doctrine of the Trinity is to provide a description of God, a picture of the divine, a deep understanding of the way God really is, then the reading of Aquinas I have given would have to be considered a reading of his failure. But I have tried to argue in the previous chapter that the doctrine can have an important grammatical and structural role within Christianity whether or not it carries any insight. If in fact the doctrine of the Trinity is simply beyond our grasp, then it may be better, more helpful, for theology to display this quite clearly, than to skirt the issue, to bluff its way along. And this, I am suggesting, is what Thomas is doing – simultaneously displaying the grammar, the pattern of speech about the Trinity, and displaying it as beyond our comprehension.

In *The Phantom Tollbooth*,[21] a classic American children's novel, the protagonist finds himself in a land where many things have gone awry ever since the two beautiful young princesses, Rhyme and Reason, were banished. The doctrine of the Trinity, one might say, is an aspect of Christian theology which has a relationship to one of these two princesses but not the other – it has rhyme but not reason. By this I do not mean precisely that it is poetic rather than logical, but that orthodox Trinitarian speech follows a pattern, a rhythm, which can be learned, but does not necessarily deliver *understanding* of God. The sense of a pattern or rhythm comes through very strongly in something like the Athanasian creed – those who read or recite the Athanasian creed do not necessarily understand it, but they get the hang of it, they catch its rhythm. They could go on speaking in this pattern. In the first books of Augustine's *De Trinitate* one finds quite explicitly an exploration of the rules of Trinitarian discourse, an investigation into how we must speak in various contexts. Augustine, of course, goes on to ask about what all this means, to try to get some understanding of it. What I am proposing is that Aquinas, even though he makes use of some of the material from the second part of Augustine's work, is doing something which is in spirit more like the first part; in greater detail, and in a changed intellectual context, Aquinas is exploring a pattern, setting out

---

20. Levering, *Scripture and Metaphysics*, 240.
21. Norton Juster, *The Phantom Tollbooth* (New York: Epstein and Carroll, 1961).

a grammar, for the way we speak about God as three and one – he is exploring in detail the rhyme of the Trinity.

There are a number of questions that a position along the lines set out is likely to provoke, and I want to clarify the position by attempting to offer answers to three of them. A first question, or perhaps objection, is this: why should we suppose that a grammatical exploration, an exploration of the patterns of Trinitarian speech, is *different* from an exploration where understanding, genuine knowledge of God, is sought? Is this not to set up a false opposition? Would we not aim to arrive at knowledge and insight precisely through and in a careful exploration of how we must speak of God? Or would the latter not lead to the former? To this what must be said I think is that in general that may perhaps be true, but whether or not it is so in general, there are points in a discussion of the Trinity where it is not true. There are times where *all* we have is a pattern, points where grammatical knowhow and an understanding of meaning diverge. But again, one might ask, what does this mean: how exactly would one know that we do not understand what we are saying if we do know how to say it? Is the distinction being used here predicated upon an unduly visual conception of meaning, so that I am supposing that we do not understand something unless we can somehow picture it? It is easy to use visual metaphors (insight, picture), but the point at issue is not fundamentally tied to them. The same point can be made without recourse to language of seeing: it is precisely when our speech hits dead-ends – when what we say naturally leads to further questions to which we have no answer, or when what we say seems to lead to inferences which we then have to deny – that we can say that we have a grammar for speaking of God, but no accompanying understanding.

Secondly, how does the not-knowing I am discussing in connection with aspects of Trinitarian doctrine relate to a not-knowing of God in general? Thomas famously affirms that we know of God not what he is, but rather what he is not. In this life we cannot know God's essence. Some of the words we use about God, such as good and wise, really do describe God, but they refer to him in a *way* which we cannot understand, since we draw our understanding of them from a created context. Some interpreters, such as Victor Preller, pursue these lines of thought to a radically negative conclusion: we are licensed to speak in certain ways about God, but we really do not know in the least what we are saying.[22] And if this is the case, then it follows rather trivially that when we speak of processions, relations and persons in God, we cannot possibly know what we are saying. Herbert McCabe in fact argued quite explicitly that although the Trinity is a mystery, it is not as though things get any *worse* for our understanding with the introduction of the doctrine of the three persons – God is entirely a mystery from the beginning.[23] Though I

---

22. Victor Preller, *Divine Science and the Science of God: A Reformulation of Thomas Aquinas* (Princeton: Princeton University Press, 1967).

23. Herbert McCabe, 'Aquinas on the Trinity', in Oliver Davies and Denys Turner (eds), *Silence and the Word: Negative Theology and Incarnation* (Cambridge: Cambridge University Press, 2002).

have a good deal of sympathy for these lines of thought, what I am arguing here is something slightly different. Whatever account one wants to give of our not knowing God in general, the situation gets worse, or at the very least more *clearly* bad, when it comes to certain kinds of statements in Trinitarian discourse. When we say God is wise or good, for instance, we at least *think* we know what we are saying, even if a reflection on issues related to the *modus significandi* of our words means that we then have to acknowledge that our conception of goodness and wisdom are not adequate to God. But when we speak of processions in God, or subsistent relations, or the Persons in relation to the essence, we are speaking in a way which we cannot make sense of, even in an inadequate way. My suggestion is, then, that there are some areas of theological speech where we run aground more dramatically and more obviously than others.[24]

A final question has to do with contemplation. As was mentioned above, one of the themes of some current retrievals of Thomas' trinitarian thought is that it needs to be seen as ordered to contemplation. The point is particularly insisted upon by Matthew Levering, who thinks that we need to rediscover, in Thomas, theology as contemplative wisdom, that we need to understand that in Thomas's treatment of the Trinity what is at stake is forming the reader to 'enable the reader to experience, through contemplation, the God of salvation history'.[25] Where is there space for contemplation if, as I am suggesting, at some key points Thomas is simply leading the reader into an absolute dead-end?

My answer to this question is two-fold. First, even if I am right about the function of some of the most technical discussions in Aquinas's treatment of the Trinity, this does not mean that there is nothing in the discussion as a whole which could be significant for a contemplative ascent. Attentive readers will have noticed the words 'Father', 'Son' or 'Holy Spirit' have made only brief appearances in the preceding discussion. My argument has been focusing precisely on the most abstract dimension of Trinitarian reflection, and it is this dimension that I maintain provides no illumination. There is however much more than this technical dimension in Thomas' thought, and much of this may well have significance – more than a negative, cautionary significance – for contemplation.

Secondly, it is worth thinking about how exactly Trinity and contemplation are related. One can distinguish, roughly, between something like contemplation *of* the Trinity and contemplation *in* the Trinity. That is to say, on the one hand one can think of contemplation in terms of the one who contemplates standing outside of the Trinity, so to speak, trying to see and comprehend the Trinity as a whole, and all the relations involved in it; on the other hand one can think of contemplation in terms of the Holy Spirit working within the one who contemplates, both enabling

---

24. This, I should make clear, is my distinction rather than Thomas's, and it need not correspond precisely to a reason/revelation divide.

25. Levering, *Scripture and Metaphysics*, 36. In the conclusion to this work, Levering makes his point about the need for rediscovering theology as contemplative wisdom through an exploration of what is wrong with my own essay 'Perichoresis and Projection'.

him and drawing him to contemplate the Father in the Son. On this second version, the whole of the Trinity is involved in the act of contemplation, but it is not as though what is being contemplated is itself the three-in-oneness.

If one thinks primarily along the lines of a model of contemplation *in* the Trinity, then one can think of the one who contemplates as beginning to be, by grace, involved with, taken up into, the life of the Trinity. And it is not entirely unreasonable to suppose that the nature of this involvement is such that the one so involved cannot also stand outside it all in order to get a clear vision of the Trinity as a whole, and of the relations of Father, Son and Holy Spirit abstractly considered. The abstract rules of Trinitarian discourse may still be necessary – to ensure that one does not fall into a heresy such as Arianism or Sabellianism, for instance, and so mistake the nature of that with which one is involved – but it is not the rules themselves that form the substance of our contemplation.

An advantage of an emphasis on contemplation *in* the Trinity rather than contemplation *of* the Trinity is that it avoids what I take to be one of the dangers of Trinitarian theology, which is to give an implausible kind of advantage to the theologian. I think it is important to presume, not precisely that the theologian has *no* advantages over other believers, but that she has no really significant advantages. The person who cleans the church benefits from certain perks, one might suppose, as regards her spiritual life – being around such things as pews, altars, crosses, candles, or indeed the reserved sacrament might perhaps provoke moments of prayer – and similarly I presume there may be certain benefits to being a theologian – coming across theological ideas might from time to time provoke one to prayer, and so on. Even if one maintains quite a rich view of theology as a discipline integrated into and directed towards the spiritual life, it seems fundamentally wrong to construct any conception of the relation between Trinitarian theology and contemplation which would mean that those who can understand really difficult, elusive, technical theology are able to get more of a foretaste of the beatific vision than those who are not. And this is what, on some accounts of Thomas on the Trinity, seems to be suggested. If however Aquinas's most technical discussions of Trinitarian themes are understood as I have been outlining, then the only advantages accruing to the theologian, in this area at least, are a more decisive knowledge of the limits of their understanding, and perhaps an added protection against falling into heresy.[26]

The point can be made in a slightly different way. There is, one could say, a spectrum within theologies of the Trinity as regards mystery – a spectrum as

---

26. For a related discussion, cf. Bruce Marshall, 'Quod Scit Una Uetula: Aquinas on the Nature of Theology', in Rik van Nieuwenhove and Joseph Wawrykow (eds), *The Theology of Thomas Aquinas* (Notre Dame: University of Notre Dame Press, 2005). Marshall concludes that, for Thomas, 'The theological master simply strives to make explicit, to recapture *in modo cognitionis*, what the faithful heart of any old woman already knows' (26). If this is right, then the idea that difficult technical discussions can yield an insight into the inner nature of God which is *not* available otherwise would seem unlikely.

regards how knowable or unknowable the doctrine is held to be. At one end of the spectrum we have many contemporary thinkers, particularly those who espouse a robust social Trinitarianism, who do not find the matter mysterious at all. They speak of the Trinity, and of the inner life of the Trinity and its qualities, with great enthusiasm; they draw all kinds of social, political and metaphysical conclusions from it; they confidently contrast the Christian understanding of God to other less satisfactory ones. In the middle of my spectrum are those who show considerably more reserve. The doctrine of the Trinity is indeed mysterious, and we cannot fully grasp it. But we can nevertheless try to gain some dim glimmer, some elusive bit of an understanding, even if we will always have to acknowledge that our minds fall short. Something like this is how many read Aquinas. My reading, by contrast, puts him at the far end of the spectrum. There are at least some aspects of what we must say about the Trinity of which we can have no grasp whatsoever.

Those who take their position at either end of the spectrum do not privilege the theologian in any dramatic way above other believers. If the social trinitarians are right, then they really can explain the Trinity to people in a way that people really can grasp. Their approach has become influential in part precisely because it is so very preachable. And if, at the other extreme, Thomas is understood as I propose, then the theologian no more than any other believer can understand what they mean in talking about the Trinity. The position in the middle of the spectrum, however, though on the face of it very cautious, modest and moderate, is the one to give what is really a rather serious privilege to those who have the time, inclination and ability to engage in sophisticated technical theology. Come and read theology at a top university, one could say, and if you do really very hard papers with a suitably prayerful attitude, and do really very well in them, you will be that much closer to the beatific vision. It might be good for boosting recruitment to the discipline, but it does not quite ring true.

Chapter 3

IS AN APOPHATIC TRINITARIANISM POSSIBLE?

But in my opinion it is impossible to express Him, and yet more impossible to conceive Him.

—Gregory of Nazianzus, Second Theological Oration[1]

Systematic theology over the last few decades has often been marked by a certain self-conscious *robustness* when it comes to the doctrine of the Trinity. There has been concern from many sides to reaffirm its importance at the very heart of Christian theology and life; to insist that the God Christians worship is not just any God, and not an abstract God, but a Trinitarian God; to insist that the doctrine of the Trinity is not a puzzle and a difficulty for Christian theology, but its rich and vital heart. Many books have appeared on the Trinity, and much asserted in tones of insistence, confidence and enthusiasm.[2]

This robustness can be understood partly as a reaction against an Enlightenment deism that continues to lurk in certain kinds of philosophy of religion and also perhaps in the wider intellectual imagination – it is a reaction, that is, against the notion that 'God' is something whose contours can be determined by abstract reflection from first principles, whose nature can be largely deduced if one starts from, say, the notion of a maximally perfect being. Against this context, to make much of the Trinity as at the heart of one's thought is to insist on the real distinctiveness of Christianity and the genuine 'theologicalness' of theology.

---

1. Gregory of Nazianzus, 'Second Theological Oration', in *Nicene and Post-Nicene Fathers of the Christian Church, Vol. VII* (New York: The Christian Literature Company, 1894), 289–90.

2. Particularly clear examples can be found in the work of social Trinitarians such as Jürgen Moltmann, Colin Gunton and their followers, discussed in the first chapter of this book. But robust Trinitarianism is not confined to social Trinitarianism. One of the things that many readers find particularly attractive in Hans Urs von Balthasar, to give just one other example, is his powerfully Trinitarian reading of the cross, which is in turn supported by a surprisingly detailed and confident discussion, particularly in the fifth volume of his *Theodrama*, of the inner life of the Trinity.

A robust approach to the Trinity can also be understood within the context of a widespread anti-liberalism. If theological liberals are hesitant to make claims which extend beyond ethics and the nature of experience, claims which extend into the realm of actual affirmations about God, champions of the Trinity are not. Where liberals are concerned to show that what Christians believe is accessible and reasonable and meaningful to all those around them, many contemporary Trinitarians want to lay emphasis on and forcefully proclaim the very thing which may seem most odd to the surrounding culture. The Trinity should be the point *from* which we take our norms, our sense of what is meaningful, our deepest judgments about the nature of being itself. It must not be shuffled off in an embarrassed way to the appendix, but boldly placed in the prolegomenon.[3] Altogether, then, confident talk about the Trinity has become a badge of authenticity, something which establishes the distinctively Christian character of one's theology.

It is possible to ask whether there are not certain dangers associated with the robust Trinitarianism of our time. If this is indeed, as I have suggested, a reaction – whether to a thin rationalism or a limp liberalism – then it is arguably not simply a return to the tradition, but rather a distinctive reshaping of it,[4] and there is the question whether in some instances this reshaping ought to be deemed a distortion.[5] Or again, one might ask whether some versions of Trinitarian robustness presuppose a rather elevated conception of the role of both theology and the theologian: it can sometimes seem that only someone who has sat at the feet of contemporary theologians is in a position to perceive what it was – perhaps the concept of perichoresis, for instance – which was all along the true meaning of Christian revelation, the central thing it has to teach us. And ultimately of course one might wonder about the danger of idolatry – about the possibility of being so robust, so confident that we know what we are talking about when we talk about the Trinity, that we are in fact projecting our most pleasing ideas onto God and making those the object of our worship.

---

3. The reference here is to Karl Barth in reaction against Schleiermacher. The relationship between what I am calling the contemporary Trinitarian robustness and Karl Barth is in fact quite complex, however. On the one hand, many of those who speak in robust tones have some sort of a Barthian lineage, and in general a robust rhetorical style is not hard to find in the writings of Barth. On the other hand, when it comes to the presentation of the doctrine of the Trinity itself, Barth is often far more cautious than many more recent Trinitarians.

4. One might object that robust Trinitarianism is not new at all: Athanasius, for instance, was surely nothing if not robust. But fighting on one side in an ecclesial dispute, at a point when the 'orthodox' position is not yet determined, is a different thing from forcefully championing the importance of a doctrine which is not in fact in dispute within the tradition. However robust and however Trinitarian Athanasius may have been, he was not in fact doing the same thing as contemporary robust Trinitarians.

5. There is now a significant body of scholarship surrounding social Trinitarians' misreading of the Cappadocians, for instance. There is also a question about whether some social Trinitarianism veers towards tritheism.

It is possible to ask such questions, but I will not proceed here primarily through criticism of some of the most confident kinds of Trinitarian thinking. Instead I will sketch an alternative, something which goes right against what seems to be the grain of contemporary Trinitarian sensibility, a kind of programme of Trinitarian theological modesty.

Apophatic theology and Trinitarian theology normally sit in different parts of our theological textbooks, and indeed of our mental landscape. We usually imagine apophaticism as something which is an issue, if at all, when God is considered abstractly, when questions are posed in a very general way about divine transcendence and knowability, and not when central Christian doctrines are at play. Some indeed may hold it against apophaticism that it seems to forget, or at least to bracket, that God is known through revelation not in some sort of abstract transcendence but concretely as Trinity.[6]

What is to be explored in this paper, however, is whether it can make sense to propose something like an apophatic Trinitarianism.[7] Is it possible to suppose that reflection on the doctrine of the Trinity might intensify rather than diminish our sense of the unknowability of God? Is it possible to accept that it presents us with a pattern which we cannot understand, rather than giving us some new understanding of God? What if we were to suppose that how the three are one, how to relate divine persons to the divine substance, what the inner relations between the persons are, are all questions which are quite simply beyond us? On such an account, the doctrine of the Trinity would confront us with these questions, in some sense force them upon us, but leave us without any resources with which to answer them. What answers we may appear to have – answers drawing on notions of processions, relations, perichoresis – would be acknowledged as in fact no more than technical ways of articulating our inability to know.[8]

---

6. Cf. Denys Turner and Oliver Davies, eds, *Silence and the Word* (Cambridge: Cambridge University Press, 2002) for a collection of essays which in various ways attempt to revise this mental landscape.

7. The qualifier 'something like' is necessary here, although I will not continue to repeat it. Strictly speaking, apophatic theology involves the negation of language, 'unsaying' things about God, denying claims about God, and on the face of it orthodox Trinitarian claims are not negative but positive. One is not denying, for instance, that God is three hypostases in one *ousia*, or that the Son proceeds from the Father, but affirming these truths. But if at issue in the negations of apophatic theology is the acknowledgement that God is beyond the grasp of our concepts, then I will be suggesting that Trinitarian language, though on the surface a language of affirmation, does just this same work. It proceeds, not by direct negation, but instead by the presentation of patterns of affirmation which immediately defeat us. Even if concepts of God are not denied, they are used in a way which make it directly clear that God is beyond our conceptual grasp.

8. That terms such as processions, relations and perichoresis may be technical ways to articulate our inability to understand rather than rich conceptual resources which shed light on the Trinity is a point that I have tried to develop in the two preceding essays.

Is such an approach to the Trinity possible for Christian theology? Is it possible to suppose that the doctrine of the Trinity, as a doctrine, gives us no depiction of God, no insight into God's inner nature, God's inner life? I am deliberately couching the question in terms of whether this is a *possible* approach, because it is a rather difficult position to argue for directly – one might find oneself obliged, if one tried to make a direct case, to take on and discuss *every* variety of Trinitarian theology which lays any sort of claim at all to any sort of insight at all. In what follows I will in fact do no more than sketch the contours of such an approach a little further and consider if it can be defended against some of the more obvious objections. Would this amount to a denial of the reality of the Trinity, or at least a denial of the reality of the immanent Trinity? Is it effectively a side-lining of the doctrine, a relegation of the Trinity once again to Schleiermacher's appendix? Does it amount to a return to the abstraction of the Enlightenment or to the nervousness of liberalism?

I

We can begin with certain perhaps over-familiar points, staples of most undergraduate teaching in this area.

First, one does not find the doctrine of the Trinity directly in the Bible. Not only does one not find the technical terminology of the Trinity – the language of persons and substance, the term 'Trinity' itself – but one does not find any attempt in some other terminology to isolate and formulate a three-and-one pattern.

Secondly, in the patristic period, the doctrine of the Trinity emerged fundamentally from Christological controversy. It was not the result of any kind of general reflection on what should be said about the inner life of God, or of any kind of general reflection on three-and-oneness, on what ontology of the divine must lie behind various threefold patterns of speech to be found in the New Testament. It was the result, primarily, of the effort to insist upon a high Christology, a strong account of the divinity of Christ, against the never-questioned commitment to the oneness of God.

The starting point for an apophatic approach to the Trinity, then, is that these two very familiar points matter for the way we think about the Trinity. The order of discovery and development are permanently significant. They give a non-reversible direction to the doctrine. Neither the function of the Trinity, nor its meaning, can be detached from the context of its development.[9]

What is at issue here can be brought out by way of contrast with the nature of mathematical reasoning. In mathematics it is possible to begin from the natural

---

9. I am here taking a position very similar to that of John Behr, who suggests at the opening of his *The Nicene faith* that 'the proper order, the taxis of theology must be maintained if it is to retain its proper coherence', and that if this is neglected 'we risk ... taking something other than Christ and his cross as constitutive of the identity of Christianity'. John Behr, *The Nicene Faith* (Crestwood: St Vladimir University Press, 2004), 1–2.

numbers (1, 2, 3, 4 …) and out of these construct other things such as, for instance, the fractions. One might in turn note the impossibility of expressing some things, such as pi or the square root of 2, as a fraction, and move on to a broader notion of real numbers. And from there, if one goes a little way beyond the mathematics familiar to most from secondary school, one might notice certain qualities, certain structural features that the fractions, taken as a whole, exhibit, and that the real numbers, taken as a whole, exhibit, and so introduce notions of fields, rings, groups. And from there, too, although perhaps now only after leaving behind undergraduate mathematics, one might – and mathematicians do – abstract yet again to the still more general concept of a 'category'. Now by the time one gets to thinking about fields and rings (or to some extent even to real numbers) one has left behind one's starting point – one has gone quite a long way, that is to say, from the experience that taught one to understand and begin to use numbers in the first place; and yet, for the competent mathematician, it is possible to operate with just as much ease, confidence, certainty, and clarity as one ever did in discussing numbers. There is no need to look back to one's starting point to guide one in understanding, interpreting, developing one's thought on fields and rings and so on: the abstraction is complete. Once the notion of a field, say, is in place, once it is securely understood, the mathematician can work with it with the same precision and legitimacy as she once might have dealt with fractions, and she can deduce new truths, prove new theorems, without even needing to remember that she first learned of fields from reflecting on fractions. The end point of one process of reasoning and abstraction can become the beginning point for a new one. The mathematician can so to speak kick away the ladder, forget where she came from, and there will be no loss to the truth or usefulness of what she does.

In theology there can also take place a process of abstraction – to describe God as three persons and one substance, for instance, must surely be counted as sitting at a level of abstraction higher than describing God as Father, Son and Spirit, which in turn may well be a rather abstract formulation in relation to the gospels, epistles and so on.[10] But in theology, unlike in mathematics, if one follows the approach I am suggesting, one can never kick away the ladder. One cannot understand the higher level of abstraction in any other way than always in relation to what it is abstracted from – and indeed it has no purpose, no interest, except in relation to what it was first abstracted from. Whereas a mathematician who understands the definition of a field can forget the concrete examples of fields they first encountered, the theologian who is thinking about the meaning of 'Father, Son and Spirit' cannot forget, say, the narratives from which they (or at least from which the church) first learned to speak of God in these terms. Still less can the

---

10. It is possible to notice that one kind of statement, or one piece of language, is at a higher level of abstraction than another, incidentally, without extending that observation into a system. I am not suggesting here, for instance, that everything in Christian theology has an identifiable level of abstraction, nor that there must therefore be an identifiable foundation for the system in an original, pure, pre-conceptual concreteness.

theologian begin to play around with notions of one and three (or one and many), of 'person', of relation, of procession and mission, or perichoresis, while forgetting the contexts and concerns which gave rise to these notions. The doctrine of the Trinity had its origins in the need to ensure the right reading of Scripture, the right kind of thinking about Christ in relation to the Father (and even more to rule out certain *wrong* versions of each) and my proposal is that it is useful and meaningful *only* insofar as it retains its connections to these origins.[11] It cannot break free and become an independent source of ideas and intellectual insights, an independent object of contemplation. Unlike the abstracted object of the mathematician, it cannot become the *beginning* of a new enquiry. Or at least it ought not.

So on such an account theology does not 'progress' in the way that mathematics does, and the doctrine of the Trinity which is the conclusion of a long hermeneutical struggle should not itself be taken as a fresh starting point for a new enquiry. But now we come to the problem. The doctrine of the Trinity, the end point of a long struggle, does have the unfortunate property that it seems to *look* as though it precisely sets a new problem in motion, sets itself at the beginning of a new and different struggle, namely the struggle to work out what on earth it might *mean* to call God three persons and one substance, how this three-and-oneness can be imagined, understood, made sense of. What is the picture of God which will accommodate and make sense of the rather puzzling formula which the fourth century bequeathed us?

The proposal that we might need an apophatic theology of the Trinity, then, is precisely a proposal that we might need to resist embarking on this second struggle – that the best response to this so obvious question ('What then does it *mean* to be in three-in-one?') might in fact be a distinct intellectual asceticism. The doctrine of the Trinity did not arise out of the desire to get a grasp on an elusive concept of God's inner working, and its purpose, meaning and significance ought not be divorced, I am suggesting, from its original function.

II

What about the immanent Trinity? If the doctrine of the Trinity gives us no depiction of God, no insight into God's inner nature, God's inner life, does this mean that the doctrine is confined to the economy, that it guides us in thinking about God in God's dealings with us but says nothing about God in God's self?

A rejection of the immanent Trinity does not in fact, I think, follow from what I am suggesting. One of the purposes of the doctrine of the Trinity is certainly to say something about the immanent Trinity, or perhaps more precisely about the relationship of the economic to the immanent Trinity. The doctrine affirms, for

---

11. This sort of connectedness is not necessarily established by having an elaborate retracing of the Biblical and historical origins of the doctrine in *one* chapter of one's book, and then moving off happily into abstraction in the next.

instance, that the Son is not the Father and the Spirit is not the Father or the Son, which is to say that Sabellianism is wrong, and the threeness that we meet in the economy is not illusory. But to affirm this does not require one to suppose that we have some grasp of what the threeness is *like* in the immanent Trinity. Or again, one thing the doctrine affirms is that there really is only one God, and to say this is to say something about the immanent Trinity, but this does not mean that one has a comprehension of – or even a feeling for – how the oneness of God fits with the threeness. Or again, one thing the doctrine affirms is that God does not *need* to be involved in the economy to be fulfilled or to be who God is, and that God's involvement in the world does not exhaust who God is; the immanent Trinity cannot simply be collapsed into the economic Trinity. But to say this is not to say that one has some *idea* of what the Trinity looks like apart from the economy. So to accept the doctrine of the Trinity is to hold a range of beliefs about the immanent Trinity, about how God really is, but it is not therefore to have any *insight* into the immanent Trinity. We know we must say each of these things about God, but we do not know how to understand them, and most particularly we do not know how to understand them all together. We cannot integrate them and derive a unified picture, a grasp, a 'concept', a vision, or a holistic Trinitarian *understanding* of God.

III

Fair enough, one might say, the Trinity is a mystery, and no one would want to deny this. But surely it is right to want to *contemplate* the mystery. Surely this is precisely the role of theology: if the Trinity is at the heart of Christianity, then how could one deny that gazing upon it, trying to gain some grasp, however dim and imperfect, must be one of theology's highest aims?

There are I think very interesting questions surrounding the place of mystery in theology. Should mystery recede just a little bit if we do our theology well? Is God a little bit less mysterious after doing theology than before? Is the Trinity, to put it another way, less mysterious to the theologian than to the less intellectually sophisticated lay person? At the very least one can say that this is not the only way to think of the function of theology. Perhaps God should be *more* mysterious if we do the theology well, or perhaps to do theology well is simply to become clearer about exactly how mysterious God is.

In any case, it would seem odd to put contemplation of the Trinity, contemplation of God's being three persons in one substance, anywhere very near the heart of the Christian life. Is there not something unsettling in the notion that the church required a number of centuries to arrive at the doctrine, and then a good deal longer to work out how to think about and interpret this doctrine, before it could be in the position to live out a key contemplative dimension of its existence?

To raise doubts about the importance of contemplation of the Trinity, contemplation of the meaning of the doctrine, contemplation of the three-in-oneness itself, is not to raise doubts, it is important to say, about contemplation as such. It is rather to raise a question about what the *focus* of such contemplation should be. The Spirit allows us to contemplate the Father in the Son. This is the fundamental structure of Christian contemplation. If we add that the Spirit who draws us into contemplation, and the Son who reveals the Father, are themselves fully divine, and so God is both three and one, this does not mean that the focus of our contemplation must shift to the very fact of three-in-oneness. The three-in-one is a commentary on the reality, the truth, of what is going on in our contemplation, rather than the object of the contemplation itself. To put it very briefly, if I am raising doubts about whether contemplation *of* the doctrine of the Trinity is really to be conceived of as central to the Christian life, I am not thereby calling into question the place of contemplation *in* the Trinity.

Here it is perhaps also worth raising the issue of what might be taken to be the unduly *negative*, the unduly dry and dismal, take on the apophatic I have been presenting. Have I not, with my simple insistence on what *cannot* be understood, on lack of insight, on questions that cannot be answered, missed the point of true apophaticism? Is it not itself bound up with contemplation? Surely denial and negativity are never employed for their own sake, and it is not a matter of a sheer blank, of simply hitting a wall, in thought and speech about God. Surely something much richer is gestured towards in apophasis: it is a response to excess, to God's superabundant richness. Where is this, one might ask, in the account I have been giving of an apophatic Trinitarianism?

Richness, excess, this overwhelming quality of what we cannot comprehend should, on the view I am developing, be located precisely at the level of our contemplation *in* the Trinity, rather than at the level of contemplation *of* the Trinity. It is enough to acknowledge infinite depths that exceed our grasp in the Father who is contemplated through the Son – we do not need to look for such infinite depths and dazzling darkness in the very notion of three-in-oneness or perichoresis. And it is precisely *because* of the sense of excess and transcendence associated with contemplation in the Trinity that there ought properly to be, on the view I am exploring, a resistance to, a fundamental reticence and reserve, surrounding speculation on the Trinity.

IV

It is beyond the scope of this essay to make the case fully, but I think it can be argued that the Cappadocian approach to the Trinity is in fact fundamentally apophatic – 'fundamentally', in the sense that the apophatic element should be seen not as a peripheral cautionary note to their Trinitarian theology, a bit of reverence and reserve softening an otherwise quite clear and confident proposal, but as something more like the heart of the proposal itself.

Consider, for instance, Gregory of Nazianzus' *Theological Orations*. Should we dismiss it as mere padding, merely a slow start before Gregory gets to his true business, that the first oration is devoted to cautionary remarks about who should engage in theology, and the second is focused on the unknowability of God? And is it merely an extrinsic and irrelevant flourish that the fifth and final oration ends with a discussion of the inadequacy of even the most well-established images of the Trinity (source, spring and river, sun, ray and light)? Or might these things in fact be part of the substance of Gregory's Trinitarian thought?

One might protest that between the apophaticism of the beginning and the caution of the end we have Gregory's substantive discussion of the Son and Spirit in relation to the Father. And what do we learn here? In the third oration we read that the Son is identical to the Father in all things, except that the Father begets and the Son is begotten. And so finally, one might think, one gets to the heart of things, the really Trinitarian bit – how is Gregory going to tell us to think about this Father-Son relationship, this business of begetting and being begotten?[12] The answer is clear, and, to anyone looking for some rich and robust content, surely frustrating:

> How, then, was he begotten? This generation would have been no great thing, if you could have comprehended it who have no real knowledge even of your own generation....[13]

And again

> ... How was he begotten? – I repeat the question in indignation. The begetting of God must be honoured by silence. It is a great thing for you to learn that he was begotten. But the manner of his generation we will not admit that even angels can conceive, much less you. Shall I tell you how it was? It was in a manner known to the Father who begot, and to the Son who was begotten. Anything more than this is hidden by a cloud and escapes your dim sight.[14]

We have to say, at the very least, that an insistence on the unknowability of God is at the beginning, the end, and the very heart of the *Orations*.

But do the Cappadocians not set us off rather more positively in the direction eventually taken up by modern social Trinitarians? Must it not mean something that they ask us to think of the Trinity along the lines of three human beings sharing a single human nature? It is arguable here again that they ought to be read apophatically. Consider Gregory of Nyssa's *Letter to Peter* 'On the difference between *Ousia* and *Hypostasis*', whose explanation begins by appealing to the difference between the common nature shared by many men and their individuality. Striking here is how laborious and in a sense indirect the discussion is. Three men sharing a common humanity are *not* here proposed as an analogy. Nor even is the relation of the individual to the species more generally proposed as an analogy. Rather, the way

---

12. There is of course no notion here that there might be some relationship *in addition to* the relationship of begetting and being begotten.

13. Gregory of Nazianzus, 'Third Theological Oration', in *Library of Christian Classics, Volume III: Christology of the Later Fathers* (London: SCM, 1954), 164.

14. Ibid., 165.

words are used in discussing what is common to many men and what distinguishes them is proposed as a model for the way the *words hypostasis* and *ousia* may be used. Indeed, we do not, in this explanation, find Gregory saying anything directly about the divine *ousia* or *hypostases*, but rather about how we are to speak. Consider, for instance, the rather dry way he sums up his recommendations:

> Whatever your judgment suggests and however it suggests as to the essence of the Father (for it is impossible to superimpose any definite concept upon the immaterial because of our persuasion that it is above every concept), this you will hold for the Son, and likewise for the Holy Spirit. For, the term 'Being Uncreated and Incomprehensible' is one and the same in meaning regarding the Father and the Son and the Holy Spirit.... But, since it is necessary, in the case of the Trinity, to keep a clear distinction [of persons] by means of individualizing marks, we shall not include in the determining individual mark that which is observed to be common....[15]

It would not be plausible to put this laborious indirectness down to clumsiness of style on Gregory's part, given all else that we know of him. If he chose to make his point only in such carefully constructed linguistic ways, then perhaps we ought to presume that he is not setting up, but in fact very specifically avoiding, any analogy.

V

I have argued elsewhere that St Thomas, when engaged in his most technical Trinitarian discussions, is also susceptible of an apophatic interpretation.[16] In questions 27–32 of the Prima Pars of the *Summa Theologiae*, where the investigation turns to processions, relations, and the persons of the Trinity in relation to the divine essence, it is at least possible to read him as laying out, in a very careful and precise way, patterns of affirmation which neither he nor his reader can understand. His intricate and technical treatment of the Trinity, in other words, is not designed to resolve the kind of difficulties that one confronts when one meets Trinitarian language, but to lay these difficulties out as clearly as possible.

But what of Augustine? The question here is a little more complex. The second half of Augustine's *De Trinitate* is markedly different from its first. In Book VIII Augustine makes a transition from the task of exploring the grammar of Trinitarian orthodoxy, exploring what must be said about the Trinity and how various Scriptural texts are to be construed, to something rather different,

---

15. Basil of Caesarea, *The Father of the Church, Volume 13: St Basil's Letters* (Washington, DC: Catholic University of America, 1951), 86–7.
16. In the preceding chapter of this volume.

something he describes as 'discuss[ing] in a more inward manner' the things that had already been treated.¹⁷ What follows is long, rich, complex, and defies simple summary. It might rather crudely be construed as a search for an appropriate model, an appropriate way to understand the Trinity, but there is a strong theme of the progressive training and purifying of the mind in its search, as well as a focus on the mind's activity in the search itself, so that the whole might almost as much be construed as a search for an understanding of the mind in its search for God, as a search for an understanding of the Trinity. Again and again, furthermore, Augustine undermines himself, undercutting anything he seems to achieve in finding analogues to the Trinity, so that the apophatic element here again is quite strong – certainly a great deal stronger than in much of the Trinitarian writings of our day. But there is some sense in which, on the simplest level, the very effort he makes to go *beyond* the first part of his treatise, to go beyond the exploration of how the doctrine works to govern our speech and our exegesis, to go *on* to some sort of search for a way to contemplate, to see, the Trinity – all this sets a kind of precedent, sets in motion a great hunt for the right analogy, the right model. Augustine's procedure, complex and elusive though it is, seems to give some comfort to the notion that once one has arrived at the doctrine of the Trinity, at the end of a long struggle, one can then safely use it as the *starting point* for a new investigation, and this is precisely what I am suggesting must be resisted.¹⁸

VI

A neighbor once offered the following analysis of the difference between our faiths: 'We Muslims believe in one God, but you Christians believe in God and Jesus.' One response to this comment might have been to say that my neighbour was just demonstrating a theological naivety: she failed to understand that Christians worship one God because she lacked any grasp of a Trinitarian

---

17. Augustine, *The Trinity*, trans. Edmund Hill, O.P. (New York: New York City Press, 1991), 242.
18. Note that what I am proposing as the salient difference between Augustine and the Cappadocians is *not*, as has too often been proposed in recent systematic theology, that Augustine begins with the oneness of the divine substance and the Cappadocians with the threeness of the Persons. The important difference is rather that Augustine takes the conclusions of the Trinitarian debate as the beginning of a new search in a way that is foreign to the Cappadocians. This conception of the difference is close to that of John Behr, who, after sketching what he thinks is wrong with much modern Trinitarian theology, suggests that Augustine seems to have been the first to move in the false direction, and that this had something to do with his having 'inherited the results of the fourth-century debates rather than living through them' (*The Mystery of Christ: Life in Death* (Crestwood: St Vladimir's Seminary Press, 2006), 174).

conception of God. My own view, however, is that Christians, too, lack any grasp of a Trinitarian conception of God. We learn to worship the Father through the Son in the Spirit, but we do not have some very sophisticated *idea* with which to put all this together, with which to envisage or explain or understand that the three are one, with which to put to rest on a conceptual level worries about the coherence of a claim to monotheism. This is why attention to the doctrine of the Trinity should serve to intensify rather than diminish our sense of God's unknowness: believing in the Trinity, we are not so much in possession of a more fully textured concept of God than a mere Enlightenment deist has, but in fact much less than any deist in possession of any sort of manageable concept of God at all.

By this point it should be clear that while Trinitarian robustness may be a reaction against theological liberalism, the Trinitarian apophaticism I am sketching should not be seen as a mere return to it, at least not if one understands one of the central concerns of liberalism as the need to make sense of Christian belief for the surrounding culture: I am suggesting that in fact Christians are, and ought to be, at a loss in making sense of their belief at all. To put it another way, robust Trinitarianism is concerned to be confident, *unapologetic* in its Christian specificity – but on slightly closer inspection the claim to have a distinctive, particular vision of God at the heart of one's thought is actually very well suited to a kind of apologetics, since one has something new, something special and concrete, to present in the marketplace of ideas. Trinitarian apophaticism is arguably more counter-cultural.

VII

But why, one might ask, dwell so heavily on the negative – on all that is *not* known, on all that is *not* within our grasp? Many theologians with similar instincts about the doctrine of the Trinity would in fact present them quite differently – they might gently steer their readers and listeners away from certain kinds of speculative questions, steer them towards the role of the Trinity in shaping exegesis, prayer, liturgy, the Christian narrative. Why not, after all, attend to what the doctrine *does* do for us, rather than what it does not?

Partly my opting for the latter is a response to the situation with which I began – to the prevalence in our time of a certain sort of self-conscious Trinitarian assertiveness. To deal with the problems that this sometimes poses it is not enough to go about things slightly differently, to lay the focus elsewhere. Because of the very *robustness* of the robust Trinitarians, theirs are the voices that will tend to be heard. If someone were to set out in our contemporary theological climate to learn about the Trinity, in other words, most likely it is some form of robust Trinitarianism they would hit upon, not just because there are in fact so many robust Trinitarians, but because these are the ones speaking most clearly, confidently, and distinctly about the Trinity.

There is, then, a danger with the doctrine of the Trinity, a danger particularly strong in our time,[19] a danger which exists both in relation to God and in relation to our fellow human beings. In relation to God, there is the possibility of idolatry, and in relation to our neighbours, of a kind of theological hubris, a theological one-up-man-ship. And the best protection, on both fronts, is as much clarity as we can muster about what we do not know.

---

19. The danger is particularly strong in our time, but not *unique* to our time, in my view. The doctrine of the Trinity has always had a potentially misleading surface grammar, since it so easily *looks* as though it offers a technical and difficult description of God, if only we can be clever enough to grasp it.

Chapter 4

THE TRINITY AND POLITICS

AN APOPHATIC APPROACH

'The Trinity is our social programme'. So Miroslav Volf entitled a 1998 paper in *Modern Theology*.[1] Volf, who was a student of Jurgen Moltmann, finds a place on most people's list of social trinitarians; indeed he works with a breadth and sophistication which make it plausible to look to him as one of the most substantial and serious proponents of the approach.

Volf's use of this phrase as a title is a little more complex than it might first seem. 'The Trinity is our Social Programme' is a quotation from the nineteenth century Russian thinker Nicholas Fedorov (originally Nikolai Fyodorovich Fyodorov, but Volf uses an Anglicised version of the name), and nearly the first thing Volf does in the essay is to distance himself from Fedorov: 'No arguments need to be wasted on showing that Fedorov's proposal is specious and his vision chimerical'.[2] These are surprisingly strong words, but not so surprising when one learns that the Russian thinker proposed that not only immortal life but also the resurrection of the dead were to be achieved through scientific progress. Whatever his excesses, however, he was, according to Volf, onto something. Even if Fedorov's own social programme was manifestly mistaken, and even if his slogan needs to be hedged around and used with great care, still Volf does in fact make the slogan his own.

And one can see why he would want to. To say the 'the Trinity is our social programme' is to capture, in a pithy and powerful way, a significant part of the appeal of social trinitarianism. The attractiveness of social models of the Trinity has not just been that they make the obscure clear, but even more that they make what had seemed arcane relevant and practical: the doctrine of the Trinity is not a point of difficulty deep in the technical bowels of theology, but something useful, applicable, motivating – it provides us with a social programme. Right at the heart and centre of the Christian faith, we can say, is something with deep and wide practical application.

---

1. Miraslov Volf, *Modern Theology* 14, no. 3 (1998): 403–23. The full title is '"The Trinity is Our Social Program": The doctrine of the Trinity and the shape of Social Engagement'.
2. Ibid., 403.

Social trinitarianism has been criticized on a number of fronts, and it has been criticized, it seems to me, to great effect.[3] But I am not persuaded that all of these attacks have made it go away. If one wants to dislodge an approach which has gained a wide grip on the theological imagination of a generation, criticism alone may not be enough: a more positive and constructive alternative is needed. In addition, it is important to get some sense of the appeal of social trinitarianism, to understand its power. And I think much of this power is captured precisely in the phrase 'The Trinity is our Social Programme'.

My own view is that the proper alternative to the promotion of a social model of the Trinity is not the promotion of some *other* model of the Trinity – with perhaps even more impressive social and political consequences – but rather a certain asceticism as regards models, deriving from a shift in our understanding of what the proper task of theology with regard to the Trinity is. The Christian life is lived *in the midst* of the Trinity, drawn by the Spirit into the movement of the Son towards the Father, and this is also where Christian thought is most fundamentally situated. We do not find ourselves in a position, then, I think, to view the Trinity as though from a distance and to develop an intellectually satisfying model of it.

I will call this an apophatic trinitarianism, and what I want to explore in this essay is where such a brand of trinitarianism stands in relation to politics, in relation to having, to use Volf's language, a social programme. If one's approach to the Trinity is all about *mystery*, about what we cannot know and what we do not understand and what we cannot form a satisfactory grasp of, is it bound to lack the appeal and the relevance of the social trinitarians and their social programmes? Will we have to say that theology, or at least Trinitarian theology, caught up with policing the boundaries of its own unknowing, can have no relevance to political struggle and political reform? Will an apophatic trinitarianism be part of an inward looking, politically neutral, perhaps even escapist approach to theology? Must it encourage the church into passivity and disengagement, and therefore, by default, an implicit support of the status quo? These are the questions I hope to explore in this paper.

I will begin, however, with a little more on Volf, because he offers an unusually careful and qualified exploration of the practical consequences of the doctrine of the Trinity, conceived according to a social model.

---

3. The historical work of Michel René Barnes, Lewis Ayres and others has been significant here. Stephen Holmes' recent *The Holy Trinity: Understanding God's Life* (Milton Keynes: Paternoster, 2012) serves both as a historical introduction to the doctrine and a decisive critique of claims by social trinitarians to be retrieving the tradition. From a more conceptual angle, Kathryn Tanner's 'Trinity' chapter in Peter Scott and William T. Cavanaugh (eds), *Blackwell Companion to Political Theology* (Oxford: Blackwell, 2003) develops a forceful criticism of social trinitarianism, at least insofar as it is put to work for practical purposes. It might be argued that the kind of social trinitarianism discussed by analytic theologians is largely untouched by these critiques. Historical rootedness – a thick connection to tradition – has so far carried less weight in this school of thought, and the concern for relevance and practical import is less marked.

4. The Trinity and Politics

As we have seen, nearly the first thing Volf does in his paper is to distance himself from the thinker from whom he derives its title. In fact he locates his own position by setting up a contrast between Nicholas Fedorov on the one hand and Ted Peters on the other. Each is taken to represent an extreme position: Fedorov attempts 'to imitate the Triune God in blatant disregard for the fact that we are not God';[4] Peters insists absolutely on creaturely *difference* from God. But we do not have to accept these as the only alternatives: 'between "copying God in all respects" (so seemingly Fedorov) and "not copying God at all" (so seemingly Peters) lies the wide open space of human responsibility which consists in "copying God in *some* respects"'.[5] We need neither say that the Trinity is in every regard and entirely a model for human community, nor rule this out altogether: the real question, according to Volf, is 'in which respects and to what extent [the Trinity should serve as a model for human community]'.[6]

Human community *should* be modelled on the Trinity, then, but, a little more concretely, we should be aware of two kinds of limit to this modelling. There is an intrinsic limitation deriving from our creatureliness, which means that Trinitarian concepts can only *analogously* be applied to human community; and there is a contingent limitation deriving from the fallen and historical character of our current lives.[7]

Volf's social trinitarianism is marked, in fact, by multiple layers of caution and qualification. We have seen two so far: first, his distancing himself from his own slogan, or at least from the unfettered enthusiasm he sees for it in Fedorov; and second, his insistence on the limits of the way the Trinity can model human community. In a third stage Volf presents us with a methodological consequence from this limitation: Trinitarian theology must work from below as well as from above. It is not a one-way matter of reading off from the Triune God a pattern of human community: the 'conceptual construction of correspondences', he writes, 'must go back and forth on a two-way street', taking into account our created and sinful nature as well as the Trinity as an ideal model.[8] So we cannot pretend to read off a social programme *directly* from the Trinity: we have to acknowledge that the process is more complicated than that.

Volf introduces two further qualifications. The first is that he actually prefers 'social vision' to Fedorov's 'social programme'. This is because the doctrine of the

---

4. Volf, *Modern Theology*, 404–5.
5. Ibid., 405.
6. Ibid.
7. Volf does not, in this essay at least, distinguish particularly carefully between temporality and sin, between, that is to say, being fallen and being historical.
8. 'By describing God in whose image human beings are created and redeemed, the doctrine of the Trinity names the reality which human communities *ought* to image. By describing human beings as distinct from God, the doctrines of creation and of sin inform the way in which human communities *can* image the Triune God, now in history and then in eternity'(405–6).

Trinity, 'does not constitute ... a plan or system of action' but gives us 'the contours of the ultimate normative end toward which all social programs should strive'.[9] He acknowledges that 'the road from the doctrine of the Trinity to proposals about global or national social arrangements is long, torturous, and fraught with danger', and so keeps his focus on 'the character of social agents and their relations' rather than 'the issue of social structures'[10] – the focus, in other words, is to be on how to think of people in relation to one another rather than how to think of, say, neo-liberalism or socialism or globalization.

The final qualification arises from Volf's commitment to working with *both* immanent *and* economic Trinities, and indeed to focusing more heavily on the economic, 'build[ing] mainly on the narrative of the Triune God's engagement with the world'.[11] If proposals about the nature of human community drawn from reflection on the immanent Trinity are not somehow related to or situated within a discussion of the 'narrative of divine self-donation', i.e. the economic Trinity, he suggests, they will be 'underdetermined', 'too formal', 'overly diffuse generalities', even 'theologically empty'.[12]

Volf's own constructive proposals, then, are offered in two main sections, the first drawing from reflections on the immanent Trinity, and the second, as he presents it at least, rooted in the economic Trinity. In fact, however, it is really only in the first of these sections that Volf sounds like a social trinitarian. The focus of the second section is not on relations within the Trinity – whether immanent or economic – but on God's relation to the fallen, sinful world and what we should learn from this for *our* relations to the world. This part of the essay might in fact more easily be understood if it were entitled 'the cross is our social programme'. This is not to say that Volf here becomes somehow *un*trinitarian. What he sets out in this part of his essay is a perfectly reasonable example of Christian theology, and so it naturally has a trinitarian dimension. But one can no longer really say that he is principally focused on the *doctrine* of the Trinity at this stage.

So let us turn to the first of the sections, which starts from the immanent Trinity. Here, after briefly affirming allegiance to an egalitarian rather than a hierarchical understanding of the Trinity, Volf sets out to develop an understanding of identity from the concept of perichoresis. Perichoresis teaches us that the divine persons are 'personally interior to one another', but that their 'interpenetration presupposes their distinctions'.[13] What this means for identity is exemplified by Jesus' capacity to say, in the Gospel of John, 'my teaching is not mine but his who sent me' (7.16). The interplay of the 'my' and 'not mine' here suggest the two corresponding principles, that 'identity is not self-enclosed' and that 'identity is non-reducible'.[14]

9. Ibid., 406.
10. Ibid.
11. Ibid., 407.
12. Ibid., 412.
13. Ibid., 409.
14. Ibid., 410.

It is interesting to consider the detail with which Volf expands on these principles. In relation to identity as 'not self-enclosed', he writes of the boundaries of the self as 'porous and shifting', of the self as 'in a state of flux stemming from "incursions" of the other into the self and of the self into the other'; and he speaks of how the self is shaped in various ways by the other, including 'by re-examining itself when the other closes his or her doors and challenging the other by knocking at the doors'.[15] In relation to the non-reducibility of identity, he writes about 'the need for boundary maintenance – a certain kind of assertion of the self in the presence of the other...'. He also writes that 'Since negotiation of identities is always conflictual, non-assertiveness of the self in the presence of the other puts the self in danger either of dissolving into the other or being smothered by the other'. And so 'to ward off [the] dangers [of obliteration of the self], we must attend to the boundaries of identities by enforcing rules that protect identities and by providing environments that nurture them'.[16]

Volf's presentation of the self in relation to the other is, it seems to me, appealing. It can be a useful way to think about one's own sense of self, for instance, as it slips and slithers around in relation to interactions with spouse, friends, colleagues, parents, children, even people one meets at a conference. It's helpful both to face the reality of the instability of one's own sense of self, the way my sense of who I am is very much dependent on day to day reactions from others that I meet. And it is helpful to remember that one is not *just* these incursions, that I need to, and that I do, assert and defend myself at times. It is commendable, furthermore, that Volf notices the tension between his two principles, and acknowledges that he has no algorithm to specify how to handle this tension: 'How does one know' he asks 'when to close the boundaries of the self in order to stabilize one's identity and when to open them in order to enrich it?' His answer is that no answer can be given in advance, that everything depends on the particular cases, that one must 'seek supple wisdom rather than stable rules' (411).

It may be that the patterns of thought Volf lays out can also be useful in thinking through various kinds of group identity – this at least ought to be expected from the way he introduces the theme of identity itself into the article, pointing as he does to the importance of identity *politics* in our time. Perhaps something about being a woman over against men, or being straight and encountering gay people, is captured by this dialectic of the incursion of the other into the self and the need for boundary maintenance – although one might wonder whether the balanced symmetry of his language of self and other is truly helpful in some of these cases.

Nevertheless, on the whole his supple and evocative language of self and other is appealing and to a large extent plausible. What is not so plausible is that it is supposed to be derived from an understanding of the immanent Trinity. Can one really get from the concept of perichoresis and the biblical portrayal of Jesus in relation to Father and Spirit, to this general understanding of the self's identity?

15. Ibid.
16. Ibid.

If the sheer quantity and detail of what Volf can find to derive from perichoresis does not give pause, then some of his phrases should: in what sense can we say that from the Trinitarian perichoresis we learn of identity as a matter of *flux*, of *shifting* boundaries, of *incursions* of self into other, of the proper response to the other 'closing doors', of the danger of dissolving or being smothered by the other? All the overtones contained in this language of change, of threat and of loss are simply antithetical to the way trinitarian relations have traditionally been understood.

But perhaps this is just an expression of Volf's 'two-way street', of his conviction that in developing correspondences between trinity and human sociality one needs to work from below as well as above, from the facts of our creatureliness, historicity and sinfulness as well as from the ideal provided by the Triune God? Perhaps. It's striking, however, that for all the methodological self-consciousness which is manifest in other parts of the essay, Volf here, in the discussion of the significance of perichoresis for understandings of identity, gives no hint or signal that he is beginning to introduce considerations drawn from finitude and sin into his discussion of the meaning for identity of perichoresis. The transition is unmarked. And on the other hand it's also striking that everything which in fact gives this discussion of identity, of the self/other relation, its richness, plausibility and interest, is introduced precisely when considerations drawn from limitation, historicity and fallenness quietly find their way into the discussion – precisely when Volf leaves behind anything that could possibly apply to or be derived from the Trinity.[17]

I have spent some effort exploring Volf's essay because it is instructive to examine a social trinitarian who proceeds – on the whole – with such care, with such an alertness to the dangers and possible difficulties of the project. In fact, one might ask why, given this awareness, Volf continues at all to espouse a kind of social trinitarianism? If he realizes the limitations of modelling creaturely, historical and sinful human relations on eternal, perfect, divine relations; if he realizes the dangers of abstraction and theological emptiness that loom over general deductions about human relations deriving from the inner-trinitarian life; if he thinks that the primary weight must be given to the *narrative* of the divine engagement with the world – why then does he not simply abandon the project of gaining political wisdom from the examination of inner-divine relations?

Is the answer simply biographical? Is it that, while Volf is alert to the difficulties involved in this kind of project, he finds himself already too enmeshed in it, given his history of working in an ecumenical context on communion ecclesiologies, and given that he is a student of Moltmann? Perhaps. Certainly none of the indications Volf gives in the paper itself for why we must 'copy God to some extent' could be considered inescapable arguments pushing us towards a social trinitarian project: he mentions that we are made in the image of God (something which can be, and has been, taken in all kinds of ways), that we are made for communion with the

---

17. Kathryn Tanner succinctly suggests that the danger of a strategy like Volf's is that 'the Trinity fails to do any work'. Ibid., 327.

Trinity and that Jesus commands his disciples to 'be perfect ... as your heavenly Father is perfect'.[18]

Perhaps, then, we could look for an explanation of Volf's espousal of social trinitarianism simply in intellectual biography, but as I've suggested I think it is also important to be aware of the appeal, of the attraction, in social trinitarianism. And this is very much present, in spite of all the qualifications, in Volf's paper. There are two dimensions to this appeal. One is what I have already indicated: the very ability to announce 'the Trinity is our social programme' (or even 'social vision') is somehow deeply pleasing. It is satisfying because it implies that theology really does have something *special* to contribute, something definite and distinctive and practical to show for all its labours. 'The Trinity is our Social programme' suggests, on the one hand, that theology has something distinctive to say as against mere secular thought,[19] its own unique trove of ideas to source social and political theory. And it also carries the suggestion – maybe less consciously – that the theologian has something distinctive to say by contrast with ordinary Christians. After all, most believers who haven't been exposed to formal theological study might think to look for their guidance on social vision from the ten commandments, the prophets, proverbs, the sayings of Jesus, their understanding of the love of God and of the nature of Christian discipleship, even natural law and their own intuitions, but they wouldn't think to look, I suppose, to the nature of inner-Trinitarian relations. So if they enrol on courses of systematic and practical theology, they'll have something new to take home – they'll have gained something quite concrete. We theologians can justify our salaries.

The second dimension of the appeal has to do with the nature of some of the technical Trinitarian concepts themselves and the kinds of reflection to which they lend themselves. Kathryn Tanner, in a chapter on the Trinity in the *Blackwell Companion to Political Theology*, suggests that the Trinitarian concepts just happen to be quite well adapted to the kinds of political questions that currently preoccupy us and this explains why the Trinity is in recent years such a popular site of political theology.[20] This is right, I think, but not the whole story. There is also the enticement of having such an elusive, even paradoxical concept to work with: something like perichoresis, a notion that we don't really understand, has, precisely *because* it is paradoxical, elusive, and not really understood, a distinct flexibility. It is not hard to weave into it our best insights about the complexities of human identity, relationship, community. It lends itself, one could say, to

---

18. Volf, *Modern Theology*, 404. It is rather striking that Volf doesn't seem to notice the *particularities* of this injunction to copy – he simply substitutes '*God*' for '*Father*' in glossing the Gospel text, and then weaves the result into his general discussion of modelling ourselves on the *Trinity*.

19. Also, of course, as against Jewish and Muslim thought. For most social Trinitarians, however, Christian self-assertion over against Jewish and Muslim thought is closer to an unintended consequence than a deliberate goal.

20. Tanner, 'Trinity', 319–20.

conceptual play. Nearly *any* understanding I hold of self and other, individual and group, person and community, could be spun as perichoretic.

It is at this point, of course, that the attractiveness of social trinitarianism is also closely bound up with what can be most problematic in it. For all his care, caution and qualifications, when Volf begins to reflect on perichoresis, he seems to become enthralled with the intellectual possibilities of the concept, with the richness of thought it allows him to discover in Trinitarian theology. Careful distinctions among the sources of our knowledge and cautious attention to the ways in which God is *not* like us disappear under the force of the speculative and dialectical attractions of the notion of perichoresis. Or to put it another way, the project of discovering in Trinitarian relations the way we humans should relate seems able to bear interesting fruit precisely at that moment when the caution, the attentiveness to limits, slips away.

Volf offers what looks at first like a sober, restrained form of social Trinitarianism, one which, rather than unthinkingly assuming that the Trinity should serve as a model for human community, will instead carefully consider 'in which respects and to what extent' it should do so. But a closer look at Volf's work suggests, I think, that what we in fact need is not a restrained and careful version of this business of finding in the Trinity a model for human community, but a different approach to Trinitarian theology altogether.

As suggested above, the different approach need not involve locating some key concept which can replace community, some *alternative* master idea that we can suppose to be at the heart of the doctrine of the Trinity. I think it is perfectly possible to say that the proper stance of Christian theology in face of the doctrine of the Trinity is non-comprehension, not knowing, not being in possession of a unifying grasp, idea, or model. It is perfectly possible to say, that is, that the doctrine of the Trinity should intensify rather than diminish our sense of the unknowability of God, that it presents us with a pattern which we cannot understand, rather than with a specific set of insights and concepts on which we can draw.[21] And if this is the case, then rather than searching for the right model for understanding the Trinity, we should perhaps be seeking to resist our own penchant for making models.

'What then is the point of the Trinity?' one might ask. If it so thoroughly defeats us intellectually, in what sense can it make any difference to affirm faith in the doctrine of the Trinity – in what sense can it be significant for Christianity? Can something which so radically transcends our understanding have anything to do with us?

One way to answer this question is to consider that perhaps we cannot understand the Trinity, the three-in-oneness of God, not because it is so far from us, but because it is so near. We are caught up in the Trinity. The Christian life is a life of being brought into the Trinity – not a contemplation from a distance, nor a mimicry at a distance, but a genuine incorporation, a being taken up by the Spirit

---

21. These ideas are developed more fully in Chapter 3.

into the movement of the Son from and to the Father.[22] Perhaps we are too much in the midst of the Trinity, too close, too involved, in other words, to be able to form an overarching conceptualization.

From this perspective, in fact, the business of attempting to construct models of the Trinity can come under suspicion of idolatry. Is there not something problematic in imagining that I can lay aside my actual position in relation to Father, Son, and Holy Spirit in order to play around with ideas of triangles or three leaf clovers or psychological or social models and gain some sort of a grasp on a concept of the Trinity, as though Father, Son and Spirit can become a kind of intellectual object over which I dispose? Maybe the language of idolatry is too inflammatory. But at least it seems that one can become involved in a kind of intellectual dabbling, a game of intellectual construction, that has little intrinsic link to the life of faith.

But of course, if one has no model of the Trinity, then one has no model which one can apply to society, whether in the wholehearted and uninhibited manner of some social trinitarians or in the more cautious and selective manner of Volf. And so one seems to have cut off the possibility of a politically relevant theology of the Trinity.

One response to this objection might be simply to grant that not every element in Christian theology need have equally immediate practical relevance. We could perhaps borrow an image from the philosopher Willard van Orman Quine, and think of Christian belief on analogy with a spider's web, where, though everything is interconnected, only some parts come into contact with the realm of the practical, of the ethical, of politics.[23] Perhaps we could say, then, that the doctrine of the Trinity plays its role somewhere in the interior of the web. It is necessary to the whole; it is linked to other beliefs in various ways, supporting them and being supported by them. But it is not really close to the edge where the action takes

---

22. My language of incorporation here is not of course distinctive in contemporary theology. Similarities to Kathryn Tanner's position are discussed in note 25 below. Cf. also Sarah Coakley's trinitarian writings – most recently *God, Sexuality and the Self* (Cambridge: Cambridge University Press, 2013) – for a sustained reflection on the importance of our incorporation into the Trinity for theology. I am not inclined to give the absolutely decisive place in Trinitarian theology to either sexuality or 'deep' contemplative prayer that Coakley does, although I think that each of them can and should be given a Trinitarian framing, and that one can learn well from Coakley how to do this.

23. This is, it should be said, a fairly free adaptation of Quine's image. It is not only that the web here becomes an image for the structure of Christian belief rather than scientific thought, but that what is imagined to be at the web's *edge* is practice, whereas for Quine it is (empirically construed) experience. For a related use of Quine's web metaphor, cf. Paul Murray's 'Discerning the Dynamics of Doctrinal Development' in Simon Oliver, Karen Kilby and Tom O'Loughlin, eds, *Faithful Reading: New Essays in Theology in Honour of Fergus Kerr* (London: Continuum, 2012).

place, and so cannot be burdened with the expectation of giving rise directly to social, ethical, or political wisdom.

But a problem with this approach is that it would involve imagining the doctrine of the Trinity as a particular *fragment* of the totality of Christian belief, a localized node, a delimitable bit, and this is not quite right. It is better to think of the entire pattern of Christian belief as Trinitarian, than to suppose that it contains one particular element which is the Trinity. If we are to use something like Quine's metaphor, the Trinity is better imagined as something about the structure of the whole web, and the quality of each of its strands, than as a particular point in the web.

Still, the notion that not every element of Christian theology needs to come into *direct* contact with our thinking about social programmes and politics seems to me to have a certain plausibility, and I would think that some likely candidates for this kind of non-front line role are the technical concepts that have emerged *within* Trinitarian theology – concepts such as persons, relations, processions and perichoresis. We need these – or similar – concepts. They have a function, helping to hold patterns of belief in place and to articulate in brief form the rejection of heresies. But we should not put them under pressure to further justify their existence by supplying direct dollops of social or political wisdom. They are, we might say, back room workers who should be allowed to remain in their back rooms. This is something that Barth and Rahner implicitly recognized when each, in coming up with a replacement term for 'Persons', gave us what are, from a rhetorical point of view, utterly uninspiring suggestions ('modes of subsistence', 'ways of being').

So we do not have, on my view, a model of the Trinity that can serve as a model for society, nor should we look to highly specific concepts that have emerged in the tradition to provide us with tidy packets of practical or political insight. But I would like to propose that there are nevertheless two dimensions in which an apophatic trinitarianism has potential political significance. The two dimensions correspond to the two aspects of the approach I have been recommending: a resistance to the project of constructing trinitarian models on the one hand, and an emphasis on our incorporation into the Trinity on the other.

First of all, then, what is the political significance of resistance to the construction of models? If one cultivates an awareness of the ungraspability of God, the impossibility of finding an image or model or integrating vision of the Trinity – if one cultivates the capacity to live with questions to which we have no answers – might this be correlated, not with a particular political commitment to one form of socio-economic system or another, to one social vision or another, but with a resistance to an absolute confidence in any system, and social vision? Economic and political regimes do, after all, tend to take on a sacred aura, to demand unconditional commitment, to imagine themselves as the end and goal of history. If Christians are schooled, by the doctrine of the Trinity as well as in other ways, to know that God is not within our grasp, that we possess no concept or overarching understanding of that which is highest, then we are in a sense schooled into suspicion of systems that present themselves with a kind of sacred, all-encompassing necessity. Might we not imagine that an important political contribution of Christian thinking about God be, then, not that it provides us with something like a shortcut to formulating a distinct alternative of our own, but that it helps call in question, helps relativize, all such systems we might find ourselves enticed by? Might there not be a correspondence, in other words, between a resistance to idolatry in relation to God, and a resistance to ideology in relation to political systems?[24]

Let me now turn to the second side of what I take to be the political potential of the approach that I am advocating. The unknowability of the Trinity, I've suggested, need not just be conceived as the result of some sort of unfathomable distance between us and God, but also as a result of our involvement in the Trinity, its closeness to us, our incorporation into it. Now, if the whole of the Christian life can be thought of in terms of incorporation into the Trinity, then it follows that social and political dimensions of Christian life also have this quality. That is to say, every dimension of our life in community, with others, in society, in politics, is somehow also connected to our life lived towards the Father, with the Son, in the Spirit.[25]

That this formula sounds rather general and not very informative should not come as a surprise. I've suggested the Trinity is not best thought of as a localized element within the structure of Christian thought, one little bit from which to get some nice ideas, but as structuring and characterising the whole. So if one talks about its political significance in general terms one has to expect to say something quite formal. Furthermore, concepts of 'the social' or 'the political' are themselves very general and can be taken in many ways.

To make the discussion a little more concrete, it may be useful to focus on a particular dimension of political existence, and a particular context, and try to sketch at least one *example* of what an incorporative, rather than a mimetic,

---

24. The cautious phrasing here is deliberate. Kathryn Tanner has argued persuasively in *The Politics of God* that a variety of political programmes can be correlated with any one way of believing in God, and I think the point also holds in the apophatic case. I am suggesting here then a possible political correlate of an apophatic emphasis, but not claiming that it is the *only* possible one.

25. My position here is close to the one set out by Tanner in the *Blackwell Companion to Political Theology*. She suggests that participation in the Trinity, rather than modelling ourselves on it, is the key to thinking about its significance for politics: 'Humans do not attain the heights of trinitarian relations by reproducing them, but by being incorporated into them as the very creatures they are' (329). Two differences between what are structurally similar positions are worth mentioning. First, Tanner lays less emphasis on unknowing than I have. Secondly, she fills out the notion of 'incorporation into the Trinity' with a slightly different, and more christocentric, emphasis than I will do below. While I am not inclined to disagree with anything she proposes, I fear that her account is open to being taken as a *denial* of political significance to the doctrine of the Trinity: everything of political import seems to lie in Christology alone.

trinitarian political orientation might look like. As the context, let me take the non-poor parts of the relatively rich world, a context that includes myself and, it is likely, a considerable portion of my readers. And as a particular dimension of 'the political', let me take the question of Christian political engagement considered in the limited sense of the struggle for justice.

I will presume in what follows that the Christian commitment does in fact include a commitment to work, as individuals and communities, for justice and for the alleviation of suffering in the situations in which Christians find themselves. And I will presume that this may involve working for structural change to one degree or another. Neither of these views are universally held among Christians, but on the other hand neither of them can be thought of as representing a particularly eccentric or minority perspective.

Now it might seem that I have already begun to paint myself into a corner. I am using words like 'society' and 'justice', suggesting that I need to know what these things are, and I have talked about the possibility of working for structural change, suggesting that I need to understand how society is and ought to be structured, and yet earlier I suggested that the doctrine of the Trinity rather than giving us a social or political vision, causes us to relativize, to call into question, to distance ourselves from, all the available possibilities. But in fact I want to suggest that this is not such a problem. Even in the absence of a comprehensive socio-political ideology, derived from the Trinity or anywhere else, it is perfectly possible to look around and see that there are many things that are not as they ought to be, that there are features of the world around us crying out for change, and it is possible to do something about them.

On my reading of our context, in fact, the biggest impediment to proper political engagement is not the lack of a comprehensive analysis of social reality, or the lack of a utopian vision of the ideal society and politics towards which we ought to move; it is rather a lack of a willingness to really look around us and take what we see into account.[26] Many of us in this context, the non-poor in the rich world, live with a knowledge that we mostly want to suppress, a knowledge that the circles of comfort and stability in which we move do not reflect to us the true story of the world. To look at the conditions of life and the suffering of those in absolute poverty, unable to feed and educated their children properly, or at the suffering of those who are mentally ill, or of those who are trafficked, or those caught in the asylum system of a country like Britain, or the criminal justice system of a country like America, is something that we who live in comfort very often simply do not want to do. This brokenness and monumental injustice and suffering is part of the reality of the world, but it is hard to look at it. What Jon Sobrino calls 'honesty with

---

26. I sketched a similar reading of our context, and a similar reflection on the doctrine of the Trinity in relation to this context, in 'Trinity, Tradition and Politics', in Christoph Chalamet and Mark Vial (eds), *Recent Developments in Trinitarian Theology: An International Symposium* (Minneapolis: Fortress Press, 2014).

the real' is not easy.[27] It is a little too disturbing. We sense that it will unsettle us, call us into question, that to look and to keep looking and act in a way that is in keeping with what we see might destabilize our existence.

Now, it would be foolish to suggest that political engagement is a theory-free zone, requiring neither social analysis nor a vision of human flourishing. Clearly it requires elements of both, and the imperfections and limitations in one's analysis and one's vision will have practical consequences. But, first of all, the absolutely *generalized* kinds of vision one might hope to derive from just the right concept of the Trinity are not the intellectual tools most required in this kind of political engagement. And secondly, while it is true that incomplete or imperfect sociopolitical analysis will hinder efforts to work for justice and alleviate suffering, it seems to me that what *most significantly* inhibits proper political engagement, the *key* sticking point, is not a lack of analysis but a lack of this honesty with or fidelity to the real, a lack in our willingness to look at and really take seriously the world around us. Indeed I think that very often we do not fail to engage because we lack the right analysis, but we lack the analysis because we are not willing to engage.

This point is worth illustrating. Suppose that I hear a piece on the radio about the plight of trafficked women in Britain. I am, perhaps, unsettled and troubled to think of such misery and oppression going on near where I live. What should I do about it? I don't know. I don't really understand what global forces of capitalism and crime contribute to trafficking, and I don't know what role faulty legislation or policing play, or what reform might be necessary, or where if anywhere pressure could be applied to bring it about, or what organizations ought to be supported in working on this problem. So I go about my daily tasks, and I listen to other items on the radio. But whatever I tell myself in this situation, my ignorance is not really what blocks me from engagement – it is much more truly understood as the result of disengagement. I don't look away and do nothing, then, because of a lack of understanding of what to do – even if that is how it seems – but I lack an understanding of what to do because I have opted to look away and do nothing.

But even if this is the case, what does it have to do with the Trinity, one might ask? Well, it is not too hard to imagine that it has something to do with Jesus. Whatever temptation we might have to tell ourselves that the way to relate to God is by rising directly above the sufferings and injustices and particularities of this world, putting them out of mind – any such temptation is thwarted by the pattern of Jesus' life, incarnate and engaged as it is in a particular political moment, responsive to the injustices and sufferings of a distinct time and place. Perhaps not everyone would agree with this reading of the Gospels, but again it is at least not an eccentric or minority reading.

---

27. Sobrino introduces this concept, together with 'fidelity to the real', in his article 'Spirituality and the Following of Jesus', in Ignacio Ellacuria and Jon Sobrino (eds), *Mysterium Liberationis: Fundamental Concepts of Liberation Theology* (Maryknoll: Orbis, 1993).

We may not be able to abstract from the life and teaching of Jesus a tidy political programme and then apply it at will in any other time and place, but if Jesus is understood as the Word of God spoken into creation, then this speaking, it seems, takes place in the midst of things, in the midst of the messy, suffering, conflicted reality that is the world – this is how and where we have to listen for God. And if Jesus is understood as the fundamental pattern of human response to God, then this response, too, takes place in the midst of things, through and not apart from the engagement with the messy, suffering, conflicted reality that is the world.

This focus on the Word Incarnate, considered on its own, however, leaves us with two problems. First, if there is no concrete programme to be transferred from his time to ours, how do we know in *particular* what to do? And there is the deeper problem on which I have already dwelt, the danger that we don't necessarily *want* to know, don't want to be disturbed and destabilized from a comfortable, secure existence. Where can we find the strength, the commitment, to genuinely confront the demands of justice and love, wrapped up as many of us are in our own secure cocoons, caught in a position of both knowing and not wanting to know of the suffering and injustice that stalk our world?

Each of these questions can in fact lead to reflection on the role of the Spirit. It is a classic Christian affirmation that the Holy Spirit incorporates us, in our variety and difference, into Christ, and this is significant for the first question. Trinitarian faith legitimates a certain trust, as Christians seek to engage with the social and political demands of their time, drawing on all the resources, theological and non-theological, that they can, that the Spirit may be at work aligning them with and incorporating them into Christ's own relation to the world. If we have no algorithm for a transition from Christ's engagement to the one required of the contemporary church and contemporary Christians, there can nevertheless be a kind of confidence that this is a gap that the Spirit can bridge.

And as regards the reluctance, the disinclination to really see what is before us, we can again be led to reflection on the Spirit, although by way first of a reflection on *sin*. For surely this evasion of the real is a dimension of the sin of the rich world. Indeed what I have tried to suggest is that it is a sphere in which sin has a particularly strong grip, so strong that it can be hard to see how to escape, how as individuals or communities we could be really willing to look at the real when to do so would so discomfort and destabilize us. But it is part of the fundamental grammar of the Christian faith that where we know there is sin, we must also trust in and look for the reality of grace, the movement of the Holy Spirit. For if it is a basic Christian conviction that the Holy Spirit is at work in the world, the church and in individuals, freeing and making new things possible, then it is a fundamental Christian requirement to attend to, to listen for, the promptings of the Spirit. So in the realm of the political, faith in the Holy Spirit means not needing to remain simply trapped and frozen, caught between a half-suppressed awareness of the injustices and oppression of the world on the one hand and one's own fear of confronting them on the other: the individual or community is rather in a position, first, to acknowledge the sin of their own situation, and secondly, to seek out and attend to the movements of the Holy Spirit which, on one level or another, allow a new fidelity to the real.[28]

So I have said something of the Son and the Spirit, but what of the Father? At this point it may be useful to consider the almost inevitable frustration of political engagement. NGOs may tell supporters that they *can* end hunger, make poverty history, eradicate debt, and so on, but Christians who engage with any of these things must do so in the knowledge that in all likelihood they will not manage to bring hunger and poverty to an end or usher in a new age of justice. At best political efforts may contribute to some partial success, and they may utterly fail. What can make ongoing, sustained engagement possible under these conditions? One strategy is to ignore the complexity and ambiguity of the world and attend only to a limited problem where there is hope of seeing full success – but this would once again be a kind of escapism. What if, however, the whole of our engagement in the world is itself – and is lived as and understood as – part of an orientation and a movement towards a horizon which transcends the world, towards the Father who is the source and goal of all?

In brief, then, one can conceive of political engagement as the Spirit moving within us, working to overcome our selfish blindness, seeking to unite us with Jesus, whose own engagement with the world and 'fidelity to the real' is at the same time always also his pointing beyond the world to the Father. Or at least we can say, that is *one example* of a way to bring the Trinity and politics together.

I asked above whether an apophatic trinitarianism could in any way match the appeal of the social trinitarians, with their ability to say 'The Trinity is Our Social Programme', and whether an apophatic trinitarianism was bound to be apolitical, encouraging the church into passivity, disengagement and escapism. I am now in a position to give at least a provisional answer to these questions.

To the first question – can an apophatic trinitarianism match the appeal of social trinitarians – the answer may well have to be 'no'. There is something unavoidably elusive about the incorporative approach to thinking about politics that I have been sketching: it cannot provide a particular difference, a particular policy, a particular political proposal, which could trace its pedigree to the doctrine of the Trinity. And there is a certain intellectual asceticism required: maybe we would like to have in our grasp special concepts about God that give a special basis for our political thought, but this is a desire that on my account has to be resisted. So it is undoubtedly difficult to compete with the appeal of social trinitarianism.

But does this mean that the upshot is, on a political level, passivity, disengagement and escapism? Not necessarily. Disengagement and escapism are certainly powerful temptations for Christians, I've been trying to suggest, at least

---

28. It may be, of course, that those in the context I have been describing can properly attend to the movements of the Holy Spirit only if they allow themselves to seek out the action of the transforming grace of the Spirit from *beyond* their own context. This would be a pneumatological corollary of liberation theologians' concept of the epistemological privilege of the poor.

in some contexts. But highly generalized social and political proposals that can be derived from thinking about how we may 'copy' the Trinity don't help to counter these temptations. In fact one might see such highly generalized proposals as themselves another form of escapism. It is not difficult to play around with ideas of perfection. It *is* difficult to really look at and think about long term, massive suffering, particularly if I have to wonder, as anyone in the well-off pockets of the world does, whether I am somehow implicated in and responsible for this suffering. The doctrine of the Trinity doesn't in my opinion give us a blueprint for remaking society. But in reminding us of our true situation – disciples of Jesus, in whom the grace of the Spirit is constantly at work, in the midst of the world on a journey to the transcendent Father – it can do something to overcome our fear and passivity and escapism, to make engagement more possible in the first place, and to help sustain this engagement in the face of our imperfection and failure.

Chapter 5

THE STATUS OF THE CONCEPT

A REFLECTION ON JOHN ZIZIOULAS' *BEING AS COMMUNION*

John Zizioulas' *Being as Communion* had, and has, a powerful appeal.[1] The appeal can be explained, in part, in terms of the dynamics of encounter between Orthodox and Western theology. Catholic and Protestant theologians in the 1980s were able to listen to Zizioulas as the voice of the 'other', to feel that in listening to him they were opening their minds to a perspective and indeed a wisdom coming from beyond their own circles. They were also able, however, to listen to Zizioulas without too much trouble, because in fact he was thoroughly at home in Western theology and already very much in conversation with a range of familiar figures. It is striking how routinely Karl Rahner and Donald MacKinnon, for instance, appear in the text and footnotes of *Being as Communion*.[2]

A second source of the powerful appeal of Zizioulas' *Being as Communion* comes from the integrative power of its proposals, from the way apparently dispersed fields of study and disparate issues in theology come together in the volume. We find ourselves reading about ontology, about the eucharist, about the technicalities of historical Trinitarian theology, about ecclesiology, and find ourselves coming to see – or so it seems – that one and the same thing is at issue in each. This is theology at its most exciting: issues that might at first seem obscure and abstruse in the Trinitarian debates of more than a millennium and a half ago reveal themselves to be linked directly to the very largest of questions about the nature of being itself, and all this in turn has concrete ramifications for our understanding of the eucharist, of church ministry and order, of ecumenical relations. The historical and technical, the grand and ontological, the existential and practical, are all woven together with confidence, authority and clarity. And they are woven together to deliver a message of just the sort that we, in our out-of-balance, individualistic, modern Western societies need to hear. So it is not

---

1. John D. Zizioulas, *Being as Communion: Studies in Personhood and the Church* (London: Darton, Longman & Todd, 1985). This paper was originally presented at the Eastern Orthodox Studies Group panel discussion *The Legacy of John Zizioulas: 30 years after* Being as Communion, at the 2015 American Academy of Religion.

2. For Rahner see for instance 40n., 45n., 88, 132 For Mackinnon, 38n., 85., and 108n.

surprising that *Being as Communion* has been so influential, so much read, so widely quoted, that it has contributed to shaping the imagination of many in the fields of ecclesiology, of Trinitarian theology, of ecumenical theology, in the decades since it was first published.

Being as Communion has also, of course, been widely criticized. Zizioulas has not, a number have claimed, understood the Fathers aright; the reading he offers of Athanasius and the Cappadocians simply cannot be sustained; he has in fact, some have argued, been far more influenced by certain strands of twentieth century existentialism in his notion of 'Person' than by anything deriving from the Patristic era.[3] Many have disagreed with his proposals about the way the church is constituted; some have pointed out that he is reading the conception of 'communion' in a very particular way that happens to favour the church polity to which he is already committed. He has also been one among a variety of targets in critiques of social trinitarianism,[4] as also in an influential critique of so-called 'blueprint' ecclesiologies.[5]

I will not attempt to review or evaluate these arguments. What I want to propose instead is that even before these particular criticisms emerge, there is something that ought perhaps be troubling about Zizioulas. Even if one did not know enough about the particular texts of the Greek Fathers to dispute the interpretations Zizioulas offers of them, or if one did not have a more general anxiety about blueprint ecclesiologies or about social theories of the Trinity; even if one did not notice that Zizioulas understands the concept of communion in a very particular way, and that others construals are equally possible – even in the absence of *any* of these specific grounds for worry there would still, I think, be something that should make us apprehensive in his work.

What is troubling at the broadest level, I want to propose, is the governing status held by a concept, or a small cluster of interconnected concepts, in *Being as Communion*. Consider communion, *koinonia*. Communion is at the heart of the Trinity – we read that 'God's being is identical with an act of communion'.[6] It is at the heart of being – 'substance', Zizioulas suggests, 'inasmuch as it signifies the ultimate character of being, can be conceived only as communion'.[7] It

---

3. For instance, Turcescu argues, 'Zizioulas ends up using modern insights of person [sic] which he then tries to foist on the Cappadocian Fathers,' in Lucian Turcescu, '"Person" versus "Individual", and other Modern Misreadings of Gregory of Nyssa', in Sarah Coakley (ed.), *Rethinking Gregory of Nyssa* (Oxford: Blackwell, 2003), 98.

4. For example, Holmes, *The Holy Trinity: Understanding God's Life*, 12–16.

5. Cf. Nicholas M. Healy, *Church, World and the Christian Life: Practical Prophetic Ecclesiology* (Cambridge: Cambridge University Press, 2000), especially ch. 2.

6. Zizioulas, *Communion*, 44.

7. Ibid., 84. This particular phrase is embedded within a question, and the question within an exposition of Athanasius. But it is clear that the question is rhetorical – its only proper answer is 'yes' – and equally clear that no distance is intended between what is here deduced from Athansius and the position of Zizioulas himself.

explains, of course, what is happening in the eucharist. It is crucial for how we should understand the relation of bishop (and priest and deacon) to the laity.[8] It is the key to how we should understand the relationship of local churches one to another.[9] It is also at the centre of an understanding of the difference between church and world, between death and resurrection. Zizioulas uses the concept of communion to lay out what is fundamentally involved in salvation, since it is the key to understanding the difference, on his account, between the 'individual', the biological hypostasis, and the 'person'.[10] So the existential truth of baptism, Zizioulas can write, is simply 'the truth of communion'.[11]

Communion seems to be something, then, close to a super-concept, an organizing idea into which everything else is tied. My question is whether, even if we didn't or don't have other reasons to worry about particular aspects of Zizioulas' proposal, we should keep our antennae out for the dangers of something like a conceptual idolatry at work?

The relevant issue, it should be said, is not the relationship of philosophy to theology. If there is danger in falling too much in love with a particular concept, or a particular cluster of concepts, and allowing this improperly to govern one's theological vision, it can be a danger whether the concept or thought pattern is derived from philosophical or from theological resources, or from any other. In some Catholic theologians, for example – most prominently Hans Urs von Balthasar – one sees something similar happening around the theme of 'nuptiality': a certain conception of masculinity and femininity, and of the sexual-reproductive relationship between them, is used to describe the relation of the Father to the Son in the Trinity, the relation of God to creation, the relation of Christ to the church, the relation of clergy to laity. It is also used to inform an understanding of mariology, and to inform the understanding of what is going on in both cross and eucharist.[12] This is not a takeover of theology by a particular philosophical argument or philosophical school, but simply the capture of theological imagination and enthusiasm by a particular conceptual pattern.

The worry about conceptual idolatry is not, then, a worry about the role of philosophy in theology. Nor indeed is it tied to any fundamental hostility towards conceptual work in theology in general. 'Faith seeking understanding' requires that one develops concepts, and that one uses them for all kinds of purposes, including that they sometimes allow illuminating connections to be made between aspects of the faith not previously closely linked. If a concept, however, ceases to be used to clarify and articulate and illuminate, and begins to be an end in itself, a primary focus of theology, its central concern, something into whose orbit and under whose order the whole of faith and tradition and church life are to be brought,

---

8. Ibid., 214–24.
9. Ibid., Ch. 7.
10. Ibid., 49–65.
11. Ibid., 113.
12. Cf. my *Balthasar: A (Very) Critical Introduction* (Grand Rapids: Eerdmans, 2012), ch. 6.

then something has gone wrong – something like a conceptual idolatry needs to be feared.

But who is to say? How do we determine when concepts are properly being used to serve and illuminate faith, and when they have taken over and become the goal in their own right? How do we judge when the legitimate enthusiasm for a powerful idea spills over into the illegitimate capture of theology by a super-concept?

I have no general rule to offer, no procedure which would allow the drawing of a line demarcating the reasonable and helpful use of concepts on the one side from the problematic emergence of a governing super-concept on the other. Indeed, I cannot claim to have the means to establish beyond doubt that such a conceptual capture has in fact occurred in *Being as Communion*. But there are a few of features of the work which suggest that it is at least a worry at least worth raising.

The first feature is simply the *frequency* with which the concept is deployed, the number of contexts in which it turns out to be the key idea. It would be an exaggeration to say that whatever the question is, the answer is going to turn out to be communion, or persons-in-communion, but one can get something of this feeling reading Zizioulas. One might protest, perhaps, that there are not a lot of independent, separate uses of the notion of *koinonia*, but really a single *koinonia* that Zizioulas is exploring – everything flows from and to, and is ultimately found in, the Persons-in-Communion of the Trinity. But even if this reading can be defended, the anxiety would remain, or rather become an anxiety about the elaborate tidiness of the single pattern of nested *koinonia*s we encounter in *Being as Communion*. We find patterns within patterns, communions within communion. The vision we are offered has something of the quality of a fractal, where the whole is one pattern but at every level within the whole encounter exactly this same pattern again.

A second point to consider is the way church is related to world, and the rather sharp dualism that marks this distinction. On the one hand of course Zizioulas wants to reject dualism – the church is not engaged in attacking or opposing or criticising the world but in offering it back to God, in taking up and sanctifying, in transfiguring it.[13] But on the other hand, because, so it seems, of the way the communion-concept functions to unify Zizioulas' thought, the divide between what goes on in the church and what goes on outside it takes on a certain absolute quality. Apart from the church, we have the individual, not the person, the biological hypostasis, not the ecclesial, subsisting apart from relations and so cut off from communion.[14] Only in the church can there be persons. This improbably sharp church/world divide seems almost an unintended consequence of the systematizing impulse. If one is going to use communion as the decisive idea which links Trinity, church and eucharist, *and* which gives one (through contrast)

---

13. Zizioulas, *Communion*, 186.
14. Cf. Ibid., 52, 58.

an account of the nature of human fallenness, it is hard to imagine how a really sharp church/world contrast could be avoided.

Finally, and more generally, there is the way the whole vision of the church *Being as Communion* presents seems to float a few feet above the ground. It gives us a beautiful, orderly ideal, but does not offer room for thinking about the boredom, the conflicts, the inadequacies, the sheer ordinariness that marks so much of most Christians' experience of being a Christian and being in community with other Christians.[15] There is a beautiful sense of 'fit' built into *Being as Communion*, but it is perhaps a fit more between one part of the system of thought and another, than between the system of thought and what most of us, most of the time, encounter in our life in the church.

I have written of a worry, an anxiety, a question, rather than articulating a more definite criticism. In part this is because the issue I am seeking to bring to the surface is an intrinsically elusive one, in part because there is danger of being unfair to Zizioulas. One might argue, for instance, that I am reading him uncharitably by failing to give proper weight to the fact that *Being as Communion* is not a monograph but a collection of essays – perhaps what Zizioulas writes must be read with careful attention to the genre in which it is written, and indeed in light of Zizioulas' own refusal to gather it together into a single system. It is safe at least to say, however, that a certain *temptation* to over-systematizing and conceptual idolatry lurks in or near Zizioulas' theology.

Alert readers may notice that what I initially suggested as a large part of the *appeal* of Zizioulas (the integrative power of his thought), and what I have pointed to as the most worrying aspect of his theology (the controlling role of a concept) are quite similar. But perhaps we shouldn't be surprised by this; perhaps in theology as elsewhere, one's vocation and one's greatest temptation lie very close.[16]

---

15. For a striking contrast, see Karl Rahner, 'God of My Daily Routine', in *Encounters with Silence* (South Bend: St Augustine's Press, 1999), 45–52.

16. I am indebted to Henri-Jérôme Gagey and his reading of Jesus' testing in the wilderness for this understanding of a link between vocation and temptation. See Henri-Jérôme Gagey, *La vérité s'accomplit* (Paris: Bayard, 2009), 200–1.

Chapter 6

EVIL AND THE LIMITS OF THEOLOGY

How ought evil to be dealt with in Christian theology? In what follows I will approach this question by reflecting on what is arguably a different intellectual tradition – the production of theodicies – and on the relationship between theology and this other tradition. What I shall try to show is that Christian theology ought *neither* construct theodicies, *nor* ignore the kinds of problem theodicies try to address. It ought instead to acknowledge itself to be faced with questions it cannot answer, and to be committed to affirming things it cannot make sense of.

In the tradition of constructing theodicies, as it can be found for instance in contemporary texts of philosophy of religion, one sets out a few propositions – that God is omnipotent and omniscient, that God is good, and that there is evil in the world – and asks how these propositions can be reconciled. One has an easily grasped conundrum, and one that presents itself as of central importance to almost any kind of religious believer. It is pedagogically useful problem as well: a simply described, intellectually tidy puzzle to present to students, a puzzle to which one can offer competing answers, or, more rarely in practice if not in theory, from which one can mount an argument for the non-existence of God.

It is not hard to argue, as we shall see below, that this pattern of enquiry as found in philosophy of religion texts and other such places is a distinctive product of the Enlightenment rather than a natural continuation of any kind of theological tradition, nor is it hard to detect in this genre of discussions of God and evil a number of problematic features, features which have been analysed forcefully by authors such as Kenneth Surin and Terrence Tilley. This still leaves open the question, however, of how a Christian theologian, recognizing both the Enlightenment derivation of theodicies, and the problems they contain, ought to respond to them. One possibility – which Surin and Tilley in their different ways have followed – is simply to refuse the whole issue which theodicies raise, to change the subject, to insist that Christians simply think and talk about evil in a different way. One can, in other words, deem the question the theodicists ask to be an illegitimate one. This is not, however, the only option, and I shall try to show that it is an unduly drastic response. Another possibility is to accept the question the theodicists raise – or rather to accept that families of questions like this do, legitimately, arise within and around Christian thinking – without following the philosophers of religion in attempting any *answers* to such questions. Even, then, if it is right to view the tradition of theodicy-making as something like a foreign body with respect to Christian theology, it may be a foreign body from which theology can learn, a foreign body which may help theology to define its own nature and explore its own limits.

This is of course an abstract way to approach a discussion of evil. I do not begin with a discussion of the 11th of September, U.S. militarism, trade injustice, human trafficking or any other contemporary horror, but turn my attention instead directly to the question of how one academic mode of discourse relates itself to another. Discussing evil is perhaps always a dangerous thing to do as an academic theologian; the accusation of fiddling while Rome burns, or indeed of actually colluding with evil in some way or another, is never far away. And yet there are things which can be said in defence of a discussion of the rather abstract question of the relationship between theology and theodicy. First, the question of theodicy has a tremendous grip on the minds of students and of many others with any (or perhaps even no) interest in theology. Undergraduates, for instance, are often very taken with the free-will defence. Many of them judge theological proposals in other areas by the degree to which these support, or fail to support, this answer to the problem of evil: if one puts to them some proposition concerning sin or grace or the nature of God's relationship to creation, that is to say, they may well reject it if they deem it to undermine free will and therefore the free-will defence. So to think through theodicy – or rather the appropriate theological response to theodicy – is at least pedagogically important. Secondly, although the position which I will be proposing is ultimately not particularly gratifying on a practical or pastoral level – that there are legitimate questions to which we have no legitimate answers – it is better than either of the alternatives, better, that is, than either offering the wrong kind of answer, or than using a form of theological intimidation towards people who ask the question.

In what follows, then, I will say a little more what I mean by theodicies, review a number of reasons why they ought to be avoided (some of the reasons are those laid out by Surin and Tilley, others my own), and finally turn to the question of where this leaves theology. There is, it should be noted, already available a very common answer to the question of what theology ought to do if not engage in theodicy, namely that it ought instead to proclaim the suffering of God. Almost as appealing as the free-will theodicy seems to be with students, so the notion of the suffering of God is to professional theologians. In the contemporary theological world, that is to say, if one finds a theologian maintaining that Christian theology ought not construct theodicies, one can have a strong expectation that the next sentence or paragraph will contain something about the suffering of God. This is a route that will not be followed here, however, for reasons to be sketched below. The question to be asked, then, is what one should do if one *neither* aims to construct theodicies *nor* thinks that an appeal to God's suffering is helpful.

6. Evil and the Limits of Theology

I

A classic articulation of the 'problem of evil' is put by David Hume into the mouth of Philo in Part X of *Dialogues Concerning Natural Religion*:

> Is he [God] willing to prevent evil, but not able? then he is impotent. Is he able, but not willing? then he is malevolent. Is he both able and willing? whence then is evil?[1]

Posing this or a closely related problem, developing answers to it, discussing and dissecting other people's answers, are staples of the trade of philosophy of religion – the so-called problem of evil comes second only perhaps to the study of proofs of the existence of God as a centrepiece of courses and textbooks in the subject. Many of those who have proposed the most influential theodicies in recent decades – Hick, Plantinga, Swinburne – are those who have been the most influential philosophers of religion.[2]

Although contemporary philosophers of religion sometimes point back to various earlier figures or themes in the tradition – Hick famously discusses Augustinian and Irenaean theodicies, for instance – there are a number of reasons for considering what they do as in fact a practice shaped primarily by the Enlightenment. Most obviously, the God whose compatibility with evil they discuss is presented as an abstract entity with a number of characteristics, a God

---

1. Philo describes these as 'Epicurus' old questions'.

2. There are a number of distinctions that can be made, both in the way 'the problem of evil' is presented and in the kinds of solutions attempted. The problem can be set up as a logical one (is the claim that God is perfectly good, omniscient and omnipotent logically compatible with the existence of evil) or as an evidential one (does the existence of a large quantity of pointless evil count as *evidence* against belief in God, rendering the proposition that God exists less probable). The problem can furthermore be presented atheistically (as something which counts either decisively or significantly against belief in God) or aporetically (as a puzzle to be pondered by believers). Those who attempt answers, finally, can try to give an account of God and the world that genuinely explains the existence of evil, or more modestly, can offer arguments to the effect that evil does not rule out or render improbable the existence of God. In Plantinga's presentation, only the former are properly called theodicies: the latter, which he engages in, are 'defences'. I am for the most part using the term theodicy in a broader sense, to cover all attempted answers to the so-called problem of evil. Cf. the Introduction of Marilyn McCord Adams and Robert Merihew Adams (eds), *The Problem of Evil* (Oxford: Oxford University Press, 1990) for a fuller discussion of some of the distinctions I have mentioned. For the most part such distinctions will not be central to this discussion. It might be supposed that the kind of defence Plantinga develops, which does not try to make any claims about the way the world actually is, but only about how, logically, it might be, is less vulnerable to some of the criticisms developed below, but it does not entirely escape them.

who can be described without reference to any particular narratives, without any discussion of incarnation, Christology, Trinity. It is, in other words, theistic belief in general whose coherence they are exploring or defending; Christianity is generally seen as one of the things you can get by adding a few supplementary beliefs to the basic starter kit of theism.[3] And not only is the God discussed detached from traditional patterns of Christian thinking about God,[4] but the way evil is discussed, and the way evil is discussed in relation to God, are also detached from any wider theological context. Theodicy is presented as a problem studied on its own, a simply stated philosophical conundrum which a theist must face, rather than an issue which might arise in a discussion of, for instance, creation or God's relation to history or Christology.

None of these points in themselves automatically constitutes a reason to reject the business of offering theodicies as practiced by philosophers of religion. What I have said so far points to the fact that these discussions have a different texture from most traditional Christian theology. Certainly the strong Enlightenment overtones of theodicy are enough to make a Christian theologian begin to wonder whether something *might* have gone wrong here – to raise the theological hackles, as it were. But the alien approach of the philosophers of religion does not, at least not without further argument, conclusively demonstrate that what they are doing could not be useful to theology. The philosophers might argue that they are merely abstracting the central logical structure of the problem in order to be able to focus on it more effectively – this is, after all, how intellectual progress is often achieved – and that whatever answers they arrive at can then be fleshed out again if necessary in traditional theological clothing. For the moment we can however leave to one side the question of whether such a procedure could in principle be legitimate, because there are, in any case, *other* reasons to reject the kinds of arguments theodicists offer.

Kenneth Surin, in *Theology and the problem of evil*, and Terrence Tilley, in *The Evils of Theodicy*, develop vigorous attacks on the whole business of offering

---

3. To put this more technically, philosophers of religion distinguish between 'restricted' and 'expanded' theism. Christianity is one kind of 'expanded' theism.

4. It might be objected that there are prominent examples of pre-Enlightenment Christian thinkers quite happy to discuss God in a similar abstraction – Thomas Aquinas in significant portions of the *Summa Theologiae*, for instance. It is beyond the scope of this piece to go into the question fully, but I think a case can be made that in spite of superficial similarities, Aquinas and others like him were in fact engaged in a very different kind of project – in terms of its context, purpose, presuppositions, and overall shape – than Enlightenment figures or most contemporary philosophy of religion. For a related argument, see Nicholas Wolterstorff, 'The Migration of the Theistic Arguments: From Natural Theology to Evidentialist Apologetics', in R. Audi and W. J. Wainwright (ed.), *Rationality, Religious Belief & Moral Commitment* (Ithaca: Cornell University Press, 1986). Cf. also Kerr, *After Aquinas: Versions of Thomism*.

theodicies.⁵ At the heart of the various criticisms these two authors make is the claim that theodicies tend to put both the author and the reader into the wrong kind of relationship with evil, or, more to the point, with particular evils. They try to reconcile us to evils, that is, in a way which we should not be reconciled. If one takes the long enough view, if one really gets the right perspective, the theodicists seem to say, everything is not so bad. One of the ways this is done is by discussing evil abstractly, as a generality, and thereby allowing us to avert our gaze from particular evils. If the theodicists move away from the absolutely general level, they usually only go so far as to distinguish between two categories of evil, moral evil and natural evil, and this is a distinction itself which, as Tilley argues, allows us to forget about, or not quite see, the many things which go wrong which cannot be attributed either to an individual's bad choice or to a force of nature.

Furthermore, most theodicies invoke, though sometimes with a degree of tentativeness, the notion of a greater good – God permits evil because it is somehow necessary to a larger whole which is very good, whether conceived of as a world in which free will and therefore love, relationships, moral development, and the growth of character and so on are possible, or simply as a world which is in fact the best of all possible worlds. The theodicist's central task is to show that the greater good really is not conceivable, not in any sense possible if the evil were removed, so that God's omnipotence is not impugned. All this may well seem reasonable so long as one is able to confine one's thoughts to evil considered as an abstraction. It begins to fall apart, however, when one confronts particular kinds of evils.

One by now standard way to drive this home is to point to the Holocaust, or to particularly harrowing stories from the Holocaust: can any but the morally insensitive treat this as acceptable, allowable, in view of some greater good? Another classic move is to bring in Ivan Karamazov, with his insistence that no final harmony of any kind can justify the cruel suffering and death of children, or indeed of a single child.

The most thorough, and also, perhaps, the least manipulative, development of this kind of point of which I am aware is to be found in some of the writings of Marilyn McCord Adams.⁶ Adams makes two key moves: first, she draws a distinction between God's goodness to the world viewed globally on the one hand and God's love of and goodness to individuals on the other; secondly, she introduces the category of 'horrendous evils'. To produce a successful theodicy it is not enough, she maintains, to show that God produces sufficient *global* goods to 'overbalance or defeat' evil on the global scale, so that looking at the world as a whole one could say that goodness sufficiently outweighs or overcomes evil: one also needs to show that

---

5. In the case of Surin the attack is limited to what he terms theoretical theodicies – by contrast the so-called practical theodicies he considers more legitimate. This is a distinction to which we shall return.

6. Cf. for instance 'Horrendous Evils and the Goodness of God', in *The Problem of Evil*, and especially the book of the same title, *Horrendous Evils and the Goodness of God* (Ithaca and London: Cornell University Press, 1999).

God loves, and is good to, *each person*. And this becomes particularly problematic, she argues, for the standard theodicies, when one considers the existence of horrendous evils. Horrendous evils, as she defines them, are evils which, if they are part of one's life, give one prima facie reason to doubt whether one's life could be a great good to one.[7] Some of the paradigmatic examples she lists are 'the rape of a woman and axing off of her arms, psycho-physical torture whose ultimate goal is the disintegration of personality, betrayal of one's deepest loyalties, … parental incest … participation in the Nazi death-camps, the explosion of nuclear bombs over populated areas',[8] cannibalizing one's own offspring and being the accidental agent of the death of those one loves best. Such evils 'devour … in one swift gulp', she says, 'the possibility of positive personal meaning'.[9] It is not just that they outweigh other good or meaningful things there might be in a life, so that you would need a whole *lot* of nice things to make up for them: such evils defeat, engulf, destroy any positive value to the participant's life – or at least they seem to do so on the face of it.

If one focuses one's attention on horrendous evils, Adams argues, the usual theodicies come apart. The existence of human free will, no matter how great a good that is supposed to be; the possibility of loving relationships and of growth in character for many people in the world at large; even the idea that of all the possible worlds there could have been, this one is the best; none of these things can actually help. That is to say, none of these things would give a person involved in a horrendous evil reason to see her life as a great good to herself. God could not be said to have been good to such individuals; and, again, a theodicy which can show that God has been good to the world at large but *not* good to particular individuals is inadequate.

If one accepts this line of reasoning, there is, at the very least, a central intellectual failure in the usual theodicies.[10] They simply cannot appropriately address quite a large range of very *particular* evils that occur in our world. What critics like Surin and above all Tilley do is to push the idea that such intellectual failing also has a moral dimension. If theodicies operate in such a way that they encourage us to be reconciled to evil, to become complacent about it, and perhaps even not to see the worst evils because they do not fit into the scheme, then they are bad for us and a bad thing altogether.

Whether it is fair to accuse theodicies not just of an intellectual failing but also of a moral one is an interesting question. Philosophers of religion will no doubt believe themselves to be unjustly condemned here by critics who misconstrue the nature of

---

7. This is a paraphrased version of her somewhat more technical definition, given on 26 of *Horrendous Evils and the Goodness of God*.

8. 'Horrendous Evils and the Goodness of God', 211–12.

9. Adams, *Horrendous Evils and the Goodness of God*, 27.

10. I use the word 'usual' here because Marilyn McCord Adams' own positive proposals need to be exempted. Adams presents her work as a solution to the logical problem of evil, and so in some broad sense one might include it as a theodicy. She is insistent, however, in refusing to attempt to find a 'morally sufficient reason why God would … permit evils' (53–4), but concentrates instead on making the case that God can 'defeat' horrors and so be good to individuals.

their efforts. Plantinga, for instance, acknowledges explicitly that his theodicy is not designed for pastoral purposes – he knows that it is not the right way in which to talk to someone who is suffering. He is not engaging in pastoral work; he is doing something different. By extension, it could easily be maintained that it is not the job of the theodicists to school us in appropriate practical responses to particular evils – struggling against injustices, comforting those who suffer, confessing and repenting our own sins, and so on – nor even is it necessarily to allow us to identify or describe particular evils well. What they are engaged in is a more theoretical enterprise, one from which they would not expect us to take our moral and practical bearings in the world. They might acknowledge that all these other things – being able to see particular evils and knowing how to respond to them – are necessary, more important even than constructing theodicies, but might not think that that need undermine the legitimacy of their own production of theodicies. Whether this could be accepted as a legitimate defence is bound up with larger issues concerning the nature of academic reflection and its political and practical engagement. In any case it is safe to say, at the very least, that if the overall tone, the final note, that emerges from a theodicy is complacency, the sense that all is really alright with the world as we know it, then there is a problem: even if one does not go so far as to actively condemn it as morally inadequate, it runs the risk of being distasteful to anyone who does not completely shield himself from the world around him.

In addition to the kinds of objections I have so far sketched from Surin, Tilley and Adams – that theodicies cannot deal with various particular evils, and that they encourage us into the wrong sorts of relationship towards evils – I want to add one further objection. Almost all contemporary theodicies are closely bound up with a widespread but unfortunate theological assumption about the implications of human free will. This concept is in one way or another central to almost all contemporary theodicies, whether directly or clothed in broader notions of soul-making and character-development. God cannot bring about a world in which a good exercise of human freedom, correct moral choices, loving actions and relationships, a positive turning towards God, are possible, without giving human beings (and perhaps other moral agents) a freedom which inevitably they can use to do ill.

Lying behind this almost universal feature of contemporary theodicies is the assumption that divine and created agency are and must be in a kind of competitive relationship. The more God does, the less we are able to do. The more God acts, the less free we are. If we are to be genuinely free to do good things, to relate to each other, to respond to God, then at some level, at some point, God must back off. Human freedom requires God's non-involvement, at least at the moment of choice, and this great good of human freedom is also where one major source of evil comes in.

All this is for the most part taken as self-evident in much of modern thought.[11] An action cannot be free and determined at the same time; it is either free, or it is caused, but not both. Such a contrastive approach is not in fact, however, the

---

11. Cf. Kathryn Tanner, *God and Creation in Christian Theology* (Oxford: Blackwell, 1988) for an argument concerning the characteristic modern distortion of traditional Christian ways of relating God's sovereignty to creaturely agency.

only option when it comes to thinking about how God relates to God's creatures. One might alternatively say that the more God, as creator, acts, the more fully we come into being, and that the more God is involved with us the freer we are. It may be true that to the extent that my actions are determined by created causes, they are not free, but it does not follow that *God's* role in my action plays the same part. Again, it may be true that as a parent I have to back off to give my children appropriate freedom, but it does not necessarily mean that God must move away from us in order to allow our freedom. On the view that I am sketching, to think that this is the case is to confuse God with a created being, to suppose that God is acting on the same plane as us and that God's action inevitably competes and interferes with the actions of created beings. On the view that I am sketching, although my mother may need to keep her distance in order to allow me as an adult to develop fully into myself, God rather needs to keep as close as possible to allow this same development.[12]

It would go beyond the scope of this paper to examine the premodern theological sources of this kind of thinking, in St. Thomas and others, or look at its contemporary exponents such as Herbert McCabe or Kathryn Tanner, or to explore whether a non-Pelagian understanding of grace is possible without such a view. It is possible, however, briefly to point to two reasons for preferring this view to the alternative. First, it usefully helps to preserve a distinction between creator and creature, between God and humanity, not by making God distant and alien to us, but by insisting that God is more intimate than we can even conceive. And secondly, it avoids the danger which the contrasting view can very easily fall into of distancing God from much that we in fact deem most valuable and hold in greatest respect in our world. This is something that Nicholas Lash points to in a series of questions in *Believing Three Ways in One God*: 'Does not God make cities as well as stars? Is God's self-gift, the Spirit's presence, less intimately and immediately constitutive of promises and symphonies than of plutonium and silt?'[13] If we assume that what is most freely human must be done somehow away from and independently of God, then we will have to say that whereas the natural world is clearly God's creation, all that civilization produces has to do with the creator in only a very distant and derived way.

---

12. It should be noted that philosophers of religion are well-aware that a free-will defence depends on what is called an 'incompatibilist' view of freedom – on the assumption, that is, that freedom is incompatible with determinism – and that there are those who defend the opposite view of compatibilism. While the view that I am sketching here might be taken as a kind of compatibilism, it is not compatibilism in its usual philosophical form. One taking the view I have outlined would, or at least could, still be an incompatibilist within the realm of created causes, insisting that to be free means precisely not to be determined by any created cause. So although I may be proposing a kind of compatibilism, it is not compatibilism as usually conceived.

13. Nicholas Lash, *Believing Three Ways in One God* (London: SCM, 1992), 51.

What we have seen, then, is that the role of human and possibly other created beings' freedom is central in almost all contemporary theodicies, and this freedom can only play such a role, for the most part, because it has an assumed *independence* from God's control – God limits God's intervention in order to allow us our freedom. If one assumes that when we act most freely God is in fact also most fully bringing about our actions, then the introduction of our freedom into the theodicy discussion cannot help – it only makes matters worse. Why, if God can bring about our free actions, and in particular our good actions, does God ever allow our freedom to go wrong?

The argument here could of course be played in reverse. Many a modern thinker might respond to the noncompetitive understanding of divine and human agency just outlined as follows: that is all very well – if it makes any sense at all. But what then about evil? How can you possibly explain where sin comes from if you say that God is so intimately involved in free human action? Where I have pointed to a problem with theodicies in that they must presuppose a competitive understanding of divine and created action, others will see the fatal weak point of the non-competitive view of God's agency precisely in that it cannot contribute to a theodicy, in that it can only fall silent when confronted with how things have gone wrong.

II

We are now in a position to consider the question mentioned at the outset. If there are reasons not to adopt any, or any modification or combination, of the available 'answers' to the 'problem of evil',[14] what then should Christian theology do in the face of the problem itself? I want to suggest that there are fundamentally two options. One is to reject the legitimacy of the question, to refuse to address the issue at all, and so essentially to change the subject. This, in slightly different ways, is the approach taken by Kenneth Surin and Terrence Tilley. There is much to be said for this approach, but ultimately I think it ought to be seen as an overreaction. The second option is to accept the question and its legitimacy, but to acknowledge that Christian theology is utterly incapable of offering even an approximate answer. Or, to be more precise, what needs to be accepted may not be precisely this question, but that questions in this family, questions structurally akin to this one, do legitimately arise, both in people's lives and in systems of theology. They ought

---

14. There is an exception, as already noted above. I have drawn on Marilyn McCord Adams' criticisms of the theodicies of other contemporary philosophers of religion, but have in fact given no reason to reject her own positive proposals. However, while she is in some sense giving an answer to the problem of evil – offering a way of showing God to be logically compossible with evil – she avoids offering an 'answer' in the sense that others do, in that she refuses to answer the question of why God permits evil.

perhaps not have the centrality in either Christian life or Christian theology that they are given in the philosophy of religion, but they are nevertheless legitimate.

Terrence Tilley's rejection of everything to do with theodicy is the most aggressive. Theodicies are destructive discourses which efface and perpetuate evils. What then should we do instead of theodicy? On the one hand, Tilley councils struggling against theodicies themselves: they ought to be resisted, interrupted, counteracted, and abandoned. On the other hand, we ought to be working to uncover evils ('identify their multiple forms'), to find their causes ('understand the processes which produce them') and to get rid of them ('empower the praxes of reconciliation which will overcome them').[15] Abandon the issue as an abstract and general one, in short, and concentrate on what can be done in relation to concrete evils.

Surin, by contrast, does not reject theodicy absolutely, but rejects 'theoretical' theodicies in favour of what he calls 'practical theodicies'. Theoretical theodicies he deems those which are preoccupied with questions of the intelligibility of evil, the logical compatibility of the existence of evil and the existence of God, or the evidential significance of evil (ought it count as evidence against belief in God?). Practical theodicies are those which try to answer the question, first, what does God do, and second, what do we do, to overcome evil and suffering.[16] For examples of such practical theodicies, he looks to Dorothee Sölle, Jürgen Moltmann, and P. T. Forsyth. Here there is no question of explaining evil or explaining how it is possible in a world made by a good God, but rather of exploring how God responds to evil – how God identifies with and suffers with his creatures and brings about salvation.

Surin presents what he is doing as a kind of change in strategy and emphasis, from an abstract, theoretical, metaphysical approach to a way of dealing with the problem which is concrete, situated, and centred on a theology of the cross. It cannot be denied that the things Surin takes up – theological reflection on the cross, on salvation, the question of what God does in response to evil – that these things are critical in a full Christian response to evil, and indeed that they play a more significant role, overall, than the questions of origin (how did evil get here, how is it possible, why did or does God allow it in the first place). On the other hand, however, Surin has not in fact simply changed strategy or emphasis, as he seems to suppose: he has changed the subject. He is not giving a better answer to the question than the usual theodicies raise, a better approach to the problems with which they grapple. He is abandoning their question, their problems, and taking up different ones.

One reason Surin may not think of himself as changing the subject is that within the so-called practical theodicies a central role is played by the notion of the suffering of God. Neither Surin nor the authors he discusses claim that the fact that God suffers makes evil, or even suffering, into a good in itself, nor

---

15. Terrence Tilley, *The Evils of Theodicy* (Washington, DC: Georgetown University Press, 1991), 250.

16. Kenneth Surin, *Theology and the Problem of Evil* (Oxford: Basil Blackwell, 1986), 67.

that it explains why God permits it in the first place. This notion is often taken, nevertheless, to go a long way towards *justifying* God in a suffering world. Thus we have Surin citing with approval the view that 'a God of salvation would be justified in creating a world which contained so much pain and suffering only if he were prepared to share the burden of pain and suffering with his creatures'[17] and similarly, in reverse, that 'the God who disengages himself from the afflictions of victims cannot be justified, either by human beings or himself'.[18] Here, then, is a connection between Surin's two groups of thinkers. All alike are engaged in theodicy in the sense that all are engaged in the business of justifying God.

Does the introduction of the notion of God's suffering in fact help to justify God? One might argue against it on rather general grounds – that theologians who take this line are rejecting a tradition which is misunderstood and misrepresented, and which in fact offers, at least in places, a richer and more adequate approach to thinking about God than the one they replace it with – but it would be well beyond the scope of this essay to do so.[19] More to the point, in any case, it is hard to see how the suffering of God can in fact help when it comes to dealing with evil. Most fundamentally, if God does stand in need of justification, then to say that God suffers cannot provide it. If I mistreat my children, then the fact that I mistreat myself as well does nothing to make it acceptable. If one wants to say that there is any level on which God is responsible for evil or suffering, whether that be by causing it or by permitting it or by creating a world in which it occurs, it is hard to see how God participating in the suffering would diminish the responsibility.

Furthermore, there is at least some danger of the proponents of a suffering God falling into the same trap as theodicists, in diminishing the scandal of evil, offering a perspective from which all is, on some level, already acceptable. At the very least they seem, like the theodicists, to be trying to bring God and evil into a kind of intellectual resolution, so that the dissonance between our conception of God and our awareness of the evil in the world around us is done away with,

---

17. Ibid.
18. Ibid., 149.
19. C.f the thorough and impressive argument in Thomas Weinandy's book *Does God Suffer?* (Edinburgh: T&T Clark, 2000). To his arguments I would add the comment that when a contemporary theologian asserts that God suffers, and a traditional theologian asserts that God is impassive, they are not necessarily talking on the same plane, and so the one is not necessarily asserting precisely what the other denies. To maintain that God is impassive and beyond change is, arguably, to maintain that certain categories cannot be used to speak of God at all, rather than to paint a kind of picture of what God is like. It is a grammatical rather than a descriptive affirmation. And therefore it would be equally inappropriate, from such a traditional position, to describe God as static as it would be to describe God as moved. If this is right then contemporary theologians are not so much affirming what earlier theologians rejected, as breaking a grammatical rule to which earlier theologians believed they were constrained to adhere. I return to this issue in the final essay in this volume.

the two reconciled in the notion that the suffering is all already there within God. Something like this seems to be going on in Jürgen Moltmann's references to Auschwitz. Indeed, Moltmann speaks not only of God suffering in Auschwitz but of God in his suffering as a source of comfort to those in Auschwitz.[20] On reflection, this is a rather interesting claim. Moltmann was not himself in Auschwitz. He does not appeal to any specific testimonies that anyone did find this notion a comfort in Auschwitz.[21] He wants to take Auschwitz with full seriousness; and yet in effect he diminishes our vision of the suffering there by asserting that those in Auschwitz were comforted. To put God into the middle of evil and suffering, then, somehow starts to make things acceptable, makes Auschwitz something that can be integrated into and dealt with in our Christian theology; the Christian has put his God in the midst of it and now it is a little tamed, no longer threatening to stop the theological enterprise.

In various ways the insistence that God suffers, especially when presented as something new and important, is in danger of being a cheap move. What Moltmann does might be taken as an illegitimate Christian takeover of Jewish suffering.[22] But it is not only in Christian-Jewish relations that something may be going wrong here: it is also in Christian-atheist relations. Asserting the suffering of God offers the theologian too easy a way to wrong-foot the protest atheist: God is made invulnerable to blame since God is now suffering more than anyone.[23] It does not of course cost the theologian anything to attribute any level of suffering to God that she pleases, but it does give her an easy way to be taking suffering seriously and even perhaps to feel that she herself is siding with the victim.

These criticisms are only sketched, and they are highly controversial. Whether one thinks that they work or not, however, one point that is not controversial is that to bring in the suffering of God does not *directly* answer the theodicy question, at least in its standard Enlightenment version. And so Surin's shift from theoretical to practical theodicies does indeed amount to a change of subject.

20. 'As a companion in suffering God gave comfort where humanly there was nothing to hope for in that hell,' *History and the Triune God* (London: SCM, 1991), 29.

21. Moltmann does, it must be said, make this comment about God as a companion in suffering giving comfort in the broad context of 'points which have emerged from Jewish and Christian discussion of theology after Auschwitz'.

22. For related criticisms of Moltmann's highly influential use of a story of Elie Wiesel, cf. J.-B. Metz, 'Facing the Jews: Christian Theology after Auschwitz', in Elisabeth Schliisser Fiorenza and David Tracy (eds), *The Holocaust as Interruption* (Edinburgh: T&T Clark, 1984), cited in *Theology and the Problem of Evil*, 124, and also Marcel Sarot, 'Auschwitz, Morality and the Suffering of God', *Modern Theology* 7 (1991): 135–52.

23. Certainly in the context of human relationships such a move would often appear highly manipulative. Consider the parent who, accused of having done some very particular kinds of harm to his or her children, responds with a discussion of how much he or she has suffered for the children over the course of their lives.

Surin does, however, offer, or at least hint at, a justification for his change of topic – a justification for ignoring the question which goes beyond the fact that all the answers to it are highly unsatisfactory. The question itself, as a product of the Enlightenment, is problematic. From the point of view of a theology of the cross, which Surin champions, 'the true deity of God is revealed on the cross of the crucified Jesus of Nazareth', and if this is true, then it may be, says Surin, that

> the true divinity of the triune God ... is in actual contradiction with the theodicist's essentially *metaphysical* conception of the essence of God, the kind of conception that allows the theodicist to talk about the divine attributes of omnipotence, omniscience and benevolence in isolation from the event of the cross, and from the triune life of (the Christian) God.[24]

In other words, the very terms in which the problem is posed rely on a misconceived philosophical theism. One may change the subject not only because the question cannot be answered, but because it is so problematic a question that it ought never to have been asked.

Is it legitimate, then, to see the problem of evil as posed by the philosophers of religion as a mere product of the Enlightenment, and therefore something which Christian theology can properly ignore? Much can be granted to this point of view. It is clear that asking this sort of question about evil took on with the Enlightenment a prominence, an intellectual centrality and self-evidence, which it never before had. It is clear that the problem of evil as presented by philosophers of religion is not an ahistorical, timeless question, a universal human conundrum, but that in different societies and in different parts of the Christian tradition people have, in the face of various evils, asked very different kinds of questions. And, as has already been granted, there is something very foreign to Christianity in the abstractly conceived God of the Enlightenment with his or its abstractly conceived and fixed number of attributes.

In spite of all this, however, simply to turn away from the problem of evil as the Enlightenment focused on it is too easy a response. Many a Christian theologian will want to agree with Surin that Christian theology does not work in terms of an abstractly conceived God with a number of properties, but whether they make this point by insisting on the centrality of narrative for Christian thought, or with Surin on the christological and cross-centred nature of a Christian understanding of God, or in some other way, it is still very likely that a ghost of the Enlightenment problem, a version of it, something with a family resemblance to it, will come back to haunt them.

Thus, for instance, suppose it is said that Christian reflection does not, when properly understood, involve playing around with the postulates of a statically conceived theism, but rather focuses on, and indeed places itself within, a story of God's dealings with the world. And suppose one adds that this is a story that points

---

24. Surin, *Theology and the Problem of Evil*, 67.

our thoughts to things such as covenants between the Lord and Israel, human rebellion and divine fidelity, rather than to abstractions such as omnipotence, benevolence, and the permission of evil. All this may be true, but it must also be said that this is a narrative which extends not only forwards to an anticipated eschatological resolution but also backwards in time to the creation of the world. And, at least if the narrative is construed in a traditional Christian manner, the scattered references in the Old Testament to something like an original conflict between God and watery, monstrous forces of chaos are resolutely subordinated to the image of God creating in sovereign serenity, utterly in charge and unopposed. Now, though the narrative primarily revolves around the question of how God *deals* with disorder, disruption, chaos, disobedience and rebellion, the narrative is nevertheless put together in such a way that it is at least not unnatural to ask, how could these elements have made their way into the plot of a story with such a serene and unruffled opening? The narrative is not structured *around* such questions, but it is structured in such a way as to make such questions, close cousins of those of the theodicist, askable.

Or again, suppose we were to say, rather like the thinkers of whom Surin approves, that Christian theology ought to be centred on the cross, and that it must be resolutely Christocentric. This theology of the cross and Christocentrism, however, only get their significance if the Christ on the cross is also the one who was there at creation, the one 'through whom all things were made'. Once again there is room here for a close relation of the theodicist's question to make its entry – how have things got to such a state where the cross is necessary if Christ is the sovereign creator in the first place? Surin seems to say that this is not the right question to ask, but unless one is a follower of Marcion, and simply detaches the creator from the redeemer, it seems that this is a question to which the theology of the cross is going to be open.

Thus, even if the canonically formulated 'problem of evil' does not come up within Christian theology, something rather like it seems often to be lurking in the wings. To give a final example, suppose one were to say, Christians do not place themselves, as the theodicists' theists seem to, in a timeless and abstract situation characterized by 'there is evil' and 'there is (or might be) a good, powerful, all-knowing God'. Rather they locate themselves at a particular time in salvation history, between the incarnation, cross and resurrection (when a victory over the powers of death and darkness is decisively won, a reconciliation between God and the world established in principle) and the eschaton, when all this will be brought to definitive completion. But this vision leaves open the possibility of the question, why the delay between these two moments? Why this long period during which there are wars and famines and soul-destroying sin and suffering, in which the victory of Christ is so often not apparent?

If one moves away from the abstract theism of the Enlightenment and towards specifically Christian ways of speaking, then, the notion of evil will take on new kinds of shapes, as does the way one talks about evil in relation to God. The 'problem of evil' as formulated by philosophers of religion might not arise, but analogues to it, more concretely textured and contextualized variants of this question still remain askable. And this is not only the case for theological systems; such questions arise equally for ordinary believers, particularly when they look on at other people's suffering, degradation, despair and untimely deaths.

Admittedly such questions do not have the centrality within Christian thought and practice that the problem of evil does in the philosophy of religion. One might be suspicious of a theological system constructed primarily around them, and if an individual was *entirely* paralysed by such questions, one might want them to begin to turn their attention to the kinds of things Surin points to – what God does, and what we ought to do, in response to evil. Nevertheless, the reality and legitimacy of these questions ought not be denied. Indeed, given the legacy of the Enlightenment, one could say that while for pre-modern theologies such questions need not always arise or be addressed, in the contemporary context they *do* arise and *must* be addressed. One cannot wish away the impact of the Enlightenment.

My proposal, then, is that these questions, these concrete and theological versions of the so-called 'problem of evil' ought to be acknowledged as completely legitimate *and* as utterly unanswerable. Christians believe God is working salvation, and trust that ultimately God will bring good out of all conceivable evils, but this does not make these evils goods, nor render their presence explicable, nor allow us to understand how they can take place in the good creation of a loving and faithful God. Sometimes of course we can already see, and must look for, good coming out of evil – suffering can bring growth, sin is an occasion to turn back to God's forgiveness with trust, dependence and gratitude. But we cannot turn these things into explanations, in part because suffering can also, through no fault of the sufferer, bring about degradation and corruption, and sin can build on itself and perpetuate itself. When we see good coming from evil, we can see this as the beginning of the hoped-for work of God, but not the beginning of any kind of explanation.

I have said that questions arise which should not be pushed aside and cannot be answered. Another way to articulate this is to say that it is of the very nature of Christian theology to make affirmations, or patterns of affirmations – about the goodness, faithfulness and creative power of God on the one hand, and the brokenness of creation on the other – that it cannot co-ordinate or make sense of. There are points, then, at which systematic theology (if there is such a thing) ought to be, if not systematically incoherent, then at least systematically dissonant. Just as believers may have to live with evils they cannot make sense of or integrate into any larger positive picture, so too theologians may have to live with points of systematic dissonance that they cannot make go away, not even by dismissing the problem and changing the subject, and that we cannot resolve, not even by saying that God suffers.

Standard discussions of theodicy set up three apparently incompatible propositions – God is powerful, God is good, evil exists. What is at stake here can be summed up with a variant on this trilemma. One might say instead that there are three features of a Christian theology, all of which are desirable, but not all of which can be achieved; a theology ought to provide a fully Christian picture of God; it ought to give, or at least leave room for, a full recognition of the injustice, terror and tragedy that we participate in and see around us; it ought to be clear that it hangs together. And I am suggesting that not all of these can be achieved.[25] Something has to be sacrificed. Process theology sacrifices the traditional picture of God to achieve an intelligible system that allows for evil. I have outlined how theodicies tend to sacrifice the full recognition of evil to hang on to what is at least thought to be a traditional conception of God while maintaining visible coherence. The option I am recommending is to sacrifice neither the picture of God nor the recognition of the range and depth of evils in God's world, but instead the possibility of a manifestly coherent theological vision.[26]

III

The proposal I have made has been set out against the background of a variety of exclusively contemporary positions – theodicies offered by philosophers of religion in the last few decades and recent theological criticisms of them. It is worth saying something, however briefly, about how such a position is related to classic (pre-Enlightenment) discussions of evil, such as those of Augustine or Aquinas. These thinkers do, it must be conceded, offer larger explanations of why God permits evil, in terms of a conception of what might be called the completeness of the universe. But one can also find, in the way they deploy the notion of the *privatio boni*, if not a systematic incoherence, then at least a systematic inexplicability entering into their theology. Evil is a privation of good, but it is difficult to work out within these schemes where the privation as such comes from. According to Aquinas, for instance, God is the first cause of all that is, but that does not make God the cause of evil, since evil is precisely *not* something which is, but a lack. But why is there this lack – why are some things not all that they should be? If one hunts within his system for an explanation of where then the lack itself comes from, how it comes to be that there is this lack, especially as regards *voluntary* evil, one meets only with frustration.[27] Now, one might say that Aquinas has a blind spot here, that he simply forgets to explain the ultimate cause of sin; or one might say that he is being

---

25. I am not advocating the assertion of *logically* incompatible propositions, but rather the holding of a set of beliefs which, somewhat more broadly, *we cannot make sense of*. There may be some other perspective in which they all make sense together, but if so this is something of which we cannot even begin to conceive.

26. In *Church Dogmatics* III, Karl Barth prefaces his treatment of 'nothingness' with a discussion of the brokenness of theology, and the fact that theology must be a report of the way things are which does not 'degenerate into a system' (*Church Dogmatics* III,3 295). He himself seems in danger of doing so, however, in his subsequent discussion of the 'right' and 'left' hands of God, and in the notion that nothingness is that which God does not will, so that 'what really corresponds to that which God does not will is nothingness' (352).

27. An evil action, an action which lacks some good it should have, comes from a deficient will, which is deficient because it 'does not subject itself to its proper rule' (*Summa Theologiae* I 49 a.1 *ad* 3). Whatever is good and has being – the will itself – is caused by

slippery and sophistical.²⁸ But it is also possible to construe the non-explanation as deliberate and up-front; there is a hole in the fabric of Aquinas' account, and there ought to be a hole there, because the thing in question is inexplicable.

IV

The position I am proposing, one might say, is nothing more than the rather common theological cliché: evil is mysterious. But if this is a cliché, then like many clichés it is often not taken seriously, not thought through fully. One sign of this is that an appeal to mystery is often made in a rather half-hearted way – I do my best to explain evil, but then in recognition of the fact that my explanation is not very good, neither intellectually satisfying nor pastorally appropriate, I add that of course it is essentially mysterious.

To say that evil is a mystery in fact raises its own interesting questions: how, for instance, should *this* use of the word mystery be related to its use in other places in theology, and in particular, to its use in discussing God? Should we say that evil is mysterious *in the same way* that God is mysterious? Surely we cannot do that. Should we say that evil is mysterious in the *opposite* way that God is mysterious? This too may have its dangers – evil is being given undue status. How is it then that our words falter before, and our minds cannot grasp, either evil or God? Should we perhaps relate the two not as positive infinity and negative infinity, but as infinity and zero, both of which can wreak havoc in mathematical equations? We cannot understand the one because there is too *much* meaning, and the other because there is too *little*? Perhaps. But how then account for the fact that an encounter with the mystery of evil sometimes brings people to a deeper awareness of the mystery of God?

There is clearly much to be thought through. The appeal to the mysterious nature of evil ought not be simply a matter of theologians throwing up their hands when they notice just how pathetic and tangled their explanations are becoming. If theology acknowledges itself to be up against its limits here, there might in principle be things it can learn about itself by examining the nature of its limitation. It is important, in other words, to be clear about what cannot be made clear.

It is not only, however, that there might be interesting theoretical consequences if one takes fully seriously the mysteriousness, the inexplicability, of evil. It is also pastorally important to be as clear as possible that evil, or particular evils, do raise questions and these questions cannot be answered. When someone asks, confronted with things gone horrifically wrong, where is God, why does God

---

God, but not its deficiency. Where then does its deficiency come from; why does the will not subject itself to its proper rule? We are given no answer.

28. Carl Jung considered the doctrine of *privatio boni* 'a regular *tour de force* of sophistry', *Collected Works of C.G. Jung*, Volume 11, 313, cited in David Burrell, *Aquinas: God and Action* (London: Routledge and Kegan Paul, 1979).

allow it, they should not be told their question is mistaken, that even to be asking the question means they have the wrong conception of God or the wrong way of approaching God. Nor should they be fobbed off with inadequate answers, made to think that they are just not quite intelligent enough or detached enough to appreciate the free-will defence. To be clear that there is a problem with no solution may not be very satisfying, but it avoids creating further problems

Chapter 7

SIN, EVIL AND THE PROBLEM OF INTELLIGIBILITY

Theology and philosophy of religion, from a distance, look very similar: an outsider would expect the two disciplines to be intellectually close.[1] In fact, however, theologians and philosophers of religion often seem to inhabit different intellectual worlds. There can be a gulf between them, a gulf not much diminished by the emergence in recent years of analytic theology.[2]

What exactly is the nature of the difference? One can approach this question on a broad, methodological level, considering the weight given to history and hermeneutics in each discipline, what is at stake in a univocal as against an analogical understanding of theological language, or the nature of rigour and clarity as it is conceived on each side.[3] Another approach, however, is to turn towards particular issues and areas where there tends to be a clash of disciplines, a disparity in sensibility and judgment. This essay will focus on one such area: engagements with questions of sin, suffering and evil.

---

1. The philosophy of religion under discussion in this chapter is philosophy of religion in the broadly analytic tradition, i.e. in what remains, despite some shifts, its dominant form in the English-speaking world.

2. Analytic theology brings the intellectual habits and style of philosophy of religion to bear on theological questions and has experienced vigorous growth in recent years. On the face of it, analytic theology offers a bridge between the two disciplines. There has not been, however, a very strong interchange between analytic and other kinds of theology – or at least, not an especially strong reception of analytic theology by other forms of theology. So while the territory of philosophy of religion has in a sense expanded, the gulf between it and traditional theology has not thereby become smaller.

3. Cf. Chris Insole and Harriet Harris, eds, *Faith and Philosophical Analysis: The Impact of Analytic Philosophy on the Philosophy of Religion* (Farnborough: Ashgate, 2005), for explorations of the tensions, possibilities and limitations of analytic method for theology and philosophy of religion. For a more recent discussion, see Simon Oliver's review of *Analytic Theology: New Essays in the Philosophy of Theology* in *The International Journal of Systematic Theology* 12, no. 4 (2010): 464–75. For a discussion of the way the understanding of clarity may differ in the two contexts, cf. Karen Kilby, 'Seeking Clarity', in Mike Higton and Jim Fodor (eds), *The Routledge Companion to the Practice of Christian Theology* (London: Routledge, 2015), 61–71.

I

One of the most widely anthologized and well-regarded essays by a philosopher of religion on the problem of evil is William Rowe's 'The Problem of Evil and Some Varieties of Atheism'.[4] In it Rowe shows strikingly little interest in anything one might call sin. The concrete example of evil he offers for our contemplation is an example of animal suffering from natural causes. He goes out of his way, indeed, to eliminate human involvement in this example: he imagines the agony of a fawn who dies slowly and painfully 'in some distant forest' from burns inflicted by a fire, a fire he is careful to tell us was caused by lightening striking an old, dead tree.

Philosophers of religion do not always stay *quite* so resolutely away from issues of human responsibility. Sometimes they consider so-called 'moral evil' alongside 'natural evil'. But this does not mean that most take more interest than Rowe in *sin*, for when they do consider moral evil, the emphasis still tends to fall on the evil *suffered* as a consequence of wrongdoing rather than the evil *done*.[5] The significance that human wrongdoing has in their arguments, in other words, tends to be the way in which it contributes to the totality of suffering in the world. Among theologians, on the other hand, it is very different: in the *Cambridge Dictionary of Christian Theology*, for instance, one finds a substantial entry under the title 'sin', but none whatsoever under either evil or suffering.[6]

One way to understand this contrast would be as follows: while philosophers of religion are concerned with the justification of God in light of suffering, theologians are concerned with the justification of humanity in the context of sin. The one group, we might say, is preoccupied with a theoretical challenge to the rationality of belief in God, the other with a central practical problem of human existence. And so we might conclude that theological reflection on sin and the philosophers' discussions of the problem of evil simply pass in the night – they have nothing to do with one another.

In this essay, however, I will explore a different way of thinking about the relationship between the two camps. In the first parts of the essay I will consider the possibility that, at its best, theological reflection on sin does not lead away from the philosophers' problem of evil, but rather to a more intense and more decisively insoluble version of it. If this is so, if theologians find themselves facing a more difficult problem of evil than the one the philosophers grapple with, what are the

---

4. William L. Rowe, 'The Problem of Evil and Some Varieties of Atheism', in Eleanor Stump and Michael J. Murray (eds), *Philosophy of Religion: The Big Questions* (Oxford: Blackwell, 1999), 157–63.

5. The contrast between 'evil suffered' and 'evil done' is borrowed from Herbert McCabe. Cf., for instance, *God Matters* (London: Continuum, 1987), 34. McCabe, together with some who are influenced by him such as Brian Davies and Denys Turner, to be discussed below, are an exception to the general tendency described here.

6. Ian McFarland et al., eds, *The Cambridge Dictionary of Christian Theology* (Cambridge: Cambridge University Press, 2011).

consequences? Is it an intellectual disaster? To approach this question, I will turn in the latter parts of the essay to consider the way sin has the quality of something dark, something mysterious, something which eludes our understanding. I will attempt a kind of map of the unintelligibility of sin, then, in order to provide a context for reflecting on the significance of this intensified problem of evil.

II

Why should theological reflection on sin lead to an intensification of the philosophers' difficulties? It is because of an absence of any satisfactory answer to the question, why does God permit sin, at least within the broadly Augustinian tradition – a tradition that includes not only Augustine himself but also Anselm, Aquinas, Luther and many other theologians of the pre-modern west. Various deep and central commitments mean that at this point this tradition faces a question which it fundamentally cannot answer. It is a difficulty which is often not recognized, often glossed over, but it is no less a real difficulty.

At first glance it might appear that there is no problem at all here for the Augustinian tradition. The conception of evil as *privatio boni*, which accompanies the doctrine of creation *ex nihilo*, seems to offer a quick solution. There is no other source for all that is except God, and all that is, is good. Evil, then, does not have being; it is not some separate kind of thing. It is a lack, an absence, a missing-ness of the good. It cannot be said to have been made, or caused, or brought into being by God, because there is nothing there to have been made, or caused, or brought into being. And the lack of being, it can be argued, leads to a block on any need for explanation: how can you give an account of that which isn't? There is a certain unintelligibility to evil associated with its status as an absence, a privation. Augustine makes the point with word plays and paradoxes: 'Let no one, therefore, look for an efficient cause of the evil will; for it is not efficient, but deficient, as the will itself is not an effecting of something, but a defect.' To try to understand the cause of the deficiency is like trying to 'to see darkness, or hear silence'. Just as we are aware of darkness by our inability to see, and of silence by not hearing anything, so too in the case of evil, we are aware of it by an inability to understand: 'For those things which are known not by their appearance, but by their lack of it, are known (if the matter can be expressed and understood this way) only by not knowing them.'[7]

One might be tempted to take privation theory to mean, then, that there is no question about evil to answer, that any purported question about the 'why' of evil is ill-formed, misconceived. The issue cannot, however, be so easily dissolved. Consider again Augustine's analogies with silence and darkness. We cannot see darkness or hear silence, it is true, but we can wonder, and even perhaps know,

---

7. Augustine, *The City of God against the Pagans* 12.7, ed. and trans. R. W. Dyson (Cambridge: Cambridge University Press, 1998), 507–8.

what has contributed to an absence of light or noise where we might otherwise have anticipated it – the electricity is out, for instance, and that is why all the lights are off, or the children are away from home, and that is why it is so quiet. Similarly, we cannot understand nonsense, it is true – we conclude that it is nonsense precisely because of our inability to comprehend – but we might be able to ask and answer the question, why is there nonsense on this piece of paper? It might be, for instance, because the person writing was inebriated, or fell on a keyboard, or was engaged in an act of political resistance. So even if sin, wrongful willing, cannot in principle be explained on one level – even if it has a kind of unintelligibility at its very heart – this does not mean that there are not, on another level, still questions to be asked, an understanding to be sought. To deem evil privation, then, does not really quite give one grounds to dismiss the view that an explanation of its origin in a good creation is called for.[8]

The issue emerges most sharply, in any case, if we begin not with the Augustinian tradition's understanding of the doctrine of creation and evil as privation, but from the Augustinian understanding of grace and its relation to human freedom. Through his encounter with Pelagianism Augustine eventually arrived at the position that we – fallen humanity – can make no good and salvific use of our freedom whatsoever apart from grace. We *can*, that is to say, freely do good works which merit our salvation, but we can only do so if our freedom is itself drawn and moved by grace.[9]

Augustine's position is not to *deny* freedom in order to emphasize the importance of grace. There is not a trade-off between grace and free will, but something more like a coincidence of the two.[10] This can be a difficult idea to come to terms with,

---

8. See Kathryn Tanner's 'Human Freedom, Human Sin, and God the Creator', in Thomas F. Tracy (ed.), *The God Who Acts: Philosophical and Theological Explorations* (University Park: Pennsylvania State University Press, 1994) for a careful and rigorous discussion of this issue: Tanner maintains that commitment to an understanding of God as creator makes the origination of sin 'properly a mystery, properly inexplicable' (112).

9. 'But good persons will also receive their reward in accordance with the merits of their own will; they have attained this good will, itself, however, through the grace of God.' Augustine, *Letter 215.1* in *Letters*, The Works of Saint Augustine: A Translation for the 21st Century, Part 2, Vol. 4, trans. Roland Teske, S.J. (New York: New York City Press, 2005), 40.

10. Thus in *De gratia et libero arbitrio* and the letters prefacing it Augustine is constantly exerting himself to demonstrate *both* that scripture will not allow us to deny free will *and* that all the good that we will is properly attributed to grace. One falls into the error of the 'new Pelagian heretics' if one 'supposes that it is according to any human merits that the grace of God is given to us' but one is 'no less in error' if one imagines 'that the grace of God … is given according to any human merits', Augustine, Letter 215.1, *Letters*, 40. Augustine anticipates that some may find all this difficult, but instructs them then simply to follow scripture and 'believe … that there exist both the free choice of a human being and the grace of God, without the help of which free choice can neither turn back to God nor make progress toward God'. Augustine, Letter 214.7 in *Letters*, 39 (emphasis added). Augustine's

because we have a persistent instinct to imagine some sort of division of labor, where God's grace does part of what is necessary, and the human agent is left to freely choose either to do the rest or not. So we might think, for instance, that if we make the first move and 'do what is in us', then grace will not be denied;[11] or that the offer of grace comes first but it is still up to us to freely accept and remain faithful to it.[12] But this is not the position of the Augustinian tradition. Grace is prevenient – it does not come second to anything we do first – and if we accept grace, if we co-operate with it, then the acceptance itself, the co-operation itself, is, to use a word of Karl Rahner's (whom I would take to stand clearly within this tradition) *borne* by grace.[13]

It is important to insist once again that it is not a matter of the *rejection* of free will, though Augustine can often be presented as guilty of this, but of a fundamentally different *patterning* of the relationship of grace and freedom than most of us tend instinctively to reach for. The pattern can be articulated with the help of Kathryn Tanner, who writes of a 'non-contrastive' understanding of the relationship between divine and human agency. It is part of the fundamental grammar of Christian discourse, until something shifts in the modern period, Tanner suggests, that one does not oppose divine and creaturely agency, one does not set them in competition with one another.[14] In general God's activity in us

---

seemingly baffling position is faithfully replicated in Thomas Aquinas' 'Treatise on Grace' (*Summa Theologiae*, 1a2ae.109–114) where we read, for instance, 'Man's turning to God is by free-will; and thus man is bidden to turn himself to God. But free will can only be turned to God, when God turns it. ...' Thomas Aquinas, *Summa Theolologiae*, 1a2ae.109.6.ad 1, in *Latin English Edition of the Works of St. Thomas Aquinas*, Vol. 16, ed. John Motensen and Enrique Alarcón, trans. Laurence Shapcote, O.P. (Lander: The Aquinas Institute for the Study of Sacred Doctrine, 2012), 447.

11. The formula echoed here ('*facientibus quod in se est Deus non denegat gratiam*'), is a later, medieval one, but the notion that we do our bit first – we believe – and then grace follows, was precisely the position Augustine rejected in his later writings, a position which has subsequently been termed semi-pelagianism.

12. This is, roughly, the position Augustine argues against in *De Dono Perseverentiae*. Why do some persevere in the faith and in the life of virtue and continence to their death, and others fall away? Just as much as the possibility of an initial conversion of the will from evil to good, the perseverance of the will in good is entirely dependent on the help of God: 'The perseverance by which we persevere in Christ up to the end is a gift of God.' Augustine, *The Gift of Perseverance* 1, in *Answer to the Pelagians, IV*, ed. John Rotelle, trans. Roland J. Teske (New York: New York City Press, 1999), 191.

13. 'In order to accept God without reducing him, as it were, in this acceptance to our finiteness, this acceptance must be borne by God himself,' Karl Rahner, *Foundations of Christian Faith*, trans. William Dych (New York: Crossroad, 1982), 128.

14. Kathryn Tanner, *God and Creation in Christian Theology* (Minneapolis: Fortress, 2004). Tanner's analysis is offered at a fairly high level of generality. She writes not just of the Augustinian tradition, but of pre-modern theology more generally; and she writes not

empowers rather than threatening. The closer God is to me, the more God acts in me, the more fully myself, and the freer, I become. On this account, God does not have to divest Godself of anything, to retract, to hold back, to do anything like self-emptying, in order to make room for creation's being and flourishing and freedom. God's involvement and creaturely freedom exist in a relation of direct rather than inverse proportion.

Even if we set aside the weight of tradition, there is a great deal to be said for the pattern of thought around sin, grace and free will which is to be found in Augustine and those who follow after him. First, insofar as it resists a trade-off between divine and creaturely activity, it allows for an understanding of God's transcendence which is not understood as distance or alienation from the world. Secondly, it is allied with an understanding of true freedom as freedom to do the good which, while strange to the mindset of our period, is in fact a better fit with the ordinary successes and pathologies of our lives than is the concept of a freedom poised neutrally between good and evil. And thirdly, it coheres with ordinary Christian speech about grace, in which the working of grace is always seen as something positive and *never* as that which needs to be kept in check for the sake of some other, pure sphere of freedom. No one, it seems safe to suppose, ever prays, 'Please help me be more charitable towards my mother-in-law, but only if this is the kind of thing, Lord, that is part of your sphere, that you can legitimately intervene in, and not if this is one of those things which is up to me to sort out on my own.' One does not, to put it another way, in begging for grace, ever feel the need to add the rider 'but thy will be done'.

While there is a good deal to be said in favour of this understanding of grace, however, it must also be said that it leaves us with a severe intellectual difficulty around the 'why' of sin. If, without the help of grace, we can only choose sin, and if, when we freely choose the good, our ability to so choose needs to be understood as through and through the gift of grace, then how do we explain why God should ever withhold grace? Why is there sin? Why does God not *always* ensure that we choose the good? On the understanding that we are considering here, we *cannot* say that God allows the possibility of sin, and so in fact as it happens the actuality of sin, in order to ensure our freedom, since on this view, on the one hand, the true freedom is the freedom not to sin, and on the other hand, God precisely *can* ensure that we freely do not sin.

To the degree that we take sin seriously, then – to the degree that we see it, not as a mere transgression of a more or less arbitrary rule, but as something which deeply distorts and damages the fabric of creation and its relation to God – to

---

just about grace and free will, but about the relation of divine and creaturely agency more generally. The position of Augustine, and those who follow him, on grace and free will can be taken as one case study – albeit a very major case study – of the broader pattern. For a more recent quite similar articulation of the same pattern, but worked out specifically in relation to Augustine's late writings on grace and predestination, see Susannah Ticciati, *A New Apophaticism: Augustine and the Redemption of Signs* (Leiden: Brill, 2013), 54–66.

just that degree the contemporary theologian seeking to work in this tradition has a *more* severe theodicy problem on his or her hands than does the (typical) philosopher of religion. Not only have we, it seems, added a new layer to the heap of all that needs explaining and justifying – sin now is there as well as suffering – but we have removed what is typically one of the key strategies deployed to deal with *any part* of this heap, namely the free-will defence.

III

Some of what I have suggested about the Augustinian tradition is not especially distinctive. One can find similar points made about the relation of grace and free will in a range of recent commentators on this tradition or some aspect of it – not only Kathryn Tanner and Susannah Ticciati, but David Burrell, Herbert McCabe, Nicholas Lash, Denys Turner, Brian Davies, and others. However, the final point to which I've been driving – that the theologian in this tradition ends up with an *intensified* problem of evil – is much less frequently raised.[15]

In part this may be because many of these commentators, sharing in the widespread theological instinct that something is off-key in contemporary theodicy debates, shy away from a discussion of anything like the problem of evil. But this is not the only reason. It must also be admitted that this intensified problem of evil is not something by which the majority of pre-modern figures themselves showed much sign of being troubled. That God should graciously choose to save only some and not all – that God should graciously enable some to freely will the good, and leave others enslaved to their sin – made sense, both for Augustine, and for many who followed him, in terms of the fittingness, the appropriateness, of God's demonstrating both mercy (in freely saving some) and justice (in condemning the rest). Mercy is more clearly seen to *be* mercy through the contrast.[16]

Interestingly, while Augustine was very conscious that there is something inexplicable, something impossible to understand here, the inexplicability and impossibility do not attach to the fact *that* God leaves some in their sins, destined for condemnation, but to the question of *who* is left to judgment and who saved. He touches repeatedly on our inability to know why particular people are chosen to receive the gift of grace and to persevere in the faith and others are not – the frequency with which he returns to this point in fact suggests a certain unease about it. But as regards the general truth that some only and not all are recipients

---

15. One exception is Denys Turner, who in his excellent *Julian of Norwich, Theologian* (New Haven: Yale, 2011), Ch. 2, does discuss precisely this kind of issue.

16. Cf. *De dono perseverantiae*, 28: 'The Lord gives his grace to human beings to whom He wills to give it, because He is merciful ... and He does not give his grace to those to whom He does not will to give it, in order that He may might known the riches of His glory toward the vessels of Mercy.'

of grace and salvation he was untroubled. It seems to have been simply obvious to him that God must show judgment as well as mercy.

So pre-modern thinkers in the Augustinian tradition presumed they had a solution to the 'why does God permit sin' question: judgment and condemnation were appropriate so that both the gratuity of mercy and the justice of God could be expressed. Perhaps it would be wrong to describe it as a solution, indeed, for in most cases there is little evidence that it was even felt as a problem – but if the question was ever raised, the answer was to hand.

This is an answer which no longer seems so obvious to everyone, even to many who are drawn in other ways towards the retrieval of this tradition. If God could enable all to turn from sin and freely co-operate with grace in order to merit their salvation, why would God not do so? It is important to notice, however, that this presumption, the presumption that the proper display of God's justice and mercy requires leaving some in their sins, is not something which must be taken as part of the *core* of this tradition of thought, in the way that the Augustinian understanding of grace and freedom, or the Augustinian understanding of the goodness of creation and the privative nature of evil, are. What one might call the 'fittingness-of-condemnation' thesis was neither the starting point of Augustine's thought nor its goal, nor was it at the heart of any of the controversies in which he engaged; it was not, in other words, something to which he gave sustained attention. Furthermore, it does not cohere particularly well with some of what *is* central in Augustine's thought, its practical orientation and its rootedness in prayer and the Christian life. This has recently been argued, with care and detail, by Susannah Ticciati in *A New Apophaticism*.

So while there is a very difficult question right at the heart of the tradition, for much of its history the question has been ignored, not felt as a question, or else answered in a way that now appears to many rather flimsy and unsatisfying. There is at least one exception, however, one figure in whom the full weight of the problem implicit in the Augustinian position does seem to be felt. This is the fourteenth century anchorite Julian of Norwich.[17]

Interestingly, the contrast between Julian and William Rowe could not be sharper. Julian seems to be rather untroubled, as a theologian, by suffering. In some ways it might even be said to play a positive role in her text.[18] The problem of sin, however, is for her very much to the fore. Along with Augustine and Aquinas, she could not consider sin as simply the price that must be paid for

---

17. I will be drawing on the 'Long Text' from Julian of Norwich, *Revelations of Divine Love*, trans. Barry Windeatt (Oxford: Oxford University Press, 2015). Julian does not cite Augustine, or any other ancient or medieval theologian. Nor, indeed, does she cite Scripture. It is clear, nevertheless, as Denys Turner argues, that she was well versed in this tradition, and her thought deeply patterned by it. Turner is one of a number of scholars in recent years who have made the case for approaching Julian seriously as a theologian, and his reading of her in particular has influenced my own. See his *Julian of Norwich, Theologian*.

18. This point is discussed more fully in chapter 10 of this volume.

allowing humanity freedom, since she does not conceive of the domain of human freedom as a domain which God keeps out of: she tells us, for instance, that in one of her visions she saw 'that God does everything, no matter how small', that 'he is in the centre of everything and he does everything'. She concludes the discussion of her third revelation with the explanation – in case we missed it – that God's meaning was 'See that I am God. See that I am in everything. See that I do everything. See that I have never stopped ordering my works, nor ever shall, eternally. See that I lead everything on to the conclusion I ordained for it before time began, by the same power, wisdom and love with which I made it. How can anything be amiss?' Now if one maintains, as Julian does, that 'everything which is done is done well, because our Lord God does everything', then in the Augustinian tradition there is only one way one can go with sin, and this is the way Julian does go: 'sin is really not something which is done' she writes, 'for in all this vision no sin appeared.' Just as, if one says that God creates everything which is, one has to deny evil the status of being, so, if one says that God *does* everything which is done, one has to deny that sin is a genuine act, that it is genuinely something done.

But in spite of its lack of stature, sin – and in particular the 'why' of sin – is very much a central problem of the *Revelations*, one to which Julian keeps returning, as Turner has argued persuasively.[19] She presents herself as troubled, made anxious, by the question, as repeatedly raising it with the Lord even in spite of a sense of impropriety, even impiety, in doing so. The text circles around the question, worries at it. In the end we learn various things about sin – how we are to live with our own sin, how God looks upon it, how we will be treated in heaven as a result of it – but we never receive an answer to this fundamental 'why' question. What is important to note, however, is that what has become the best known saying in the *Revelations* – all shall be well, and all shall be well, and all manner of thing shall be well' – is closely connected to the 'why sin' question. It is not so much an answer, as part of what one might call God's non-answer. Julian is told, rather shockingly, that 'sin is behovely' (befitting, appropriate – Turner has suggested behovely is an equivalent of the medieval Latin *conveniens*), without being given any hint of the *way* it is befitting, behovely, and it is immediately following this that she receives the threefold affirmation that all shall be well.[20] God refuses to answer her question, then, but in place of an answer simply gives her this assurance.

What I am suggesting is that we can read Julian not just as an oddity but as a high point of the Augustinian tradition, a theologian who sees where its logic leads, and follows it through more fully than most of those who came before. Where it leads is to an intense problem, one which she is utterly unable to resolve, over why it is that there is such a thing as sin.

---

19. Turner, *Julian*, esp. ch 3.

20. Julian of Norwich, *Revelations*, 74: 'Sin is befitting, but all shall be well, and all shall be well, and all manner of things shall be well.' Cf. Turner, *Julian*, 35–8.

IV

I have argued, until this point, for a reading of the Augustinian tradition according to which it leads to a deep problem around the 'why' of sin: it drives us towards a question we cannot answer, and in doing so it effects a kind of redoubling of the philosophers' problem of evil. Should this redoubling of the difficulty give us reason to think again? Is it an intellectual disaster to adopt an understanding of sin, and of God's relation to sin, which rather than helping understand the problem of evil, leaves us with an intensified version of it? Should what I have outlined above, in other words, be taken as grounds for abandoning the Augustinian tradition? To be in a position to address this question, it will be helpful to take a brief tour around some of the aspects of what one might call the darkness of sin, the ways in which it defeats our understanding, the ways in which it eludes us.

The first thing to note is that, on phenomenological grounds, it seems reasonable to propose that sin blinds in such a way that one cannot think well about one's own sinning. When I am in the midst of sinning, it will not be clear to me, or I will not be clear to myself. In Augustinian terms, we might say that when I sin, I choose the lesser good in place of the greater – my desire is disordered. But I cannot, presumably, be fully, clearly aware of what I am doing, I cannot genuinely see my desire *as* disordered. In my sinful state, with my sinful desires, I cannot in fact see the lesser good as lesser, the greater as greater. Disordered desires, in other words, are on this view by their nature bound up with disordered perception, disordered understanding. While lucid dreaming may be possible, lucid sinning is not. I have at best a kind of divided awareness of my sin, perhaps a sense that this is the kind of thing people usually call sloth or gluttony or whatever it is, but at the same time I will feel that for some reason such a judgment doesn't really apply in this particular case. What I am doing in this case will, whatever the general theory of the matter, somehow seem the right or natural or the only possible thing. In more biblical language we might talk about the connection between sin and the darkening of the mind and heart, about Satan as liar and father of liars.

The difficulty of thinking about my own sin is significantly amplified if we consider the relationship between personal sin and what liberation theologians term structural sin.[21] Structural sin, first of all, is hard for those in the midst of it to see, in a way analogous to the difficulty of an individual thinking about her sin – societies will be set up to blind, to confuse, to obfuscate the sin woven into their structures. The order of things that society presents to its members may be fundamentally disordered, but it will be hard to escape the sense – conveyed

---

21. What follows is written on the assumption that 'structural sin' is a coherent concept. This is not a universally shared assumption. In a Catholic context, for instance, the use made by liberation theologians of the term has been criticized by Ratzinger and others. For the purposes of this chapter, with its fairly rapid survey of a variety of different issues, it is more practical to use (and illustrate, in using) the concept, than to offer a full discussion and justification of its use.

socially through a multiplicity of channels – that this nevertheless, somehow, is just the way things must be.

Furthermore, there is a deep *entanglement* of structural and personal sin, and so an irreducible opacity to the relationship between them. This is not to suggest that personal sin is swallowed up by the concept of structural sin, as critics of liberation theology have worried.[22] Indeed, to suggest that two things are entangled, that there is an opacity to the relation between them, is already to presume that they are two. It seems to me necessary to maintain a distinction of personal sin from structural not only because some sins have little to do with social and political structures, but also because even in relation to structural sin, personal participation in, and personal relationships to, the structures can differ. If, for instance, we suppose that there are elements of structural sin in global capitalism, then clearly we are all enmeshed in it, but we are not all enmeshed in exactly the same way: the man whose chief aims are to maximize his income, and his tie collection, in a career in international finance, stands in a different relationship to global capitalism than the man who works for a church development agency, for instance. Nevertheless, while there is a distinction between the personal and the structural, and a distinction that must be made, it is a distinction that cannot be made *clearly*.

This could perhaps be shown in relation to a contemporary individual's relationship to global financial capitalism, but in keeping with the principle that that which we are in the midst of is hard to see, I will approach it by way of a different example.[23] Imagine a person born into a slave owning family in a society

---

22. See for instance *Libertatis Nuntius*, the Congregation for the Doctrine of the Faith's 1984 'Instruction on Certain Aspects of the "Theology of Liberation"', especially paragraphs 14 and 15.

23. I have not found a way to unfold this point about entanglement without resort to example, but there are difficulties associated with deploying an example of structural sin. First, there is a question of distance: it seems that I ought focus on a form of sin in which I and my audience are likely entwined, so as not to encourage myself and those who read what I write into the complacent supposition that really serious wrong only happens elsewhere, far away in time or space or social location. But on the view that sin blinds, it is precisely such situations that I will find difficult to describe or to persuade an audience to see clearly. There is also a question about level of detail. Anything which might count as a site of structural sin will be a complex phenomenon, with multi-layered consequences, affecting real people in deep, ongoing and multi-faceted ways. It is not clear, for instance, that one should write of slavery without mentioning some of the things which accompany it, e.g. murder, mutilation, rape, dehumanization; without allowing it to become more real to the imagination through concrete history and particular narratives; without recognising the centrality of the perspectives of the enslaved; without attention to the many ways in which a past history of explicit slavery continues to shape and distort present societies. But a properly textured and serious approach to the reality of slavery as structural sin and evil, as distinct from to a *concept* of slavery as structural sin, is not practical as a single element in the confines of a relatively brief essay. I have not, then, found a way in essay format to touch

in which slavery is an explicit, recognised part of the economy, in which it has been in place for generations and has accordingly shaped the culture. He grows up surrounded by the system of slavery, being served by slaves and seeing slaves work the family business. The wealth and the livelihood of his family is closely linked to the slave system. The world view, the language, the patterns of seeing and not seeing, into which he is raised are also bound up with the system. Suppose he somehow comes to realise that something is very wrong with this world in which he finds himself. It is unlikely that he would be able to conceptualize fully the evils of the reality he had lived in, but even supposing he could be brought to this point, would it be possible for him to choose a course of life which would enable him to be, henceforth, free of *personal* responsibility for the horror and evil of slavery?

We might imagine he could do the right thing by simply tearing himself out of the fabric of his life, moving to another society with a different economic structure, and devoting all his energies, all the benefits of his education and any wealth he has, to the cause of the abolition of slavery and the welfare of freed slaves. But this might not be a possibility, or it might not be the right thing for him to do. He may be constrained for one reason or another – perhaps he needs to tend to an ailing parent – to remain where he grew up, living in the midst of an economy and a society intimately shaped by slavery.

It seems impossible to imagine a person maintaining a personal innocence as regards slavery in the midst of this structurally sinful system. A person might try. Perhaps he always carefully considers how he spends his money, knowing it to be his only because of the injustices inflicted on others: he lives the life of an ascetic and never spends except what would be justifiable under these circumstances. Perhaps, in all his contacts with slaves, he always does his best to overcome the sense of superiority which he finds instilled deep in his bones. Perhaps, if we don't imagine that he manages his role perfectly, we might suppose that a tally could be kept, with clear distinctions drawn between where he – his life, his thoughts, his habits – is non-culpably shaped by the system and where he avoidably and therefore culpably contributes to and colludes with it. Perhaps one could keep an exact tally, for instance, of where his condescending or superior reactions are unavoidable, given his upbringing, and where they begin to become his fault. There is perhaps an instinct, at least in Catholic thought, shaped as it is by the practice of individual confession, to suppose that such a manner of distinguishing *must* be possible – but even if it is, it would be a mode of reckoning that would be impossibly complex, and it would not be an *illuminating* way to approach such a life. The general case is made very powerfully in Alistair McFadyen's *Bound to Sin* that the language of sin functions well descriptively precisely when it is *not* tied up neatly with individual moral accountability.[24]

---

on structural sin innocently. For a sustained exploration of 'the sins of sin-talk', see Stephen G. Ray, Jr, *Do No Harm: Social Sin and Christian Responsibility* (Minneapolis: Augsberg Fortress, 2003).

24. Alistair McFadyen, *Bound to Sin: Abuse, Holocaust, and the Christian Doctrine of Sin* (Cambridge: Cambridge University Press, 2000).

Trying to sort out the precise relationship between the personal and the structural would not help us describe what is going on, and more importantly, it would also not be conducive to the good conduct of such a life. A focus on how to maintain one's own innocence, how to know exactly where one is and is not responsible, when the entanglement in evil is so widespread and multi-layered, would be a distraction at best, and a selfish turning inwards at worst.

In short, then, the descriptively most plausible, and the practically most fruitful, position to take is that I both can and cannot distinguish my personal culpability from the larger structural evils around me: to live well in a context of structural sin requires a willingness to acknowledge this opacity; to refuse the opacity is to live less responsibly. I might refuse the opacity by saying that the system is so all encompassing that there is nothing I can do, no scope for particular individual responsibility, no better or worse ways of responding. Personal sin then disappears as a useful concept. Or I might refuse the opacity by determining that I will only accept personal culpability, personal sin, if I can identify exactly where it begins and ends, exactly where something could be said to be my fault. And because it would be impossible, or at least impossibly complex, to do this, I am likely to arrive at a severely limited conception of my own responsibility.

Critics of liberation theology have suggested that to adopt the notion of structural sin is to evade the seriousness of sin as personal responsibility before God. What I am suggesting is the reverse: to take on the notion of structural sin in its complex interweaving with personal sin is to *deepen* the notion of personal responsibility before God; it is actually the position of the critics, the resistance towards allowing for supra-personal patterns of sin which shape and entangle us, which tends to underestimate the seriousness of sin.

The *origins* of sin, too, seem necessarily shrouded in darkness, if one maintains the goodness of creation, and rejects any kind of ultimate dualism. How can one conceive of sin first entering into that which God made, and made to be good?[25] God gave humanity – or perhaps some broader set of creatures – freedom, we might say, but why would that freedom have been directed towards anything but the greatest good? Surely there would have to be something *already* wrong in one who would freely, culpably choose a lesser over a greater good. Was it pride, a desire for autonomy, the creature refusing to accept its dependence on the creator? But where did the pride come from, or the inclination to rebel against creatureliness?[26]

So on many levels we meet a darkness in sin, a difficulty in seeing it, a difficulty in explaining it. And at a number of these points, if we were to resist, to deny, the intellectual darkness associated with sin, the way in which it eludes us and

---

25. Note that this question is prior to, and distinct from, the question raised earlier in the essay, which was, assuming that we are *already* fallen, why it is that God, who could without damage to human freedom cause sinners to turn away from their sin, does not do so in every case?

26. It is possible of course to thicken and complexify the discussion of the origin of sin by locating it within a vision shaped by evolutionary biology and paleo-anthropology, but this cannot eliminate the underlying difficulty.

escapes our grasp, we would do so at a real cost. To demand that we must have a lucid, comprehensive account of the origin of sin, for instance, would push us towards a denial, on one level or another, of the goodness of creation. In the more practical realm, if we were to insist that we could only accept an account of personal sin which we could fully understand and clearly delineate, we would dull our understanding of our actual situation, and dull our capacities for morally sensitive response to this situation.

Very often, then, it seems that in matters relating to sin, to insist on intelligibility or explanation would be to take the wrong path. This does not of course dictate an answer to my original question; these considerations do not prove that it is a good thing that at the heart of the Augustinian tradition lies an unanswerable question about God's permission of sin, nor that it is a good thing to be faced with a worse problem of evil. But they do suggest one should be cautious in assuming, as philosophers of religion tend to, that one can always legitimately *prioritize* the resolution to any particular intellectual difficulty, that one can legitimately set intelligibility – in any area whatsoever – as one's goal, and then make a series of theological decisions accordingly.

On the other side, there are many theologians who would never consider allowing the problem of evil to set the terms for theological reflection, but the danger on this side, in my view, is to block certain questions altogether, to deem them simply malformed and illegitimate. If it would be a mistake to allow the search to solve the problem of evil to shape one's theological commitments, this is not because the problem of evil is in fact a non-problem. Julian was perfectly right to struggle with the question of why God, who is all courtesy and kindness and gentleness, and who does everything that is done, should permit sin. She was right to be distressed by it. And she was right to be unable to answer her own questions, except with God's threefold assurance that all shall be well, and all shall be well, and all manner of thing shall be well.

What we need, as both philosophers of religion and theologians, I would suggest, is not to block certain questions, nor to drop the search for clarity, but that they must seek greater clarity still, clarity about the reasons that in any given instance one might seek understanding, and the reasons why at times one might not.

Chapter 8

GRACE AND PARADOX

Issues of grace and justification are not, whatever may have been supposed in the past, church dividing – that this can be asserted with confidence is a tribute to the success of ecumenical scholarship in recent decades.[1] When one has said this, however, one has not necessarily said everything there is to say. There are real, enduring, ongoing *differences* in typical Protestant and Catholic patterning of thought around grace, and the differences are worth exploring: they are interesting, and theologically rich. In this paper, then, since the concern is with *on-going* difference, I will not attempt to repeat the work of historical theologians and revisit the struggles of the sixteenth century, but focus on what I take to be examples of systematic Protestant/Catholic differences in some recent theological work.

But is there anything that can be said *in general* about Catholic views of grace, or Protestant views of grace? Perhaps not. The aim in what follows will be to compare, not all Catholic with all Protestant thought, but what I take to be the best of Catholic theology, on the one hand, with a significant strand of Protestant theology, on the other – a pattern of talking about grace which is recognisably, distinctively Protestant even if not all Protestant thought falls into this pattern. One might say, by analogy, that the fast-talking New Yorker is a distinctively American type, even if not all Americans are fast-talking.

To begin, then, with a broad and perhaps familiar comparative framework. Catholic thought on grace tends to be shaped by its pairing with *nature*: much Protestant thought, by a pairing with *sin*. So for a typical Catholic thinker, how the human being is as created by God is a starting point for, or at least a significant point of reference for, reflection on grace – we have some sort of understanding of grace when we understand how grace takes us *beyond* the gift of nature; for at least some prominent strands in Protestant thought, by contrast, we understand grace to the extent that we understand that and how it is a response to sin – sin is the problem for which grace is the solution.

---

1. See the Lutheran-Roman Catholic *Joint Declaration on the Doctrine of Justification* of 1999, which was joined by the World Methodist Council in 2006, affirmed by the Anglican Communion in 2016, and signed up to by the World Communion of Reformed Churches in 2017.

What I would like to suggest is that in each of these patterns, in the sin/grace pattern and in the nature/grace pattern, there is a distinct pull towards paradox. One way to understand the Protestant/Catholic distinction, in other words, is to attend precisely to where one places one's paradox, or where one most inclines towards paradox. We might call this the lump-under-the-carpet issue: everyone has one, but it typically turns up in a slightly different place for Catholics than for Protestants.

In what follows, I will first offer a brief sketch of each of these two patterns (with their attendant lumps), and then look in a little more detail at the interaction of these patterns in some recent work by the leading American theologian Kathryn Tanner. Tanner provides an interesting case study for several reasons. While she has always done her constructive theology in a consciously ecumenical mode, deliberately drawing on a range of sources, pre-modern, Protestant and Catholic, and while her earlier works were I think equally accessible and helpful to Catholics and Protestants alike, a distinctly Protestant sensibility around sin and grace has made itself felt in her two most recent projects. In *Christ the Key* she borrows typically Catholic language of nature and grace to work out what is nevertheless a powerfully Protestant vision.[2] And in her recent Gifford lectures on theology and capitalism,[3] it becomes clear just what a far-reaching effect the commitment to a Protestant pattern of thinking on grace has: the question of where the lump under the carpet lies, of whether grace comes paired with sin or with nature, is not just a question about theological abstractions or about how to organize a text book, but a question which has a bearing on almost anything one might care to think of, including how one frames resistance to global financial capitalism.

I

Let me begin by proposing three principles which seem to govern a typically Protestant strand of the theology of grace. First, the sharpest possible antithesis between sin and grace must be maintained. For grace to be appreciated and our utter dependence on it grasped, the opposition between grace and what we are apart from grace, understood as a state of sin, needs to be as complete as possible. Secondly, there is a requirement that this radical dependence on grace can never become a thing of the past. The sin/grace opposition is always now, always contemporary, never narrated as a sequence that is receding in history. If sin did not remain a current reality, something which even now, and not just in the past, radically threatens; which even now, and not just in the past, needs to be met and overcome by grace, then grace would lose something of its power. And finally, grace can never be something in our control: it cannot be caught or held; it cannot

---

2. Kathryn Tanner, *Christ the Key* (Cambridge: Cambridge University Press, 2010).
3. *Christianity and the New Spirit of Capitalism* (New Haven and London: Yale University Press, 2019).

be supposed to reliably follow from anything which might lie in our command, anything that we might do, whether in sacrament and liturgy or good works or study or techniques of meditation or anything else.

With these three principles taken together, we are not far from the territory of paradox. On the one hand, the purpose of such a theology of grace is in large part to reinforce trust in and gratitude for what God does in Christ, to insist on the ever-present necessity of grace, to properly honour and praise it. On the other hand, because of the second principle, because our need for grace, our need for delivery from sin, must always continue to be emphasized, there is also a level on which we have to be very careful in talking about any change to who we are in ourselves being brought about by grace. It is not just that sanctification needs to be distinguished from justification, but that sanctification is somehow a source of real ambivalence, attended by a degree of nervousness. For this strand of Protestantism, there is something like a double affirmation always to be made: grace is really working, it is powerful, it makes all the difference; and grace is needed just as much today as it was yesterday, because we remain ultimately, in ourselves, unchanged, still sinners. One must be very careful about ever supposing that one has moved away from the starting point. One *must* insist that grace makes all the difference, but at the same time there is a pull towards insisting that on some level grace makes almost no difference.

Something of this pattern is I think captured in the words of the *Book of Common Prayer*, designed to be recited regularly by Anglicans at Morning and Evening prayer: after confessing, as Christians of any tradition might, that 'We have offended against thy holy laws: We have left undone those things which we ought to have done, and we have done those things which we ought not to have done', after confessing, in other words, *particular* sins of omission and commission, the Anglican faithful are led to draw a radically general conclusion: 'and there is no health in us'. So each morning and evening, in all kinds of ways the congregation as envisaged by the *Book of Common Prayer* prays for the grace of Christ and for the coming of the Holy Spirit – praying in a way that suggests that these things are real – and yet always they come back, half a day later, to the claim that they are starting from zero, that there has been absolutely no outcome, at least on the level of sanctification, from all the previous prayers: 'there is no health in us.'[4]

However, if there is, in a certain strand of Protestant thought, this proclivity towards a somewhat paradoxical account of sin and grace, this is not I think grounds for smugness on the part of Catholics. There might be a temptation, observing from the sidelines, to think to oneself, 'those poor Protestants, with their dialectical tendencies, constantly inclined towards getting themselves into a tangle over sin and grace – at least we have an intelligible account of such things, where we can tell a consistent, incremental story of a real if gradual healing of sin and

---

4. *The Book of Common Prayer* (London: Society for Promoting Christian Knowledge, 1953), 3.

a visible, if incomplete, effect of grace in our lives'.[5] Catholics need to resist such a smug response not only because there is probably some truth in the recurring Protestant worry that Catholic theology does not take sin seriously enough, and not only because we might hear something both existentially compelling and distinctly Pauline in this persisting Protestant dialectic. We also need to resist a smug response because Catholic theology of grace has its own paradoxical proclivity, its own field of recurring tension.

In Catholic theology, typically, there is an emphasis on the idea that nature, and specifically the human being as created by God, is good, to be valued and affirmed: it has its own kind of integrity, a certain wholeness, and yet it is also yearning for something more, incomplete, desiring to go beyond itself. It is whole and it is not whole. At the centre of nature is a longing to transcend nature. Or to approach the matter from the other side, grace and the supernatural are simultaneously in a sense 'natural' to us – they are what we long for, what we recognize, in encountering them, as that which fulfills us, that which we were made for – and radically *un*natural to us – they are strictly beyond us, they are that which we are, in ourselves, by our nature, *not*. Or again, if we shift to the language of divinization, the human being as divinized remains herself at the same time as she is raised above herself. One is simultaneously creaturely and raised to something beyond the creaturely; one is beyond oneself without ceasing to be oneself.

One of the most significant Catholic theological controversies of twentieth century was provoked by Henri de Lubac's *Surnaturel*, and specifically the claim within it (which I have just been echoing in various ways) that there is a natural desire for the supernatural.[6] De Lubac emerged the clear winner in this controversy from the point of view of fidelity to the tradition – he is a persuasive reader of the history of theology – and spiritual depth.[7] There is one respect, however, in which his neo-scholastic opponents undoubtedly had the advantage: they held to a position which was much easier to understand, whose consistency and coherence were clear. One way of reading the *Surnaturel* controversy, then, is that in Catholic theology if one wishes to have a clear, straight-forward, paradox-free account of nature and grace, it is possible to do so – one can construct a fully comprehensible system of the relation between the natural and the supernatural. One can do this, however, only at the cost of a kind of sterility, and only if one is willing to operate

---

5. Ibid.

6. Henri de Lubac, *Surnaturel* (Paris: Aubeir-Montaigne, 1945). For an overview of de Lubac's position, see Nicholas J. Healy Jr, 'The Christian Mystery of Nature and Grace', in J. Hillebert (ed.), *The T&T Clark Companion to Henri de Lubac* (London: Bloomsbury, 2017), 181–204. For a broader discussion, see S. Bonino, ed. and trans. R. Williams and Matthew Levering, *Surnaturel: A Controversy at the Heart of Twentieth-Century Thomistic Thought* (Ave Maria: Sapientia, 2009) and Daniel Rober, *Recognising the Gift: Towards a Renewed Theology of Nature and Grace* (Minneapolis: Fortress Press, 2016).

7. This is in any case my reading of the controversy, and one which is shared by many contemporary Catholic theologians, though admittedly not by all.

with a certain of deafness to the longer tradition. Some Catholic theology avoids any hint of paradox here, I am suggesting, but the best Catholic theology does not.

Lest such an analysis seem overly dependent on one line of argument from Henri de Lubac, it is worth briefly considering one further example, that of Karl Rahner. One of Rahner's earliest works, appearing a few years before de Lubac's *Surnaturel*, is *Encounters with Silence*, a set of ten brief prayers.[8] These prayers offer, of course, no technical exploration of the nature/grace relationship, but in them one can detect a distinctive nature/grace pattern of thought.

One way to summarize the prayers is as a series of dialogues between two characters, an 'I' and a 'You', where 'I' is full of complaints and laments, and 'You' is depicted in various ways, but above all as infinite, ungraspable, and silent. Much of the drama in these prayers revolves around a sense of struggle, of wrestling, between the I and the You, often depicted precisely as a struggle of the finite and the infinite: 'why do you torment me with your infinity,' writes Rahner, 'if I can never really measure it? Why do You constrain me to walk along Your paths, if they lead only to the awful darkness of Your night, where only You can see?'[9]

What is worth noting is that while many of the images used in relation to God might, taken in themselves, seem to have an impersonal quality – infinity, endlessness, unapproachable brightness and so on – they are presented precisely in the context of addressing a 'You'. We find written into these prayers *both* the presumption that God is utterly ungraspable, infinite, boundless, incomprehensible; *and* that the 'I' is in an immediate, intimate, intense relationship with God. It is this constantly present tension which gives much of the power and interest to these prayers. And once one attends to this tension, one can see it returning at key moments in Rahner's subsequent theology – and can see that it is, essentially, a nature-grace tension. God, in the language of the later Rahner, is the ungraspable horizon towards which all our acts of knowing and willing are ultimately directed – this much the philosopher can know, on his account, because this much is written into human nature – but in grace the horizon draws near, and communicates itself. What does this mean? What could it possibly mean – how can one think of a self-communicating horizon, or a horizon which remains a horizon while also being 'God of absolute closeness and immediacy'?[10] Rahner, who works so carefully to unpack so many ideas, leaves us without help any real help in reconciling the images he offers. My suggestion is that the tension Rahner generates here is not incidental or accidental but deliberate. These rather paradoxical patterns are precisely the *right* kind of patterns with which to talk about the nature-grace relationship.

There is a proclivity towards paradox in the sin/grace opposition in Protestant thought, or at least in one recognisable strand of Protestant thought, and there is a proclivity towards paradox in the nature/grace complementarity of Catholic

---

8. Karl Rahner, *Encounters with Silence* (South Bend: St. Augustine Press, 1999).

9. Ibid., 4–5.

10. Rahner, *Foundations of Christian Faith: An Introduction to the Idea of Christianity* (New York: Crossroad, 1989), 129.

thought, or at least in what I take to be the better examples of Catholic theology. My proposal is not that there is necessarily a contradiction on either side, but that in both camps we find a tendency to hold certain patterns of thought or affirmation together unsynthesized, rather than force them into a single, fully articulable, fully graspable, unity.

II

Let us turn now to a case study: the recent work of Kathryn Tanner. *Christ the Key*, Tanner's sixth book, offers a confirmation of the enduring nature of the Protestant-Catholic divide – and it does so precisely *as* it seeks to lay out an understanding of grace which can bridge this divide.

Tanner sets out to work in a traditionally Catholic pattern, a nature-grace rather than a sin-grace pattern, but to do this in a way which 'accords quite well with Protestant sensibilities'.[11] Within a Catholic framework, she wants to show, in other words, that it is possible to come up with something that can suit Protestant instincts. What she offers is fascinating, drawing in a way which is typical of much of Tanner's work on familiar aspects of the tradition even as she unfolds a position which is fresh and somehow unfamiliar. It is an account of grace which not only aims to satisfy Protestant instincts while working from a broadly Catholic framework, but which also, Tanner argues, has the capacity to escape the recurring difficulties into which Catholic theology itself falls in trying to defend the integrity of nature and the freedom of grace. However, in reworking the nature-grace pattern in such a way that it can make sense to Protestants, Tanner ends up transforming nature-and-grace language into something fundamentally dissonant with Catholic sensibilities. Though she speaks of nature and grace, that is to say, she in effect reproduces a *sin*-grace pattern, with its characteristic moment of tension around needing to both affirm and deny the efficacy of grace. Tanner may indeed, as she implies, have found a way to get rid of the lump under the carpet where Catholics tend to have a problem with it, but the lump nevertheless makes itself felt in a more typically Protestant location.

When we think about human nature, Tanner proposes, we should think about its plasticity: 'what is of theological interest' in human nature is its 'lack of given definition, its malleability through outside influences, unbounded character, and general openness to radical transformation'.[12] Nature is essentially undetermined. More particularly, she holds that humans are so designed as to *require* grace – they need, for their proper functioning, 'to have within themselves something which they are not':[13] 'Our faculties were made to operate as they should, to operate well, only when incorporating what remains alien to them, the very perfection of

---

11. Tanner, *Christ*, 58.
12. Ibid., 1.
13. Ibid., 22.

Word and Spirit themselves.'[14] Human nature, in the absence of grace, is not just not-quite-what-it-could-be, containing perhaps some unfulfilled longing: human nature in the absence of grace is fundamentally lost. And this is true even if we do not introduce any particular consideration of sin: nature without grace is lost, not because sin has in some way *wounded* it, but simply because we were never designed to work properly except in dependence on that which is beyond us, on grace. One might think of the relationship of a petrol-driven lawnmower to the fuel which powers it. It is not that there is a natural fuel, and then some special extra high octane fuel which corresponds to an elevation in grace, but rather that it is the nature of the lawnmower to rely on something beyond itself, something which is not part of the machinery itself, in order to be able to work. The fact that without the petrol the lawnmower goes nowhere is not a sign that it has endured any particular damage, that it has sustained some particular distortion to its original nature, but that it was never, from its origins, designed to run without fuel.[15]

Tanner's novel patterning of nature and grace is likely to jar with typical Catholic sensibilities on several counts. The goodness of nature can be affirmed here only in a severely limited way – in itself it is good as a necessary stage towards something else, but no more than that. Without grace, as Tanner puts it in one place, human nature 'seems utterly wrecked'.[16] She works with the concept of nature, but by making it so malleable, incomplete and needy, she seems, from a Catholic perspective, to have obscured its goodness just as surely as if she were operating with a more typically Protestant sin-and-grace perspective. And then there is the frequent emphasis on the *alien-ness* of grace to nature. Again and again, grace is referred to as that which we are *not*: 'what makes our lives good', Tanner writes, to give one example, 'is not anything we are ourselves but the presence within us of what we are not';[17] 'we are not good in virtue of what we are but of what we are not';[18] 'our faculties were made to operate as they should, to operate well, only when incorporating what remains alien to them';[19] Christ remains 'foreign' to us even when present to us.[20]

---

14. Ibid., 28.

15. The lawnmower analogy is mine rather than Tanner's, and is partially misleading because lawnmowers do not partake in our 'plasticity'. Furthermore, without grace, we are not *exactly* like a lawnmower without fuel: it is not quite the case that we would not move, or do anything, at all. It is just that without grace, on Tanner's account, we have no particular inclination to move in the *right direction*. Human nature was just never designed to work properly without a reliance on that which comes from beyond, on grace.

16. Ibid., 109.
17. Ibid., 76–7.
18. Ibid., 77.
19. Ibid., 28.
20. Ibid., 102.

Tanner is of course perfectly aware that she is deploying nature-grace language in a way that is at odds with typical Catholic instincts. So, for instance, within her system it can be affirmed that grace completes or perfects nature, but she points out that the statement does *not* serve, as it does in Catholic theology, as a way to 'emphasis[e] the value of creation, which the gift of God's grace respects'. Instead, the phrase, as deployed by Tanner, serves to point 'out the inadequacies that essentially mar [nature] and that account for God's own dissatisfaction with it'.[21] She is well aware that this will be, to Catholic ears, an uneasy deployment of the language of nature and grace. But part of her argument is that this Protestantizing, as one might call it, of the nature/grace pattern has the advantage of escaping from the difficulties that have plagued Catholic discussions in the area.

Tanner argues at some length that since its rejection of the neoscholastic notion of a more or less self-enclosed pure nature, Catholic thought has not been able to find a satisfactory way of showing that nature has an orientation towards grace while also defending grace's gratuity. Theologians have felt they needed to protect the latter, the gratuity of grace, by holding onto the idea that some sort of reasonable human life would in principle be possible without it, but then have wanted to stave off extrinsicism by inserting into their understanding of such a life 'the natural desire for the supernatural'. Tanner enumerates a series of difficulties this has led to.[22] In her own scheme, by contrast, there is no need to posit a 'natural desire for the supernatural' because there is never any question that any sort of a reasonable human life could be possible without grace. There is no natural desire for the supernatural, one might say, but instead just a complete mess if nature is deprived of the supernatural. She can still offer a defence of the gratuity of grace, but it comes, she argues, from a completely different angle – not through any thought experiment about the sufficiency of a purely natural existence, but through attention to what grace itself is, which is so other to everything creaturely that it could never be anything but unexacted, free, gratuitous.

What Tanner is suggesting, then, is that she has found a way to make the typical Catholic lump under the carpet go away. If one rethinks nature and grace along these radical, Protestantized lines, one can simply bypass the recurring tensions, disputes and difficulties in Catholic thought. Interestingly, though, when Tanner turns to the question of what effects on our actual, experienced lives the grace of Christ might have, a different set of tensions and difficulties starts to make itself manifest. At some moments, Tanner writes of the experienced consequences of grace in a very positive mode. As a result of the Incarnation she suggests, our situation changes radically: 'what we are given in Christ so adheres to us as to amount to a kind of redone internal constitution. Via the hypostatic union, we are wrapped around with something we cannot get rid of, something that therefore inevitably makes itself felt in all

---

21. Ibid., 61.
22. Ibid., 106–26.

that we go on to become.'²³ The gift of the Spirit is the flip side of attachment to Christ, through which comes genuine sanctification, 'Actual renovation of our lives', through which, in a progressive manner, 'we begin to do good to our fellow creatures'.²⁴ At other points, however, it seems the situation is a little more complicated: having affirmed progressive sanctification on one page, on the next she writes, 'nothing has necessarily happened to change our human character. The immediate impression made on us is a divine rather than a human one: it amounts to the presence of the Holy Spirit itself'.²⁵ So a bifurcation seems to be opening up in her portrait of the justified Christian. There is the divine level, where everything happens all at once – the presence of the Holy Spirit itself – and then the human level, which has no fixed correlation with this. So she writes that 'the Holy Spirit may be genuinely given to us, present within us, even when that fact is not made visible in our changed dispositions and deeds', and that it is possible to 'have the Spirit for our own in virtue of our attachment to Christ without drawing upon it'.²⁶ All this is perhaps summed up with her statement that 'one must carefully distinguish the holiness of the divine Spirit itself [which is "in" us, in virtue of our justification] from any holiness of ours that is its consequence'.²⁷ So it seems imaginable, on Tanner's account, that a person can be not only justified but sanctified, in virtue of the presence within them of the Holy Spirit, and yet nothing whatsoever is changed in the concrete pattern of their life or in the nature of their experience.²⁸

Tanner's reflection on nature and grace, then, is a fascinating thought experiment in the possibility of overcoming deep divides between certain typically Protestant and Catholic thought patterns, but an experiment which in the end tends to confirm the persisting power of these differences.

Discussions of grace can risk appearing obscure and technical: one can begin to wonder whether theologians twist themselves into knots over issues which do not on a practical level make any difference. It is partly for this reason that I want to consider a final example, Tanner's 2016 Gifford lectures, published in 2019 as *Christianity and the New Spirit of Capitalism*.

The starting point for these Gifford lectures is Max Weber's famous thesis about the Protestant ethic and the spirit of capitalism. Tanner's project is both a tribute to Weber and an exercise in turning him on his head. Tanner endorses Weber's method of working with ideal types, agrees with his key premise that religious beliefs 'have the capacity to provide powerful psychological sanctions

---

23. Ibid., 72.
24. Ibid., 87.
25. Ibid., 89.
26. Ibid.
27. Ibid., 90.
28. This seems to be a Protestant version of the neo-scholastic *extrinsicism* which Karl Rahner so frequently attacked, where grace can occur in some sense behind our backs, on some other plane entirely than the plane of our conscious, lived experience.

for economic behaviour',[29] and admires his instinct to undermine the inevitable, natural-seeming quality of the capitalism of his time. So in various ways she follows Weber. The overall goal of her project, however, is not to link the spirit of capitalism to a Protestant work ethic, but just the reverse: to undermine the spirit of capitalism with a Christian or Protestant *anti-work* ethic. In successive chapters, Tanner isolates key features of the spirit of our contemporary finance-dominated capitalism, especially as concerns its relation to time and the way it shapes the self, and then shows how Christian belief, or a certain *style* of Christian belief, offers a radically opposed alternative.

The characteristically Protestant tension between claiming that grace changes everything, and that grace changes nothing at all, makes itself felt in this project on two levels. It makes itself felt, first of all, at particular moments in the text. In the second chapter, for instance, Tanner contrasts a feature of contemporary capitalism according to which the past controls and in a sense sucks all life and possibility out of present and future – because of the role that both debt and target-setting play – with a Christian vision according to which the past is utterly repudiated, where that which has organized one's whole life in the past (i.e. sin) is entirely renounced. The relationship to the past is conceived according to notions of radical disjunction, rather than as a gradual process of present and future evolving out of past, and even less as past controlling, determining and limiting the future. If, however, we put this notion of radical disjunction and radical repudiation together with the proposition, which Tanner also affirms, that the moment of conversion is constantly re-initiated in the Christian life, that being *in* this moment of a break with the past is the constant state of a Christian, we seem to have something of a puzzle. There is an absolute contrast between before and after, and yet after can never actually come, because one is always beginning again in the moment of absolute repudiation of the past. This seems to mean that while grace, the action of God, makes all the difference in us, it may also make no discernible difference whatsoever.

The second level to consider is that of the project as a whole. It is all about setting up a radical opposition – between a total package, an all-consuming logic, of finance dominated capitalism, and an utterly contrasting vision of self and time derived from Christian faith. There are several things that one does not find as part of the mix here. First, there is no account offered of an underlying good of which finance-dominated capitalism is a distortion, nor of any partial goods in our current economic order. Secondly, there is nothing like a concrete plan of action offered – no suggestion of ways in which we might resist, reform, undo global capitalism, or even begin to do so, take any steps in this direction. Nor does one find, thirdly, any attention given to already existing concrete practices of resistance, to the possibility that there may be pockets of life that are governed otherwise than by the capitalist system. There is the stark contrast between finance-dominated capitalism and the Christian vision, and nothing which acts as any kind of bridge or connection between them.

---

29. Ibid., 4.

None of these points are intended as criticism. And each of the absences I mentioned can be understood in a number of ways. Tanner – and many others – would probably say that it is the nature of the current capitalism to engulf, to swallow up, to reabsorb all particular attempts to resist it, forcing its own logic on them, so that only a radically alien thought pattern has any hope of piercing its totality, and any currently imaginable and concrete suggestions would be doomed to failure. The absence of attention to already existing spheres of resistance might also be a result of not trying to do everything in one book: Tanner is a thinker who operates at a relatively high level of abstraction, and has deliberately focused the project around ideal types rather around any sort of search for exceptions.

If it is true, however, that these absences can be explained in terms of the nature of contemporary capitalism and the nature of the project Tanner undertakes, it is important also to notice how consonant they all are with a distinctively Protestant style of thought around sin and grace. What we are given is a sharp contrast, a contrast made as sharp as it possibly can be, between the economic system and the Christian vision, and no way of bringing the two together, no hint of how the grace of Christ is already making a difference, or how it could possibly make a difference. It makes all the difference, but there is a distinct hesitation to consider how it makes any particular difference.

III

Alongside questions of formal doctrinal condemnation or reconciliation, then, there are also questions of theological style: questions about where the focus and the emphasis are placed, where the intellectual tensions are endured. At this level, it is not clear that we are seeing Protestant and Catholic theology moving closer to one another. Indeed, we need not suppose that convergence, at this level, is a goal. The ongoing dualism of theological styles may rather be one of the gifts of the Reformation. It can be a difficult gift to live with at times, insofar as one tends to find the tension or paradoxes of the other side troubling, while finding those of one's own side natural and obviously necessary, but it remains, nevertheless, a gift.

Chapter 9

CHRISTIAN THEOLOGY, ANTI-LIBERALISM AND MODERN JEWISH THOUGHT

In this paper I will explore not so much the impact or trace of modern Jewish thought on Christian theology, as its absence, its absence in particular at a juncture where one might have expected to find it. I want to probe, that is to say, a point at which the influence of modern Jewish thought is strikingly *missing* from contemporary Christian theological debates, and consider what might be the value to Christian theology of a greater engagement at this point.

There are, of course, traces of Judaism, and of modern Jewish thought specifically, to be found in contemporary Christian theology. Buber, or at least a few themes from Buber, are widely quoted. Christian theologians grapple with Levinas in various ways. Hannah Arendt appears from time to time, Hans Jonas is beginning to become a presence, and one can find a theologian like Jürgen Moltmann making use of Bloch in one book, Heschel in another.[1]

There is also to be found, in twentieth and twenty-first century Christian theology, a serious wrestling with the question of Christianity's relation to Judaism. Christianity's traditional supersessionism, its traditional displacement theology, has been formally repudiated by a number of churches, and the question of how this repudiation requires a reshaping of the whole pattern of Christian narrative and doctrine continues to be a matter for reflection. Kendall Soulen's *The God of Israel and Christian theology*[2] offers an impressive example of this sort of work, and Peter Ochs in *Another Reformation:Postliberal Christianity and the Jews* undertakes an important analysis, from a Jewish perspective, of a whole series of so-called postliberal Christian theologies with respect to their position on supersessionism.[3]

---

1. The frequency with which appeal to Buber is made by Christian thinkers, and the paucity of reference of a figure like Rosenzweig, might suggest that the 'canon' of modern Jewish thinkers as perceived by Christian theologians has its own distinctive shape.

2. R. Kendall Soulen, *The God of Israel and Christian Theology* (Minneapolis: Augsburg Fortress, 1996).

3. Peter Ochs, *Another Reformation: Postliberal Christianity and the Jews* (Grand Rapids: Baker Academic, 2011).

This belated self-correction of Christian theology is very important, but engagement with Jewish thought – certainly with recent Jewish thought – is not, as far as I can see, a particularly central or necessary part of it. What is primarily at issue, if one wants to get away from supersessionism, is how Christian theology arranges its own elements: how it sees one part of its Scriptures in relation to another; how it understands one theological concept – that of 'Church' – in relation to another – 'Israel'; and so on. What is at stake, to put it slightly differently, is a reform of how Christians think about Jews – and a number other things in light of this – but not necessarily a particular focus on how Jews think of Christianity.[4]

The focus of this paper, then, will be on one recurring theme in modern Jewish thought, and particularly in modern Jewish thinking *about Christianity*, which has to my knowledge made no impact whatsoever on Christian theology, and my proposal will be that Christian theology might in fact benefit were it to pay some attention to this.

I

The theme in question revolves around the notion of paganism. A number of Jewish thinkers over the last few centuries have envisaged some form of fundamental contrast between Judaism and paganism, and many present Christianity either as poised between the two poles, or as aligned with one – with Judaism – but nevertheless subject to a distinct leaning, a distinct temptation, towards the other – as constantly in danger of sliding towards paganism.

This is a pattern that emerges in the Jewish Enlightenment, with Solomon Formstecher, to give one example, contrasting the religion of nature with the religion of spirit, where the religion of nature is termed paganism and the purest example of the religion of spirit is Judaism.[5] In the one God is identified with nature, in the other God is recognized as transcending nature. Christianity and Islam are fundamentally classified, along with Judaism, on the side of a religion of spirit, but Christianity in fact contains a mixture of the false paganism with the 'true transcendence of Judaism' and Christianity's history is construed as the history of a struggle between these elements. Or again, Samuel Hirsch presents religion in terms of paganism, Judaism, and Christianity, with paganism being valueless, Judaism representing the true religion which recognizes ethical freedom and the transcendence of God, and Christianity lying somewhere in the middle,

---

4. It is important not to exaggerate the distinction I am drawing here. Soulen, for example, is insistent that 'the path beyond supersessionism must go by way of renewed encounter with the theological claims of Jewish existence' (*The God of Israel*, 5) and himself draws upon the work of Michael Wyschogrod.

5. The account of figures from the Jewish Enlightenment in this paragraph draws from Norbert M. Samuelson's *An Introduction to Modern Jewish Philosophy* (Albany: State University of New York Press, 1989).

having corrupted its Jewish inheritance with notions of original sin and salvation by Christ.

In the thought of Franz Rosenzweig, things become more complex, but something of the same pattern seems to emerge. Paganism is no longer characterized completely negatively, nor is the term used quite so broadly as a catch-all for everything contrasted to Judaism. Paganism seems to be paradigmatically the position of the ancient Greeks, and in Rosenzweig's thought it stands in contrast to, and in a position of superiority to, religions of the East such as Buddhism – and also indeed to Islam. So Rosenzweig's presentation of paganism is at least partly sympathetic – it seems to represent something like the best we can do, the highest expression of human longing, prior to revelation. Rosenzweig also, in a certain sense, has a very positive view of Christianity – it is not understood, in its difference from Judaism, purely in terms of corruption, lack, deviation, but as having, alongside Judaism, a crucial providential role.

So the story is considerably more complex in Rosenzweig, but for all that something of the pattern of the thinkers of the Haskalah is still to be found: Rosenzweig presents Christians as always threatened by a reversion into paganism. Thus, while Jews are born Jewish, Christians always have to become Christian – they all begin as pagans, and they are constantly needing to resist their paganism.[6] Rosenzweig writes that there is a 'piece of paganism in every Christian', and it shows itself in the centrality of the incarnation, in the fact that the Christian can only trust that God wants to condescend to him if God can appear as man, in the fact that for the Christian God's vitality only becomes real if it appears in the flesh of a particular man.[7] Or again, Rosenzweig suggests that because Christianity has to be on a mission to incorporate the pagan peoples within it, it is constantly in danger of absorbing the paganism itself. Christianity hovers, then, necessarily but also dangerously and problematically, between Judaism and paganism.

In our own time we might point to a figure like Agata Bielik-Robson. Bielik-Robson is engaged in an ambitious project of intellectual reorientation, seeking to persuade us to redraw our fundamental philosophical and cultural maps so that Jewish thought can be seen not as a marginal and peculiar phenomenon, a 'Yiddish twist' on the fringes of mainstream cultural developments, but rather as both a powerful shaping force on modernity and the bearer of one of the fundamental options which now lies open to us. Her argument is woven out of an exploration of and conversation with a wide range of figures, and quite frequently we meet, once

---

6. 'This is indeed the profoundest difference between the Jewish and the Christian man, that the Christian man, innately, or at least on account of birth – is a pagan, but the Jew is a Jew. So the way of the Christian must be a way of self-renunciation, he must always go away from himself, give himself up in order to become Christian' Franz Rosenzweig, *The Star of Redemption*, trans. Barbara E. Galli (Madison: University of Wisconsin Press, 2005), 430.

7. Ibid., 371. It is worth mentioning that the discussion here concludes on a rather positive note: 'precisely that "paganism" of the Christian qualifies him for the conversion of the pagans.'

again, in her thought and in her treatment of others, 'pagan' as a category which stands in some kind of fundamental opposition to the Jewish.[8] And though the role or significance of Christianity does not (thus far, in any case) hold as prominent a place in her thought as it does in that of Rosenzweig, there are clear indications in her scheme also that some forms of Christianity, at least, are in danger of going over into paganism.[9]

II

Now, if one accepts the existence of such a strand in modern Jewish thought, one might suppose that there is in fact good reason why Christian theologians have not thus far attended to it. One might suppose that Christian theology, if it is going to remain in any sense Christian, must simply reject or dismiss this accusation of paganism; that what is at stake here is an irreducible difference between Christianity and Judaism, so that a theologian could not ask whether there might not be something worth listening to here, and in particular something worth worrying about, without thereby in fact ceasing to be a specifically *Christian* theologian.

Certainly some of the aspects of Christianity which have been associated by Jewish thinkers with paganism, such as the incarnation or the link between Christ and salvation, are non-negotiable for most mainstream Christians. But the recurring concern about a pagan temptation of Christianity seems to go beyond this, at least in some of its articulations: it is not just that Christianity is presented as *being* pagan, or partly pagan, but that it is depicted as *tempted* in this direction, as exposed to particular *dangers* of drifting off in this direction. And given that Christianity does also understand itself as holding onto an affirmation of God's transcendence, God's otherness from nature – from creation – then it ought to have its own reasons for taking seriously any suggestions that it is in fact in danger of sliding into paganism.

The issue is of course a large one, but one dimension of the Judaism/paganism pattern of thought that I will focus on here is the link that some Jewish thinkers suggest between paganism and modern disenchantment, or rather, the link

---

8. Cf. for instance the presentation of certain understandings of the sublime as pagan in 'Troubles with Divine Aesthetics: A. J. Heschel's Tarrying with the Sublime', in Adam Lipszyc and Stanisław Krajewski (eds), *Abraham Joshua Heschel: Philosophy, Theology and Interreligious Dialogue* (Wiesbaden: Harrasowitz Verlag, 2009), 67–86, or the way the category is introduced through a discussion of Rosenzweig in 'Nihilism through the Looking Glass: Nietzsche, Rosenzweig, and Scholem on the Condition of Modern Disenchantment', *Revero. Revista de Estudas da Religiao*, San Paulo (Spring, 2008): 39–67.

9. One can see this, for example, in 'Nihilism Through the Looking Glass,' and its examination of what is involved in certain understandings of the resurrection and in certain Christian theologies of participation and the beatific vision.

between the *repudiation* of paganism and the disenchantment of modernity. If paganism has something to do with the sacralization of nature, sheer awe at the greatness of being, if it has something to do with finding and worshipping something divine in the world, then the modern process of disenchantment, of stripping the world of its sacredness, its mythic qualities, its meaning even, should be understood not so much nostalgically a loss of a necessary religious sensibility, a development which makes it *harder* for the modern person to turn to God, but in a fundamentally more positive light. Modern disenchantment is something Jewish thought can be seen both to move towards and to affirm. If a mythicising paganism is no longer an option, then faced with a meaningless world stripped bare, the possibility of acknowledging the transcendence of God is enhanced rather than diminished.[10]

III

Christian theology, I have already suggested, gives no attention to the strand of thought I have been discussing. A reader of Christian theology will not meet 'paganism' as a category of critique or concern in contemporary Christian thought, much less any reflection on whether Christianity itself may be peculiarly threatened by a temptation towards it. One could perhaps point to the category of 'idolatry' as the closest approximation – idolatry as temptation and danger can appear as a concern in Christian theology, though not necessarily at the moment a particularly dominant one – but the term functions considerably more narrowly than the notion of 'paganism' and the richly textured discussion which surrounds it seems to in modern Jewish thought.[11]

It would be difficult to give a unified *positive* account of the state of contemporary Christian theology, but one thing common to many of the strongest voices, certainly in recent British and American theology – voices ranging from Hauerwasians to the followers of the so-called Yale school to the adherents of Radical Orthodoxy to the Barthians – is a *negative* point: they are united in rejecting theological liberalism, not only the nineteenth century liberalism

---

10. In 'Nihilism through the Looking Glass' Bielik-Robson highlights (in the context of a larger and more complex argument, which has a confrontation between 'the Nietzscheans' and 'the Hebrews' at its core) an affirmation of *Entzauberung*, the embracing of a modern secularizing disenchantment as a necessary religious moment, as a feature of the thought of a number of modern Jewish thinkers. So, for instance, she writes, 'For Rosenzweig (and for the whole Judaic tradition, for which Rosenzweig serves here as a spokesman and *pars pro toto*), religion … is a mature, courageous stance towards reality, actively forcing its demythologization and disenchantment.'

11. One is also more likely in contemporary Christian theology to find idolatry employed as a term of critique *ad extra* – the idolatry of capitalism or of the celebrity culture, for instance – than as tool for self-examination.

running from Schleiermacher through Ritschl, but anything which much more broadly could be said to smack of liberalism. The danger is understood to be one of accommodation, loss of nerve, loss of theological substance, loss of Christian distinctiveness. A liberal is seen as one who is so concerned to adopt to the times, or to make sense to the mentality of our age, or to speak to the modern person, or to justify the rationality or the meaningfulness of Christianity, so concerned to do all these things that they in fact distort the gospel and evacuate theology of its proper content. What is valued across at least a number of these otherwise differing groups, I think, is the capacity to articulate Christian distinctiveness, and often to retrieve pre-modern modes of thought, ways of doing theology and ways of reading scripture.

This is not intended to paint a picture of contemporary Christian theology as fundamentalist. Many in fact argue that fundamentalism is just the other side of the same coin as liberalism, equally enthralled to a modern mindset and equally mistaken. Nor ought this description of a dominant anti-liberalism suggest that current Christian theologians are simply conservative, or simply wanting to retreat into the middle ages. They may value a rediscovery of certain pre-modern ways of thinking, but it is a matter of *rediscovery*, of creative retrieval, and not simply of blind repetition. Modern and liberal values are as a matter of fact present, in my judgment, in the way contemporary theologians proceed, but their focus, and the focus of current Christian theological rhetoric, tends not to be on any of this, but on the need to preserve distinctiveness and on the dangers of liberal accommodation.

In the dominant voices of contemporary Christian theology, then – the theology of the past fifteen or twenty years at least – 'modernity' appears principally in negative guise, as danger, as that which we must avoid judging ourselves by and moulding ourselves to. It appears as that which is alien, as that which distorts. There have certainly been theologians in the last half century who have taken a far more positive approach, who have found in modernity something positive for Christian faith, something that represents an advance, a clarification, an opportunity – but such thinkers all now have the ring of liberals, and as a result they are little published, little read, little taught, little written on – they do not get much attention, except occasionally as foil.

IV

If the rejection of paganism, as I suggested above, has been linked to one of the central features of modernity – disenchantment – does it follow that *nervousness* of modernity might in fact carry with it particular dangers of paganism? The link, stated thus abstractly, sounds perhaps a little far-fetched, but experience may bear it out. I want to consider at this point a case study: two Roman Catholic theologians, Karl Rahner and Hans Urs von Balthasar, one German and one German-speaking Swiss, near contemporaries who were at their intellectual peak in the 1950s, 1960s and 1970s.

Rahner and Balthasar are often seen to indicate two very different roads down which Roman Catholic theology could go. In the 1960s and early 1970s, Rahner's star was in the ascendant, Balthasar a rather doubtful and shadowy figure, but since then Balthasar's standing in the church and among theologians has been steadily rising, while Rahner is much less in fashion. And this is true outside of Roman Catholicism as much or more than it is true within it – Balthasar is the conversational partner of choice for a whole range of Protestant and Anglican thinkers who wish to engage with a Catholic, whereas Rahner is routinely set to one side.

One point on which Rahner and Balthasar quite sharply diverge is precisely in their relation to modernity. Rahner tends to stress that we all are inescapably modern, that Christian faith must be formulated in an idiom that the modern person can understand and integrate with their thinking more broadly, and indeed that there are aspects of modernity which contribute to something like a purification of Christian faith. Balthasar's rhetoric towards modernity is, on the other hand – at least after a certain point in his career – almost entirely negative. Modernity is cast generally in terms of loss, of lack, of deficiency, of blindness: it is something whose self-satisfaction and smugness needs to be pierced.[12]

The positive, or partly positive, tone that Rahner takes towards modernity is a significant part of what has led to his marginalization in more recent theology. His thought is routinely presented as controlled, shaped, distorted, by an option for modern philosophical thought in general, or the Kantian transcendental turn more specifically. And conversely the fact that Balthasar is seen as standing apart from modernity, as presenting a genuinely different possibility for theology, seems to be a significant dimension of his appeal.

But the reason for attending to Rahner and Balthasar in this context is not just to see that Christian theologians take different stances towards modernity, and at the moment the anti-modern tone is winning more votes. What is particularly interesting is that Balthasar's anti-modern rhetoric does indeed seem to go hand-in-hand with what one might call a slide towards paganism.

I have not offered a precise conception of paganism, since the thinkers whom I reviewed above do not present paganism in precisely the same way, but on almost *any* conception of what it might be, Balthasar seems to move Christian theology in that direction. This could be shown in a number of ways – by exploring the significance of his development of theological aesthetics, for instance, or of his dramatic approach to theology – but I will take a simpler route, and focus on what might be called Balthasar's 're-mythologizing' of Christianity.

This process of re-mythologizing goes on across Balthasar's oeuvre. His much-discussed theology of Holy Saturday, with its vivid and untraditional presentation

---

12. For a more extended discussion of the relationship between the two, and their differing attitudes to modernity, cf. my 'Balthasar and Karl Rahner', in Edward T. Oakes, S. J. and David Moss (eds), *The Cambridge Companion to Hans Urs von Balthasar* (Cambridge: Cambridge University Press, 2004).

of Christ's sinking passively into hell, as one dead among the dead, and enduring the full horror of abandonment and rejection by God, can be seen as a kind of innovative mythologization of the atonement. More generally his treatment of the eternal relations between the persons of the Trinity has a distinct, and again untraditional, mythological quality: he is able to describe these relations in considerable detail, complete with references of the divine persons' gratitude, amazement, prayer towards one another, their consideration for one another, even their decision-making procedures.[13]

One can also see a remythologization at work in his presentation of the characters who surround Jesus in the Gospels – Mary, Peter, John, Paul – not as historical individuals, but as the fundamental constellation of the church, as quasi-eternal types, so that Peter, for instance, represents not just himself, a particular individual, nor even, as you might expect from a Catholic, the first in the line of popes, but actually the institutional element in the church as such, popes, bishops and clergy, hierarchy, the need for order and rules, for office in the church; and again John represents not just an individual, but love, the saints, the charismatic element, sanctity in the church. And so when Peter and John go to the empty tomb, and John arrives first but stands aside for Peter, this is an expression of the relation of the church as holiness to the church as institution. One might argue that a mythicising reading of Mary is well-established in the Catholic tradition, but Balthasar is not simply taking up familiar patterns here, but freely inventing new ones.

A particularly significant and disturbing element of remythologization appears in what is sometimes euphemistically described as Balthasar's 'nuptial theology'. Gender difference – the difference between the man, construed as active and taking initiative, and the woman, construed as receptive – plays a key role in his thought, as does also the pattern of sexual reproduction. One meets gendered conceptions of activity and receptivity, and indeed images of seeds and wombs, at almost every level in Balthasar's writings. He makes much of the scriptural image of the church as the bride of Christ, and wants to retrieve the traditional deduction from this that Mary should be viewed as the bride of Christ. But he also, going beyond anything that one can find in the tradition, so far as I am aware, views the relation of the institutional church to the laity as a male/female relation – in fact as a relation to be spoken of in terms of insemination and of 'bearing fruit' – and he conceives of relationships within the Trinity in gendered manner: the Son is feminine with respect to a masculine Father, since the Father as begetter is the initiator, and the Son receives everything from the Father. But above all, and running through nearly all his thought, is the notion that the God-world relation must be conceived in male-female terms, because God is the initiator, the active party, and the world is receptive, but able to bear fruit. The systematic way these

---

13. For a fuller discussion of Balthasar's Trinitarian theology and its extraordinarily well-informed quality, cf. my 'Hans Urs von Balthasar on the Trinity', in Peter C. Phan (ed.), *The Cambridge Companion to the Trinity* (Cambridge: Cambridge University Press, 2011).

patterns of thought permeate his work suggests that for Balthasar this is not one metaphor among other possible metaphors for speaking about something which eludes us, but that it really *is* the nature of God's relation to the world, or to put it another way, this really *is* the deepest meaning of the man-woman relationship and of sex itself. So for instance Balthasar argues that priests cannot be women, because they must represent Christ in relation to the church, and Christ was not just contingently male, but *had* to be a man because he in turn represented God in relation to the world.[14]

Unsurprisingly, there has been criticism of Balthasar's conception of 'man' and 'woman', and a certain hesitation, at least, as regards his introduction of gender into the Trinity. But in general what I have been describing as remythologizing passes more or less uncriticized in most of the literature surrounding Balthasar. Commentators note that his thought is at times 'idiosyncratic' and surprising, but generally they associate this with the originality and energy of his work, and the enviable freedom he has achieved from the constraints that modern theology usually allows itself to be put under: he is not engaged in a desiccated, spiritually dry *academic* style of theology; he is not frightened or controlled by the demands of historical-critical scholarship; he is not buying into a narrow, impoverished vision of rationality of the Enlightenment.

V

Balthasar, then, might be taken to exemplify the dangers of a slide towards paganism within Christian theology, and in particular of a slide towards paganism which may be correlated with a theology which sets its face too simply against modernity. But more than I am interested in Balthasar here, I am interested in the *reception* of Balthasar by other Christian theologians, Catholic and non-Catholic. In fact I know a number of theologians who have little time for Balthasar, who are quite troubled by him, but on the whole they simply keep quiet and avoid him. They do not have, one could say, the means of a decisive critique easily to hand. There is a widely available shorthand for what people think is wrong with Rahner – he is too liberal, too Kantian, too captive to modern modes of thought – but none for what may in fact make many hesitate over Balthasar. If the accusation of a slide towards paganism came as readily to the lips of Christian theologians as the accusation of a slide towards liberalism, a much more articulate critique of Balthasar might by now have taken hold, and more generally Christian theology might proceed with a little more balance, opposing to the fear of liberal accommodation to the times on the one side the fear of paganising sub-Christian backsliding on the other.

14. For a helpful discussion of Balthasar on gender cf. Corrine Crammer's 'One sex or two? Balthasar's theology of the sexes' in the *Cambridge Companion to Hans Urs von Balthasar*.

What I have suggested so far is that if Christian theology could in some way take on board, even in part, the suggestion that paganism may be a danger, a temptation, constantly threatening it, this might introduce a useful means of self-critique, and might bring about a certain shift in the dominant contemporary theological mood. This would also, it is worth noting, represent a significant shift on another level, a shift in thinking about what it might mean for Christian theology to take Judaism seriously. While this has been a real concern for at least some Christian theologians, on the whole the presumption has been that it is precisely in rejecting liberalism and questioning many of the presuppositions of modernity that Christian theology will be in a position to be serious about its relationship with Judaism – for only then can Christianity take its roots, its particularity, its concreteness, to be central to its identity. Only if we free ourselves, the thinking usually goes, from an Enlightenment mentality with its premium on universality and a neutrally conceived rationality can we begin to rediscover that it is precisely the God of Israel that we worship, and can we begin to notice just how thoroughly and decisively Christianity is rooted in Judaism. But what I am suggesting is more or less the reverse of this: that if Christianity focuses too heavily on purging itself of liberal tendencies and on setting its face against modernity, then it may fail to take Judaism seriously, in the sense that it will miss a significant chance to learn something it really needs to know from modern Jewish thought.

Chapter 10

JULIAN OF NORWICH, HANS URS VON BALTHASAR AND THE STATUS OF SUFFERING IN CHRISTIAN THEOLOGY

What is the status of suffering in Christian theology? Must Christianity on some level give suffering and loss a positive valuation? Such questions open up a very large, and relatively unexplored, territory. This essay is an opening foray into this territory, beginning with a reflection on the relationship between suffering and *love*.

In any Christian vision of things, it seems nearly inescapable that the relationship between love and suffering will be significant: it is difficult to operate within a system which has the cross as its central symbol without somehow thinking about these two things in close proximity. But *how* one should think about love and suffering together is not so obvious – this is not something on which the Christian tradition is clear. The aim of the first part of this essay (sections I–V) is to explore this 'non-obviousness' through a juxtaposition of the theology of Julian of Norwich and Hans Urs von Balthasar. While intriguingly similar in a number of ways, Julian and Balthasar show sharply divergent sensibilities as regards the relationship of love to suffering. They can, I will propose, be taken as representatives of two quite different strands within the Christian tradition.

The two strands do not necessarily exhaust the possibilities open within the tradition, but the striking difference between them helps to provoke thought on the question of the status of suffering. In its second part, the essay takes a more constructive turn, sketching something of what it might look like for a contemporary Christian theology which would, departing decisively from Balthasar (even if not precisely following Julian), set its face against a positive evaluation of suffering and loss. Is it possible for a theology to refuse to grant any intrinsic positive value to suffering and loss, while remaining a genuinely Christian theology?

I

While Julian and Balthasar are not usually discussed together, there are a series of interesting points of contact between them. Each, though in the longer term influential, did much of his or her writing from a position of ecclesial marginality. Julian wrote as a woman and in the vernacular, not a part of any 'school' theology, and her status as an anchoress put her on the edge of several worlds, neither a member of a monastic community nor an ordinary lay woman.[1] For Balthasar there was a more active process of marginalization. He left the Jesuits in 1950, out of commitment to his joint work with Adrienne von Speyr. Leaving a religious order was not something which, before the Second Vatican Council, was easily countenanced, and as a result Balthasar suffered ecclesial isolation. He was, for instance, the only major theologian of his generation who was *not* invited to Vatican II. He never held an academic position, and his writings, like the writing of Julian, do not take a standard academic form. That is to say that his work, like hers, was not shaped by students, colleagues, editors, or the demands of an academic curriculum.[2]

There is in both authors, too, a style that is sometimes described as 'vernacular'. This goes beyond the fact that they write in English and German rather than in Latin, and even beyond the fact that neither writes for a strictly academic or scholastic audience: one finds a kind of familiarity, an immediacy and directness with the reader, in Julian's reflections and in at least some of Balthasar's texts.

In both cases there is a blurring of boundaries between what one might call a spiritual and even visionary writing, and theology proper. Balthasar described his work as a 'kneeling theology', and set out a critique of the separation of spirituality and theology in an influential essay entitled 'Theology and Sanctity'.[3] His thought, furthermore, was deeply shaped by his association with the mystic and visionary Adrienne von Speyr. He insisted their work was two halves of a single whole, and could not be separated, and there are at least points where the interpenetration of von Speyr's experience and Balthasar's theology is very clear (in the final volume of his *Theodrama*, for instance, and in his account of Christ's descent into hell).[4] In Julian's work the influential visions and experiences are her own. But she is very far

---

1. Denys Turner draws attention, among other things, to Julian's marginality as an anchoress. He suggests that 'all these forms of marginality contribute to a freedom of vocabulary and image, an expansiveness of thought, and a singularity of theological emphasis that set her apart from mainstream styles of medieval theology' in *Julian of Norwich, Theologian*, 16.

2. In *Balthasar: A (Very) Critical Introduction* I have suggested that this set of circumstances contribute to an 'unfettered' quality in Balthasar's theology, which I take to be both its strength and its weakness.

3. Hans Urs Von Balthasar, 'Theology and Sanctity', in *Explorations in Theology Volume I: The Word Made Flesh* (San Francisco: Ignatius Press, 1989).

4. The two cases are slightly different. The final volume of the *Theo-drama* quotes very heavily from von Speyr's writings, and in this sense the influence is unmissable. Balthasar's reliance on von Speyr in relation to Holy Saturday and the descent into Hell is not so explicit textually, but most commentators presume that there must be a connection between his quite novel and idiosyncratic proposals and her annually repeated experiences during Holy Week.

from a mere passive reporter of past experiences – she is now recognized as 'one of the great speculative theologians of the Middle Ages'.[5]

So in both cases we have a theologian writing from the margins, in a vernacular style, and in a way which transgresses or at least ignores expected boundaries between mystic and visionary on the one hand and intellectual on the other. Two other similarities are worth at least briefly noting. Both have become known for the role *gender* plays in their theology. In Balthasar's thought notions of male activity and female receptivity make an appearance on many levels, coming into his treatment of everything from the inner Trinitarian life to the assent of faith to the relations between priests and laity. He is the most powerful exponent of the so-called nuptial theology which emerged as such a significant and strange development in late twentieth century Catholic theology.[6] In Julian gender and theology intertwine in a less systematic but no less striking way: in many quarters, in fact, she is principally known for statements such as 'our Savior is our true mother, in whom we are eternally born and by whom we shall always be enclosed', or 'the mother can give her child her milk to suck, but our dear mother Jesus can feed us with himself'.[7] In both figures, finally, there seems a certain leaning towards universalism, although neither of them directly asserts a doctrine of universal salvation, and in Julian's case there is a degree of dispute about what she in fact intends.[8]

II

The writings of Julian and Balthasar, then, show a range of intriguing similarities. For the purposes of my explorations in this paper, it is one last similarity which is most significant, however: in each *suffering* plays a prominent role.

---

5. Nicholas Watson and Jacqueline Jenkins, *The Writings of Julian of Norwich* (University Park: Pennsylvania State University Press, 2006), ix.

6. Cf. Fergus Kerr's *Twentieth Century Catholic Theologians* (Oxford: Wiley-Blackwell, 2006) for a discussion of nuptial theology and an indication of its striking novelty against the background of earlier twentieth century Catholic thought.

7. These statements are found in chapters 57 and 60 of Julian's Long Text. All quotations from Julian in this article are from this Long Text, and for ease of reading, they are drawn from Penguin Classics translation by Elizabeth Spearing, *Revelations of Divine Love* (London: Penguin Books, 1998). Where the argument depends on issues of detail, the Middle English text from Nicholas Watson and Jacqueline Jenkins, eds, *The Writings of Julian of Norwich* will be given in the notes.

8. Cf. Balthasar's *Dare We Hope 'That All Men Shall be Saved'? with A Short Discourse on Hell* (San Francisco: Ignatius Press, 1988) for his reflections on the question of universal salvation. Julian mentions a desire for a complete vision of hell and purgatory but then writes 'as for this desire, I could learn nothing about it' (33). However, alongside the absence of a vision of Hell, the denial of anger in God, and the radically positive affirmation of God's love, stands her repeated insistence that she accepts the faith of the church in its entirety, and this, as she understands it, includes an insistence that there is indeed a (populated) hell.

Balthasar's claim that there is something like suffering, a kind of analogical suffering, in the inner life of the eternal Trinity has attracted considerable scholarly scrutiny. Most of the attention, however, has focused on how the proposal relates to a traditional understanding of God – does Balthasar, or does he not, deny divine immutability and impassibility?[9] Something which has drawn less notice is how this proposal relates to a broader interest in and evaluation of suffering in Balthasar's work. What he says about something-like-suffering in God, in other words, should not be thought of as standing on its own, but is one expression of a positive valuation of suffering running throughout his thought.[10]

One of the places Balthasar's positive valuation of suffering makes itself felt, unsurprisingly, is in his reflections on the cross. He is driven towards a kind of maximalism here – the more that can be said of Christ's suffering, it seems, the better. So Balthasar affirms with Pascal that Christ's agony lasts until the end of the world. He writes that because of Christ's 'filial intimacy with the Father', he can 'suffer *total* abandonment by the Father and taste that suffering *to the last drop*'.[11] He represents Christ's sufferings as exceeding and in some sense containing all other suffering, writing of 'wounds which transcend all inner-worldly hurts'[12] and of Christ's suffering as 'towering far above chronological time'.[13] 'Never', he tells us in his collection of aphorisms, 'will an individual man or the totality of all humanity even approximately grasp and encompass these sufferings.'[14]

There is also a distinct focus on suffering in Balthasar's understanding of the Christian life. Self-loss and humiliation regularly appear as key elements in the Christian life. The act of faith is fundamentally understood as an act of sacrifice of the self, and love in Balthasar's writing is almost always presented in close connection with renunciation and self-abnegation.[15]

A particularly privileged form of the Christian life, furthermore, as Balthasar envisions it, is to be allowed to share mystically in Christ's passion. This is how he understands the dark night of the soul of the mystics, and the intense sufferings of Adrienne von Speyr. His preoccupation with this notion of a sharing in the passion is strong – so much so that it leads to some familiar scriptural passages being

---

9. Cf. for instance Gerard O'Hanlon's excellent *The Immutability of God in the Theology of Hans Urs von Balthasar* (Cambridge: Cambridge University Press, 1990).

10. I first drew attention to the suffering-laden atmosphere of Balthasar's theology in Chapter 5 of *Balthasar: A (Very) Critical Introduction*.

11. Hans Urs Von Balthasar, *Truth Is Symphonic: Aspects of Christian Pluralism* (San Francisco: Ignatius Press, 1987), 169, emphasis added.

12. Hans Urs Von Balthasar, *Elucidations* (San Francisco: Ignatius Press, 1998), 84.

13. Hans Urs Von Balthasar, *The Grain of Wheat: Aphorisms* (San Francisco: Ignatius Press, 1995), 70.

14. Ibid.

15. In this connection, see also Ben Quash's discussion of the role of *Gelassenheit* in Balthasar's thought, in *Theology and the Drama of History* (Cambridge: Cambridge University Press, 2005).

read in an unfamiliar way. When in the gospel of John Jesus says to Mary 'This is your son' and to John 'This is your mother', for instance, Balthasar construes this not as an act of care or provision of any kind, but as a gesture of *rejection*: Jesus here is denying Mary as his own mother. He is causing her to experience divine abandonment, in order to allow her to share in his passion. Or again, when Jesus cries at the death of Lazarus, as Balthasar reads the scene, he is weeping for the suffering of Martha and Mary. In itself this is a traditional bit of exegesis, but what is unfamiliar in Balthasar's account is that he is weeping for the suffering of Martha and Mary that *he himself has caused*. That is to say, by temporarily abandoning them – by his delay in coming to see them – he has drawn them into his own coming experience of divine abandonment, his own passion.

Balthasar nowhere writes a whole treatise on suffering, and perhaps, because it does not become an *explicit* subject for reflection, its importance in his thought can be missed. But important it is: if one begins to look, one can detect a kind of fascination with suffering at nearly every level in his writings.

In Julian's *Revelations* the prominent role of suffering is harder to overlook, even to the most casual reader. Julian begins the story of her visions by explaining how, earlier in life, she had asked God for three gifts, one of which was a vivid perception of the passion: in particular, she 'longed to be shown [Christ] in the flesh so that [she] might have more knowledge of [his] bodily suffering'. Another of her requests was to have an experience of dying: 'I longed eagerly to be on my death-bed, so that ... I might myself believe I was dying ... I longed to have in this sickness every kind of suffering both of body and soul that I would experience if I died, with all the terror and turmoil of the fiends.'[16]

In the experience which is at the center of *Revelations of Divine Love*, God grants Julian both these wishes. At the age of 30 and a half she falls deathly ill and receives the last rites of the church. She lingers on, and then, on what really seems to be the point of death, her eyes on a crucifix, she again requests to be filled with the 'remembrance and feeling of his Passion; for I wanted his pains to be my pains...'.[17] The visions which follow include some vivid representations of Christ's blood. Julian sees in her first vision 'the red blood trickling down from under the crown of thorns, hot and fresh and very plentiful',[18] and in her fourth she sees 'the body of Christ bleeding abundantly, in weals from the scourging'. She tells us that 'the fair skin was very deeply broken down into the tender flesh, sharply slashed all over the dear body; the hot blood ran out so abundantly that no skin or wound could be seen, it seemed to be all blood'.[19] Her visions also contain powerful images of Christ's thirst and the drying out of his body as his death draws closer: 'as it appeared to me, the nose shriveled and dried, and the dear body was dark and black, quite transformed from his own fair living color into parched mortification.'

---

16. Julian, *Revelations*, ch. 2.
17. Ibid., ch. 3: '... For I wolde that his paines were my paines ...'
18. Ibid., ch. 4.
19. Ibid., ch. 12.

She tells us that it seemed to her that 'Loss of blood and pain drying him from within, and blasts of wind and cold coming from without, met together in the dear body of Christ. And these four, two without and two within, gradually dried the flesh of Christ as time passed. ... So I saw Christ's dear flesh dying, seemingly bit by bit, drying up with amazing agony'.[20]

III

In each of these theologians, then, one meets a positive presentation of suffering. Julian prays to experience suffering, and details visions in which Christ's sufferings in the passion are graphically emphasized. Balthasar places self-abnegation and humiliation at the center of his understanding of the Christian life; like Julian he emphasizes the extent of Christ's suffering in the passion; and he proposes that there is something like suffering at the very heart of the eternal divine life.

If in each case there is a positive presentation of suffering, however, the two presentations are positive in *different* ways – a fundamentally different sensibility is at work in the two theologians, in spite of all the similarities.

Let us begin with Julian. She can shock the modern reader, it is true, with her intense evocations of aspects of Christ's suffering, and with her prayer to experience mortal illness. But jostling alongside her focus on suffering we find some of the most intensely, unequivocally *positive* language about God's love in the whole of the Christian tradition. She writes of his kindness and gentleness and mercy, his courteousness, his comforting, his homely intimacy, of his desire and delight in us, of his love and longing for us, of his rejoicing in us, of his joy in our salvation. When Julian writes of God's love, it is not something which is also mixed or balanced with anger, or sadness, or rebuke: its positive quality is unalloyed, linked only to joy, gladness, delight.

There is of course a role for suffering in Julian's thought, and a link between suffering and redemption. She presumes Christ's sufferings play a key part in our salvation. She presumes also that the depth of his suffering reveals something of the depth of his love, which no doubt contributes to her desire to have a fuller appreciation of the passion. And finally, she assumes that in this life we do in fact suffer, that this suffering is linked to sin, and that it needs to be accepted. But while there is a link between suffering and salvation in her vision, there is also a distinct *contrast* between them. Thus the sufferings in Christ's passion, while much magnified in her contemplation, are nevertheless finite, fixed to a particular time. They are temporal, not eternal. Christ suffered, but he does not now suffer. At a number of points in fact she goes out of her way to underline this: when she writes of her own pain at the thought of Christ's pain, for instance, she is careful to add 'though I knew full well he only suffered once' (17).[21] Elsewhere, she describes

---

20. Ibid., ch. 16.
21. Ibid., ch. 17: 'For I wiste welle he sufferede but onys ...'.

the Passion as a 'noble, glorious deed performed *at one particular time* through the action of love, love which has *always* existed and will never end'.[22] Or again, she writes that 'all that [God] has done for us, and all that he does, and ever will do, was never a loss or burden to him ... except what he did in our human form, beginning at the precious incarnation and lasting until the blessed resurrection on Easter morning; that was the only loss and burden that he bore to accomplish our redemption, a redemption in which he rejoices eternally'.[23] There is, then, a very deliberate and repeated contrast between a particular suffering in time, bounded by a beginning and an end, and an eternal and unending love and rejoicing.

What applies to the passion also applies to our own suffering in this life, which is contrasted to the joy and delight of what is promised eternally. In some passages it is true that Julian writes of a correlation between the two – the more we have had to suffer, the more we will later be rewarded – but it is still a correlation of things which stand in sharp *contrast*.

The theological atmosphere of Balthasar's work is very different. The concern with suffering here is not one element among others, but is diffused throughout his writings, present at every stage. Suffering in a sense colors the whole, in one way or another permeating almost every level of his thought, up to and including, as already mentioned, his thought on the immanent Trinity. Once one begins to notice this dimension of Balthasar's theology, it is hard to escape. In a single, relatively slim volume of ecclesiology (the second volume of *Explorations in Theology*), for example, one can find references to the church in its sinful members as 'borne by the suffering members', to the 'inner mystery of suffering' that the Constantinian church of glory hid, to the true Christian spirit as 'the will to poverty, abasement and humility', to the 'real, fruitful humiliation' of Peter, which was not a 'mere exercise in humiliation', to a humility which, because we are sinners, must be 'instilled into us by humiliation', to 'self-abnegation in the service of Christ' as the only way to reveal Christ's own self-abnegation, to a self-abnegation that liturgical piety requires – one which indeed Balthasar describes as 'this violent, this often "crucifying" sacrifice of the pious subject to the ecclesial object' – , and to 'complete self-abnegation and obedience to the hierarchy' as something Charles de Foucauld rightly commended.[24]

It is a telling mark of the atmosphere of Balthasar's thought that even when he expresses thanks to his family, suffering plays the central role. In a retrospective

---

22. Ibid., ch. 22: 'For the paine was a noble, precious, and wurshipfulle dede done in a time by the working of love. And love was without beginning, is, and shall be without ende'.

23. Ibid., ch. 23: 'Alle that he hath done for us, and doeth, and ever shalle, was never cost ne charge to him ne might be, but only that he did in our manhede, beginning at the swete incarnation, and lasting to the blessed uprising on Ester morrow. So long dured the cost and the charge about our redemption in deed, of which dede he enjoyeth endlessly, as it is befor said'.

24. Hans Urs Von Balthasar, *Explorations in Theology II: Spouse of the Word* (San Francisco: Ignatius Press, 1991), 179, 16, 14, 114, 188, 27, 30, 25.

essay written in 1965, after a paragraph on the impossibility of properly acknowledging all that one ought to be thankful for, we find the following:

> And where would a man end, if he wanted to begin thanking those of his fellow men who accompanied him on his way, formed him, protected him, made everything possible? Left and right the greetings would have to go: to the nameable and the nameless. A mother is there, who during the course of a long fatal illness dragged herself to Church each morning to pray for her children. Other close relatives, of whom (to what ends God knows) fearful sufferings were demanded. Only in the light of God will one really know what he has to be thankful for.[25]

He is of course thanking his family for nurturing, loving, and educating him – this is presumably all covered in the first sentence cited. But what particularly calls out for gratitude here is, first, the painful prayers of one suffering and dying, and then simply sufferings whose purpose is unknown.

In Balthasar, then, we find a blurring of the distinction between love and loss, love and suffering, at every level of his thought, so that suffering takes on the aura of something *intrinsically* positive. Suffering and loss work their way into the very center of the Christian vision: he is distinctly disinclined to speak positively of God, or of love, or of Christ, or of the Christian life, without always at the same time making reference to suffering and loss.[26]

Where in Julian some almost gruesomely vivid descriptions of suffering sit alongside of – and are in the end decisively outstripped by – an utterly positive and joyful evocation of God's love and God's nature, Balthasar quite explicitly rejects the possibility of a conceiving of God in a purely positive way: 'we have no right' he writes in the *Theo-Drama*, 'to regard the Trinity one-sidedly as the "play" of an absolute "blessedness" that abstracts from concrete pain and lacks the "seriousness" of separation and death.'[27]

IV

Why the difference between the two? Why do we find in Julian's writings a tone, an atmosphere, so much more vibrantly positive than we do in Balthasar? They lived,

---

25. 'In Retrospect: 1965' from *My Work: In Retrospect* (San Francisco: Ignatius Press, 1993), 88.

26. Something fundamental about his thought, in other words, is captured in the following aphorism: 'The more we come to know God, the more the difference between joy and suffering becomes tenuous: not only do both things become engulfed in the One Will of the Father, but love itself becomes painful, and this pain becomes an irreplaceable bliss,' *Grain of Wheat*, 13.

27. Hans Urs Von Balthasar, *Theo-Drama: Theological Dramatic Theory Volume IV: The Action* (San Francisco: Ignatius Press, 1994), 325.

of course, in very different eras, and one might argue that they are responding to the demands of their contexts. The argument would go something like this: since in Julian's time an intense focus on the passion of Christ was commonplace, as was an understanding of suffering as a central component of the Christian life, these elements could be woven into her meditations without becoming their central pre-occupation. Though she does not question the importance of suffering in either the life of Christ or of the Christian, in other words, she has no particular need to emphasize it, but focuses on something more positive. Balthasar, on the other hand, is reacting against what he feels to be a tendency towards a shallow modern optimism, a contemporary fear of and flight from suffering, and so is more actively concerned to stress the place of self-abnegation and loss, of humility and humiliation, in a Christian vision. In very broad terms, one might say that in a dark time Julian stressed the light, and in a flippant era lacking seriousness, Balthasar stressed the dark depths of the faith.

In fact, though, I do not think it is right to harmonize Julian and Balthasar in this way: I do not think it is possible to suggest that the different sensibilities they exhibit can be interpreted as merely the result of differing contexts and strategies. There are, rather, deep and structural theological differences between them.

One way to see this is to consider the relationship of each to the Augustinian *privatio boni* tradition. Julian does not mention Augustine, or the term *privatio boni*, or indeed any Latin or technical term, and yet in her writings the notion of evil as a *privatio boni* is clearly present. As in Augustine and Aquinas, this rests on a strong doctrine of creation and providence: everything which is, is created by God, and so everything which is, is good. In connection with Julian's third revelation, where she sees that God is in everything, she asks, 'what is sin? For I saw truly that God does everything, no matter how small. And … nothing happens by accident or luck, but everything by God's wise providence'. The problem is clear: if 'everything which is done is well done',[28] then what can we say about sin? Julian's answer here is simple, if like much in the *privatio boni* tradition, perhaps a bit frustrating to us: 'And here I saw' she writes 'that sin is really not something which is done, for in all this vision no sin appeared'.[29]

Her denial that sin is 'something which is done', it is worth making clear, is not a reflection of lack of seriousness or a naïve optimism. In fact the question of sin, and why God allowed it to arise in the first place, is, as Denys Turner has

---

28. Julian, *Revelations*, ch. 12: 'Wherfore me behoved nedes to grant that alle thinges that is done is welle done, for our lord God doth all'.

29. Ibid. The original version is 'And here I saw sothly that sinne is no dede, for in alle this, sinne was not shewde'. It might be supposed that by introducing the concept of *privatio boni*, I am changing the subject – I have shifted the grounds of the debate from suffering to sin. In fact, however, the two cannot be tidily separated in Julian's thought. Sin is in her view the greatest kind of suffering for a Christian. For Balthasar, a similar kind of intertwining applies, at least as regards the grounds of both sin and suffering in the eternal life of the Trinity.

argued forcibly, the central theological problem of the work, one around which Julian's thought keeps circling.[30] Sin troubles her deeply. But however troubling and in need of explanation she finds it, she remains within the Augustinian and Thomistic tradition – it is granted no ontological status.

In Balthasar, by contrast, the *privatio boni* tradition is quietly set aside. This happens right at the heart of his soteriology. He affirms that we need to learn of the Trinity from the cross, and since on the cross he finds alienation and abandonment, he concludes that there are, not quite alienation and abandonment in the eternal life of the Trinity, but an infinite distance, an incomprehensible separation which can then become, in the economy of salvation, alienation and abandonment. He maintains that this inner-Trinitarian distance is the ground of all created difference and – this is particularly striking – *of the possibility of sin itself*. So God does not sin, but the possibility of sin is grounded in the Trinity; and in the same way while God does not suffer in the same sense that we do, suffering is analogically rooted in God. In Balthasar's thought, then, sin and suffering are ultimately granted as much reality, as much ontological status, as God's good creation.

So the contrasting sensibilities of Julian and Balthasar around suffering cannot be described merely as difference of emphasis, I think, or ascribed merely to their differing contexts. Balthasar does not just lay a bit more stress on the darker side of things than does Julian, but gives the darkness itself a fundamentally different ontological status. This is perhaps what creates the theological atmosphere of his writings: in his thought we do not just find love and suffering close together – rather we see the distinction between them blurred. They become mutually internal to each other, so that fundamentally, Balthasar's instinct seems to be something like this: if you plumb the depths of suffering you find love, and any genuine love must have a central dimension, a central motif, of suffering.

Linked to this differing stance towards the *privatio boni* tradition is another important difference between Julian and Balthasar, a difference regarding the *intelligibility* of sin and evil. The two theologians differ not only in ontology, one could say, but in epistemology.

Trying to understand the existence of sin is, as I have already mentioned, a key theme in Julian's *Revelations*. A modern free-will defense cannot be a solution for her because, with the classical theological tradition, she presumes a very different concept of divine transcendence than do most modern thinkers, a conception of divine transcendence according to which God's causation and our freedom go together rather than standing in opposition to one another.[31] And while her denial of the reality of sin – the *privatio boni* strain in her thought – allows her to avoid

---

30. Turner, *Julian of Norwich*, ch. 3.

31. Cf. Kathryn Tanner, *God and Creation in Christian Theology* (Oxford: Blackwell, 1988) for a discussion of the general patterning of premodern Christian thought along these lines, and the second chapter of Turner's *Julian of Norwich, Theologian* for an exploration of this point specifically in relation to Julian.

any affirmation that God *causes* or *commits* sin, it does not get her off the hook, for it does not resolve the issue of where sin comes from or why God *permits* it.

But while the *Revelations* contain an intense struggle with the question of why there is sin, they contain no answer. Or more precisely, the answer they contain is no answer at all. Julian tells us that the Lord responds to her worried queries with the assurance 'Sin is befitting' and then, in the most famous of all the lines of the work 'but all shall be well, and all shall be well, and all manner of thing shall be well'.[32] Why is sin 'befitting'? That is never specified. How shall all be well, and all manner of thing be well? Again, it is not explained. True, Julian is told of a great, secret deed that God shall do at the end of time – but it is a deed which we cannot now know and which we should not seek to find out.[33]

So in Julian's thought, where suffering and love are conceptually distinct and indeed sharply contrasted, the presence of darkness in our experience, of sin and suffering, defeats explanation. Julian, and her readers with her, have no access to a unifying, integrated vision, where it can be understood *how* all things, including sin and suffering, fit together.[34]

In Balthasar's work, on the other hand, there *is* such an integrating vision, a vision rooted in the inner-Trinitarian drama he describes. For this is a drama which

---

32. *Revelations*, ch. 27. 'Sinne is behovely, but alle shalle be wele, and alle shalle be wele, and all maner of thinge shalle be wel'. 'Appropriate' might be another translation of 'behovely'. Turner argues that 'behovely' is Julian's equivalent of the (equally difficult to translate) Latin '*conveniens*', in Turner, *Julian of Norwich*, 35–7.

33. While I am in general following Denys Turner in emphasising the centrality of the (unresolved) intellectual struggle around the 'fittingness' of sin in Julian, one place where my reading of Julian diverges from his is in the significance given to this 'deed' beyond our knowing. On Turner's reading, there is nothing more to expect after the cross, which is 'the final outcome of that [final] conflict', the conflict 'between sin and love' (21). Beyond the cross, Turner asserts, 'there is no concluding Resurrection narrative in Julian, no further episode of dénouement' (20). He sees the cross, for Julian, as 'sin's defeat of love', but this is in turn sin's own defeat, 'its power being exhausted by its very success'. The *meaning* of the cross, which is the Resurrection, is 'that the vulnerability of love … is stronger than sin's power to kill' (21). Whatever one makes of Turner's account in its own right, I do not myself detect in Julian any sense of love as 'vulnerability', and while it is true that the cross is enormously central for Julian, I do not take it to be, for her, the conclusion of the whole drama: not only does her insistence on a great, secret deed work against this, but also the care which she takes, discussed above, to contain the cross and the associated suffering to a clearly finite period in time.

34. One might ask whether the parable of the Lord and the Servant does not provide precisely a kind of unifying vision. I think Christopher Abbot is right to say that the vision of the Lord and the Servant does not offer 'a rationally appropriable formula'. It may be true that in her exploration of this elusive image Julian sets out 'to produce an integrated, large-scale interpretation of sinful humanity's relation to God, and to one another, through Christ', but this does not mean she arrives at an understanding of *why* God *permits* sin. Christopher Abbot, *Julian of Norwich: Autobiography and Theology* (Cambridge: D.S. Brewer, 1999), 90.

in eternity, from before all time, combines love with something like suffering, and makes room at the very center of the inner life of God for that which can become alienation and sin.

In *both* Julian and Balthasar we find a dimension of mystery as regards the relation of love and suffering, of the light and the dark, but it is a mystery of a fundamentally different kind, a different texture. For Julian what is mysterious is how two distinct and opposing elements fit into a single narrative. Our intellectual situation as she sees it is quite straight-forward to describe: we do not know how to envisage all things together. There is a gap in our understanding. Our desire for an explanation, for a story that makes sense of both love and suffering, simply is not met. A life of faith is a life lived with a tension which, before the last day, cannot, for either Julian or her readers, be resolved.

Balthasar's theology has a more esoteric quality: the mystery is one that, if one has eyes to see, it is possible to some degree to penetrate. The mystery is that love itself, to those who truly understand it in the light of the cross, turns out to be something darker and more painful than is usually supposed. The fundamental mystery is not the co-existence of love and suffering, but their mutual inherence, perhaps even their ultimate identity.

V

Why should this matter? One reason is that Balthasar's sensibility towards suffering – as a kind of shorthand we might call it his embrace of suffering – is part of a broader phenomenon. His 'embrace' is perhaps an extreme version, as the unusual exegesis indicates, but one finds tendencies in the same direction across a range of figures, from Simone Weil to influential Anglican theologians such as Donald MacKinnon. One also finds hints of such a sensibility within quite widespread appeals to the vulnerability of God and in a current tendency to make free and wide-ranging use of the language of kenosis. So Balthasar's 'embrace of suffering' is worth considering not just because he himself is an influential thinker, but because he can help us to see a broader pattern.

But why compare him with Julian? A more expected contrast might be with Rahner. Usually, if Balthasar is going to be one of two strands, then Karl Rahner will be the other. When Rahner and Balthasar are set off against one another, however, the difference is often conceived as a difference in their relationship to modernity, which Balthasar is thought to resist and Rahner to embrace.[35] So to set up a Rahner/Balthasar contrast on this issue might be to encourage the supposition that Balthasar's embrace of suffering has something to do with an option for tradition against modernity, and I think this would be a mistake.

Contrasting Balthasar with Julian, then, is instructive for a number of reasons. First, Julian shows that a wholly positive, wholly joyful vision of love and of

---

35. I believe this common conception is as a matter of fact mistaken: see my 'Balthasar and Karl Rahner', 256–68.

God is genuinely available within the tradition – even from within a moment in the theological tradition when the Black Death is a living memory, and when a pious person can sincerely pray to undergo nearly-mortal illness. It is not merely a bit of fluffy, unserious contemporary optimism. In fact Balthasar's embrace of suffering pulls him away from aspects of the classical theological tradition to which Julian adheres. I have explored this in relation to the notion of evil as a *privatio boni*: something similar could be argued in relation to divine simplicity or to Christology. Secondly, in Julian we can see that such a wholly positive, wholly joyful vision of love and of God is not simply the result of forgetfulness or indifference to the darkness of our experience. One cannot say of Julian that she has simply not thought about suffering, or about the gravity of sin. It would be closer to the truth to say that these are the experiential starting points of her thought, its unquestioned presuppositions.

The Christian tradition, then, contains real variety, not just on the familiar level of theories of atonement and conceptions of redemption, but on a more fundamental level of sensibility, sensibility concerning the relation between darkness and light, between love and bliss on the one hand and suffering and loss on the other. While I have suggested that Julian sits far closer to the classical theological position shared with Augustine and Aquinas, this is not to deny that Balthasar's thought too has its roots somewhere in the tradition. A proper history of Christian theology and suffering is yet to be written, but Balthasar's embrace of suffering would likely need to be located within a later-developing strand, a strand which perhaps has a beginning towards the end of the middle ages, which gains some ground in the Counter-Reformation and flowers in the nineteenth century.

What to make of the existence of such different – indeed, such *opposed* – sensibilities within the tradition? A range of responses are possible. Some will see the sensibility which is aligned with the classical theological vision as the more authentically traditional; others will read the kind of instinct Balthasar represents as a necessary and important development, a blossoming of a central but previously neglected dimension of the Christian vision.

I belong in the first camp: the position I will begin to sketch in the next section, as the paper moves into its more constructive phase, is nearer to that of Julian. Balthasar's approach allows him, no doubt, to make a kind of sense of the darkness of our world, but to do so at what I take to be an unacceptable price. Better to live with unresolved questions, it seems to me, than to move, through an embrace of suffering, to the kind of integrated vision Balthasar offers – for if suffering is integrated right into the heart of love, it becomes just a little too hard to see how the good news of the Gospel can really be good.

VI

What might it mean, then, for contemporary theology to move decisively away from Balthasar, to turn its face systematically against any positive valuation of suffering and loss?

One might begin, first of all, with the affirmation that in God gift and love have nothing intrinsically to do with pain and diminishment. God creates the world without diminishing in the process, and if we speak of the Father giving everything to the Son, we should insist that this is a giving in which there is not even a hint of a becoming less, a giving which requires the introduction of no language of risk, emptying or loss.

In a second step, one might seek to allow this fundamental pattern – a pattern where giving does not diminish or deplete the giver – to govern our reflections on the nature of what is at the heart of *created* gift and love. There are many things I can give without being diminished – my friendship, my attention, even my recipes. If we do not begin by associating gift with loss, then we might take such examples – the giving of friendship, attention and recipes – not as the paradoxical examples of giving but as its *paradigmatic* examples. However frequently love, or some kinds of love, must in fact become sacrificial, furthermore, we would nevertheless be wary of the term 'sacrificial love' – for on this view it is not of the *essence* of love itself to involve sacrifice and loss, although it may well be what love in particular circumstances requires.[36]

One might ask whether there is any value to the distinction set out in this last sentence. What is the difference between speaking of love as sacrificial and speaking about love which in some circumstances needs to involve sacrifice – especially if these circumstances are likely to be widespread, perhaps even universal? To take a mundane example, what experience of parental love does not have an element of suffering and loss woven into it? Why not simply acknowledge that it just *is*, by its nature, sacrificial?

This distinction, though elusive, is real, and has real consequences. Were I to conceive of maternal love as intrinsically sacrificial, for instance, I might be tempted to think that the more I suffer in service of my children, the more truly I am loving them – and thinking this way, I might be inclined to take decisions that are bad for me and bad for my children. Or to shift into a slightly different sphere, I suspect those priests whose ministry is most appreciated are not for the most part those who communicate an understanding of this ministry as fundamentally a matter of sacrifice and loss, but those who seem to delight in and be enriched by their congregation.[37]

VII

There is a great deal that could be explored to develop this line of thought more fully. One issue is the relationship of suffering and loss to finitude: does the finite

---

36. Among the theologians who have written extensively about gift recently, this very brief account is closest to that of Kathryn Tanner. See her *Jesus, Humanity and the Trinity* (Minneapolis: Fortress Press, 2001), ch. 3, especially 75.

37. The fascinating work of Emma Percy has taught me to think in parallels between mothering and priestly ministry. See her *What Clergy Do: Especially When it Looks like Nothing* (London: SPCK, 2014) and *Mothering as a Metaphor for Ministry* (Franham: Ashgate, 2014).

nature of the created world mean that suffering and loss are inescapable ingredients within it, and does an affirmation of the fundamental goodness of creation therefore require one to ascribe some sort of positive value to suffering and loss? There is a question about whether suffering is a stable category, or whether there might in fact be different, perhaps incompatible things bundled up together in the way we use word. There are questions about what, if we refuse to value suffering, we are to think about the frequently observed relationship between suffering and learning, between suffering and growth?[38]

The most difficult and acute questions, however, revolve around the cross. Can a theology which refuses to ascribe value to suffering and loss possibly do justice to the central Christian symbol? What can one make of the Christian reverence for the cross if one refuses to consider suffering valuable? Is the line of thought I have sketched fundamentally at odds with some very basic Christian instincts?

Let me try to sharpen this question by considering two twenty-first century stories. Shabaz Bhatti, the Pakistani minister for minorities, had been campaigning against his country's blasphemy law. He was at risk and knew it; he was provided insufficient security by the government but did not go into hiding. He was gunned down in March 2011. José Cláudio Ribeiro da Silva was a campaigner against illegal logging in the rainforest in Brazil. He had predicted his death in late 2010 and spoken of his fear of it. He continued his campaign. He and his wife, Maria do Espírito Santo, were shot and killed in May 2011.

These are both stories, at the very least, of great loss. In each case we have, in particular, a life marked by fear of death followed by actual death. The life is destroyed, the years the person would have had to live are lost, the mission to which the person was dedicated thereby, presumably, weakened if not ended.[39] And yet for the Christian imagination, I believe, it is not possible to come across such stories, even in the very bare and brief form I have narrated them, without sensing in them the presence of Christ, without hearing in them at least an echo of Christ, and finding oneself somehow moved, even uplifted, by them.

It seems hard to resist the conclusion that a Christian must revere something in loss and death itself – that these are in some way good. To attempt to say the opposite – that it is what is positive in these lives, the steadfastness of commitment, which speaks of Christ, rather than the suffering and loss – would seem to fly in the

38. For further explorations of some of these issues, see Karen Kilby, 'Eschatology, Suffering and the Limits of Theology', in Christophe Chalamet, et al. (eds), *Game Over? Reconsidering Eschatology* (Berlin: De Gruyter, 2017), 279–92; 'The Seductions of Kenosis', in Karen Kilby and Rachel Davies (eds), *Suffering and the Christian Life* (London: Bloomsbury T & T Clark, 2019); 'Suffering, Mystery and Politics: A Theological exploration', in *Modern Theology*, forthcoming.

39. I have seen nothing to suggest that Bhatti's death has led to a resurgence of religious tolerance in Pakistan, nor da Silva's to a new protection of the rainforests. We might think of Archbishop Oscar Romero also in this context, whose death was followed not by the victory of his message but by a long, terrible civil war in El Salvador.

face of the evidence. For it seems to be *precisely* lives marked by the wastefulness of an early death which speak in a powerful way of Christ. If one could change the facts, so that these became stories of long and flourishing lives devoted to the cause of protection of the rainforest or of religious minorities, the accounts might provoke admiration, but they would not turn the mind so immediately to Christ, nor move their hearer in the same way. Does, then, the cross of Christ teach us to understand something fundamentally positive in suffering and loss, so that when we come across even the barest outlines of a similar suffering and loss, we are moved?

What I want to suggest is that what we respond to in these lives may not in fact be some dimly perceived and mysterious ultimate value in suffering and loss, so much as that in them we see worked out an ultimate *indifference* to suffering and loss, a refusal to be moved by suffering and loss.

Not a complete indifference, of course. On an emotional level there is clearly no indifference whatsoever to suffering and death but a straightforward reaction of fear. This is clear from what we are told of Jesus in Gethsemane, from conversations recorded with Oscar Romero, from what is recounted about da Silva. But on the level of the course of action chosen, the living out of the commitment, we do have an *ultimate* indifference, in the sense that the action taken is taken *exactly as if* there were no threat of suffering or loss. The necessary course is walked, not as a compromise between what needs to be done and the desire to avoid a backlash from the forces of death and destruction, but exactly as if there were no such forces at all.

What we might say, in fact, is that whereas in Balthasar we found a moving away from the tradition of the *privatio boni*, away from the tradition of denying substantial reality to evil, here we have a kind of *enacted privatio boni*. In those lives where we perceive the presence of Christ in this distinctive way, what we perceive is a kind of denial, in practice, of any ultimate reality to suffering and loss. These things are given no weight. They are allowed no influence. They do not dictate, or even have the slightest influence, on the choice of a course of action. They are not treated as substantial. The action proceeds as if they were not, even though, or even as, the actor is destroyed in the process.[40]

Of course this is not a recipe for all Christian action. I ought not, for instance, ignore all risk of suffering and loss every time I cross the street, so that because of my commitment to the goal of getting to the other side I am indifferent to the question of whether or not I am run over by a car. If we really do refuse to give suffering and loss a positive valuation, then in general, and as a first principle, suffering and loss are to be avoided, fought against, resisted. We ought never aim for them, on this account, never consider them a goal. And it follows that we also cannot *aim* for this pattern of life I have been describing, even if it is the case that *in* such a pattern the presence of Christ is particularly visible.

---

40. I should be clear that such an enacted *privatio boni* is not a form of stoicism. The point is not that the protagonists of these stores don't suffer, or that they somehow rise above pain and loss, or that they remain untouched.

One way of understanding this phenomenon – that in a certain pattern of life the presence of Christ is most visible, and nevertheless it is not a pattern at which we may *aim* – might be as follows. In the ordinary course of affairs, I can never be sure of the purity of my motives, the depth of my commitment. Am I visiting prisoners, or giving a theological paper, or campaigning on a political issue, because I am fulfilling my calling from God, because of concern for the prisoners, or the truth, or justice, or am I doing it because I love the recognition, the sense of achievement, the praise it brings? This ambiguity, to ourselves as well as to others – to ourselves perhaps even more than to others – is the normal state of affairs, the normal situation in which the Christian finds herself. But on some occasions it may happen that concern for the outcast, or pursuit of truth, or love of justice, requires that all else be subordinated, put at risk, even lost. And on such occasions it will become clear, to others at least, that there really was a certain truth to this person's mission, a genuine presence of Christ in them. To *seek* the suffering and loss, however, would be to seek, not the fulfilment of one's mission, whatever it might be, but the confirmation of one's authenticity, and this would in itself point to something gone wrong. This would be to seek confirmation of one's Christian status, of the presence of Christ in one's life, rather than to pursue one's actual mission, whether it be solidarity with those who are marginalized, or the pursuit of truth, or the struggle for justice. Actively to seek a life of suffering and loss, then, to dwell upon these things as things to be desired and sought, would be to misunderstand both the fundamental nature of the suffering and loss themselves – which in themselves, on the account I am giving, are simply not good, not to be sought – and also to misunderstand the nature of the Christian life.

VIII

Christianity has to grapple with suffering and loss because of the nature of the world and because of the nature of the gospels. And if Christianity is to be good news, it must say something *positive* in relation to suffering and loss. But it makes all the difference, I am suggesting, what the nature of that positive message is. Is it a positive embrace of suffering and loss, understood as ultimately bound up together with love, or a positive overcoming of suffering and loss, understood as that which cannot most fundamentally touch love?

Chapter 11

BEAUTY AND MYSTERY IN MATHEMATICS AND THEOLOGY

The relationship between theology and science is a well-established, or at least familiar, domain of inquiry. But what of theology and mathematics? Can anything useful emerge from bringing the two together?

One way to link mathematics and theology would be to ask, does what mathematicians can tell us about infinity also tell us something about God? There is precedent for this approach – reflection on the relationship between mathematical infinity and metaphysical infinity has a history stretching back thousands of years. In comparatively recent times, Georg Cantor, the nineteenth century thinker who more than any other was responsible for working out a coherent mathematics of infinity, thought that his discoveries had deep theological significance, as did a number of Jesuit scholars of the period who, under the influence of Pope Leo XIII's *Aeterni Patris*, took interest in his work.[1]

1. Some of the French philosopher Alain Badiou's work, while not precisely concerned with mathematics and theology, is so close to it that it calls for at least a passing comment. Badiou explores set theory and the mathematics of infinity in order to say something, if not about God, then at least about ontology, about the fundamental way that things are. The programme of *Being and Event* (London and New York: Continuum, 2005, trans. by Oliver Feltham from *L'être et l'évenement*, Editions du Seuil, 1988) is bold and refreshingly novel, based as it is on the presupposition that 'mathematics is ontology – the science of being qua being' (4). There are, however, difficulties with such a project in principle. Badiou puts enormous demands on his readers, who have to learn their way around set theory in order to follow the presentation of his argument. Indeed, his method of teaching his readers set theory, in spite of his best intentions, places on them a burden much greater than that borne by any ordinary student of the subject, since at every stage they need to sift through what is standard mathematics, what is Badiou's attempt to recast this in an 'easier', more intuitive way, and what are his own innovative philosophical theses. Without a prior knowledge of set theory, in fact, it is probably not possible to perceive these distinctions. This means a reader cannot be in a position to notice, much less question, key philosophical moves. An example is Badiou's deployment of the terms 'normal' and 'natural' – there is no reason whatsoever, mathematically, to understand one particular kind of set (ordinals) as more natural than others, but most of Badiou's audience would have no reason to know this. His choice of terminology here creates the impression that almost all sets have this structure, or that sets

However, to follow this path one must take up certain contested positions in both the philosophy of mathematics and theology. There are entrenched and seemingly interminable debates within the philosophy of mathematics about how any kind of mathematics, even the most simple, relates to a reality outside itself – what it is to which mathematics, even at the level of '2 + 2 = 4', refers, if it refers at all. And within theology there are of course questions about how it is possible to refer to God, and how it is possible, if it is at all possible, that God can be known. To seek to find a description of God in the proofs of the mathematicians requires both a very particular, contestable conception of what mathematics really is, and an even more contestable confidence in the possibility and propriety of getting to knowledge of God through a technically enhanced natural theology.

What I will propose in this essay is that it is not necessary to commit oneself in either of these directions in order to find in mathematics, even the mathematics of infinity, some help for theology. I will give two examples in what follows of how a more modest approach, philosophically and theologically, can yield insight. The first example centres upon the place of beauty in each discipline, the second on the relation between clarity and mystery.

I

Historically there have been strong claims about the relationship between beauty and mathematics, particularly between beauty and numbers. That beauty is somehow fundamentally about numbers is an idea that goes back to Pythagoras, and that was given forceful expression by Augustine: 'only beauty pleases; and in beauty, shapes; in shapes, proportions, and in proportions, numbers'.[2] Such views are not, however, widely accepted or influential in contemporary aesthetic theorizing, and I will not propose a wholesale revival of this strand of what has been called 'The Great Theory of Beauty'.[3] The claim I will develop is slightly different: whether or not beauty needs to be understood ultimately in terms of mathematics, mathematics, especially pure mathematics as it has developed in the last 120 years, needs to be understood ultimately in terms of beauty. Just when, philosophically, the ancient link between mathematics and beauty is almost

---

which do not are somehow strange or odd or puzzling to mathematicians – an impression which is actually quite important for the plausibility of what follows. Badiou's approach to bringing mathematics and the fundamental questions of theology and philosophy together, then, cannot be one to emulate: there is a danger here of an esotericism whose effect is to shock, dazzle and confuse, but not illuminate, one's readers.

2. Augustine, *De ordine*, II, 15, 42, *Corpus Christianorum Series Latina*, XXIX (Tournhout: Typographi Brepolis, 1970), 130; translation from Wladyslaw Tatarkiewicz, 'The Great Theory of Beauty and Its Decline', *The Journal of Aesthetics and Art Criticism* 31, no. 2 (1972): 168.

3. Tatarkiewicz, 'Beauty', 165–80.

completely abandoned, in other words, mathematics itself has developed in such a way as to bring out more clearly than ever before the centrality of beauty to its own enterprise.

Beauty is not the first thing which usually comes to mind when non-specialists think about mathematics. Many theologians, together with most contemporary intellectuals with a literary-philosophical education, are more likely to think of mathematics, alongside science and engineering, as something technical and pragmatic, and indeed as part of a way of knowing and interacting with the world which is fundamentally to do with control and manipulation, with measurement, mastery and domination.

If one considers mathematics, and in particular pure mathematics, as it is actually practiced, however, such a conception rapidly runs into difficulties. Pure mathematics is a project engaged in precisely *not* for the sake of any practical outcome, of any measurement, control or domination of nature. If a pure mathematician discovers that her work has applications, she may be somewhat pleased, but for at least the great majority, the work is not undertaken in the first place for the *sake* of such application.

Pure mathematics is, it should be said, a relatively recent term. It is only a little more than a century ago that mathematics split into pure and applied branches. So the business of pursuing a mathematics that one does *not* take to be descriptive of the natural world is an innovation.[4] But most pure mathematicians would conceive of what they do as in a strong form of continuity with the mathematics that was done before this divide took place, going back all the way to Euclid and perhaps beyond. What the development of a distinct field of pure mathematics does is to bring out more clearly some features of mathematics which were always present.

The most obvious way in which mathematical work is judged is in terms of its validity. Does the proof in fact succeed in proving what it is supposed to? But it will not do to suppose that this is all that counts. Mathematicians make all kinds of judgments about the relative worth of equally valid mathematical proofs: from some of them one turns away in disgust, others are worth doing, others are significant, and win a prize or promotion to a chair. Some mathematical papers are judged worthy of publication in prestigious journals, others only in journals lower in the hierarchy, and the difference cannot be measured in terms of how many new theorems are proven or how long and complicated the proofs are. To put the point in a slightly different way: there are infinitely many theorems a mathematician might in principle attempt to prove – how does one determine which are worth the trouble? How, in particular, is this choice made given that what is in question is precisely *pure* mathematics, where the decision will not be led by issues of what might be useful to the scientist or the engineer?

---

4. For an accessible and fascinating discussion of the shift in mathematics a little over a century ago and its broader significance, see Frank Quinn's 'A Revolution in Mathematics? What Really Happened a Century Ago and Why It Matters Today', *Notices of the American Mathematical Society*, January 2012.

It might be difficult to argue that such judgements and such decisions are made *entirely* on the basis of aesthetic criteria. There are considerations relating to how much a new piece of mathematics illuminates, extends or unifies areas already established, and these considerations may not be simply reducible to aesthetic concerns. But at least in large part judgements about which mathematics to pursue, which mathematics to fund, and which mathematics to reward, are made on aesthetic grounds, on the basis of considerations which mathematicians typically articulate in terms of interest, simplicity and elegance.

One does not find, of course, absolute unanimity as regards judgements of beauty in mathematics. Members of the different mathematical subdisciplines may make somewhat different judgements about the relative merits of certain kinds of theorems. What seems a lovely theorem, or a lovely proof, to an algebraist, may seem less than inspiring to a topologist. But the disagreements and the ambiguities involved in aesthetic judgments in mathematics are no worse than those which can be found in other spheres of life in which we speak of beauty, and they ought to be taken as an indication that talk of beauty in mathematics is 'merely subjective' only if we suppose this to be the case more generally.

What might be the consequence, then, if a theologian reflecting on beauty allows his or her thinking to be informed not only by art, music, literature and natural beauty, but also by beauty as it can be found in a subject like mathematics? One result would surely be to direct attention to the possibility of beautiful arguments and beautiful intellectual constructions. Just as a mathematical argument can be beautiful, elegant, satisfying, or else clumsy and ugly, can a theological argument, or a theological system, also be beautiful or ugly? And should this affect our judgment of it?

This notion of theological beauty needs to be distinguished from questions about language and literary style. The aesthetic quality of the mathematical argument does not depend very closely on the linguistic abilities of its formulator, and the question about the beauty of a theological argument need not be reduced simply to a question about the quality of the theologian's prose. One can convey an extremely elegant theological position in halting English, and if we find beauty in the theology of Aquinas, it is not necessarily because of any outstandingly mellifluous qualities of his Latin.

The analogy between mathematics and theology is particularly easy to see if one looks to a thinker such as Anselm. Just as mathematicians who have already proven a theorem may well seek, and if they find it then publish, a better proof – a simpler, more elegant way of establishing the same truth – so Anselm in his best-known work, the *Proslogion*, is not aiming to establish truths he previously thought uncertain, nor even primarily to demonstrate rationally for the first time truths he had previously held certain through faith. Rather, if we are to believe what he says in his preface, he is trying to find a more *elegant* way of demonstrating truths for which he had already, in a previous work, found arguments. He became, he indicates, dissatisfied with his previous effort, the *Monologion*:

> Reflecting that this was made up of a connected chain of many arguments, I began to wonder if perhaps it might be possible to find *one single* argument that

for its proof required no other save itself and that by itself would suffice to prove that God really exists, that He is the supreme good needing no other and is He whom all things have need of for their being and well-being.[5]

And once he has, after much frustration, come upon his one argument, he writes it down because he thinks it might *please* some of his readers. What Anselm finds important about his phrase 'that than which nothing greater can be conceived', then, is not so much that it makes possible his so-called ontological argument, but that it gives him a way of unifying many of the things he wants to be able to demonstrate about God, including, as it happens, that God exists. And because it introduces this unity and simplicity to his argument, it raises it to a new level of elegance.[6]

Anselm, of course, is not to everyone's taste. Aquinas, for instance, was both unpersuaded by what has come to be known as the ontological argument, and often averse to the kinds of *necessary* reasons that Anselm thought he could provide to explain God's dealings with the world. From this we can conclude, not that intellectual beauty is to be sought *only* in those who work in the style of Anselm, and is dismissed by others, but that there is more than one style of beauty to be found in theological works. Anselm's hunt for simplicity, clarity, necessity and elegance is one, but it is presumably a very different *kind* of beauty than that which can be found in, say, Karl Barth's *Church Dogmatics*, which is again to be distinguished from the deep beauty which lurks in Karl Rahner's sometimes torturous writings.

On one level I am proposing nothing new here. Most readers surely do respond to theologians and theological works at an aesthetic level, and whether they defend or criticise, whether they dismiss or read on, is in significant part determined by whether they find what the theologian presents them with to be, in one way or another, beautiful. Mostly, however, this response remains implicit. Mostly we argue about whether Karl Barth has an adequate pneumatology, whether Schleiermacher's consignment of the Trinity to an appendix is acceptable, whether Balthasar's conception of cross and Trinity is orthodox, and so on. The aesthetic appraisal, which is one of the factors that determines our fundamental orientation towards a theology, is most often kept mute. And when the importance of an aesthetic dimension *is* acknowledged, usually the discussion turns to paintings or poetry or symphonies.

It might be objected that if theology is to be concerned with beauty, it should be the divine beauty, and not its own, which it takes as its theme. To ask about the beauty of theology as such is for theology to become *incurvatus in se*, concerned

---

5. Anselm, *Proslogion*, preface, in *Anselm of Canterbury: The Major Works* (Oxford: Oxford University Press, 1998), 80.

6. That his readers may find what he has to offer 'pleasing' and beautiful is also a justification Anselm gives more than once in the *Cur Deus Homo* for the arguments he offers there, or more precisely, for the fact of his offering them.

with itself rather than its object. And ultimately this may be true. Finally, perhaps, any beauty of theology, if it has no connection to the beauty of God, is simply distraction. But it is important not to move too swiftly to this point, not to collapse, too quickly, the conversation about theological beauty into a conversation about the beauty of God. If I were to take whatever beauty I see in a theological writer, whether it be Barth or Anselm or Aquinas, as straight-forwardly and without question the beauty of God as it is given through this theologian, I would become a reader of the most sycophantic, uncritical and potentially dangerous kind. We need to be able to appreciate what is beautiful in a theological work, and yet still be able to ask, as a *further* question, what is the significance of this beauty?

A reflection on the role of beauty in mathematics, then, can suggest something of a programme for theology: to make explicit a largely hidden aesthetic dimension in our judgments of theological systems and positions; to consider whether it might be possible to classify and compare theologians in part by the *manner* in which their works are beautiful; and to begin to reflect more carefully about how theological beauty in general, or theological beauty of various kinds, relates to the beauty of God.

To pursue this programme is beyond the scope of a single essay; instead I would like to move on to a second way in which mathematics can be useful to theology. One of the most striking features of some of the best of pure mathematics – one thing which makes it beautiful – is the way in which it confronts us with that which exceeds our control, the way it opens up to us things which are beyond our ability to comprehend. It is to the significance of this that we turn in the next section.

II

A feature of almost all Christian theology is that at one point or another the theologian will suggest that we are dealing in a realm of mystery, that God or other things of which the theologian must speak (e.g. evil) are mysterious. It is part of theological piety to give at least a nod to mystery. But how does the acknowledgement of the mystery of God (and maybe other things) fit together with the fact that theologians actually *do* theology, that they talk, often at great length, about God? It seems natural to presume that a theologian thinks that if you read their treatise in some way you will know more afterwards – understanding will in some way be increased. How does the not-knowing of God (and other things) which most theologians will acknowledge relate to the *knowing* which prima facie would seem to be an aim of doing theology?

There is a stream within theology which focuses very precisely on the not-knowing of God. There are particular texts to which one traditionally turns to take up this question, the writings of the so-called pseudo-Dionysius, the works of Meister Eckhardt and so on. But if we ask, not specifically about this mystical and apophatic tradition, but about the acknowledgement of mystery in theology, then the canvas becomes much broader. Not just those whom we designate as negative,

11. Beauty and Mystery in Mathematics and Theology

apophatic or mystical theologians acknowledge mystery, but nearly all theologians; and so it is not just of the apophatic tradition that we can ask, 'What then are you doing when you do theology, and how does this relate to the mysteriousness of God?,' but of almost any theologian within the Christian tradition.

This is a question of great generality, and it would be unwise to suppose that any one simple answer is available. How the acknowledgement of mystery and the intellectual aims of theology are related to each other, whether explicitly or implicitly, is bound to vary from one thinker, system or style to another. Nevertheless, a consideration of the way knowing and not knowing, clarity and mystery, are related in at least some areas of mathematics can cast a useful light on the subject.

One might suppose that mathematics, as the realm of the certain and the calculable, is the last place to look for help with questions of mystery: it is easy, to make the point again, for those trained in humanities to conceive of mathematics as fundamentally a matter of mastery, manipulation and the subjugation of nature. But in fact very often pure mathematics does not offer calculation and control, but articulates the uncontrollability, the non-manipulability, the incalculability, of things.[7]

I will offer three examples, one ancient and two modern, to give some plausibility to this claim. First, consider Euclid's proof of the infinity of the primes.[8] At first sight it is not at all obvious how many primes there are, nor how one might go about establishing this. One might suppose one had to go on endlessly testing bigger and bigger numbers. But Euclid's proof, in a few sentences, without any calculations at all, produces a result that holds good no matter how big the numbers get, no matter how far along the list of numbers one goes.[9] In the space of a few dozen

---

7. The language of control or the uncontrollability of things, of manipulability or its contrary, is not itself mathematical language. In what follows I am engaged in an act of persuasion, trying to lead readers to understand that certain mathematical phenomenon are best seen in a certain light. In this sense I am operating in the register of the humanities, of interpretation and persuasion, rather than of mathematics itself.

8. A prime number is a whole number bigger than one which is divisible only by itself and by 1 (which has, to put it precisely, no positive integral divisors other than itself and 1). Euclid's theorem states that there are infinitely many of these – you can never have a 'biggest' prime.

9. The proof of this is by contradiction: one supposes the opposite to be the case – that there is some finite list of the primes – and then shows this leads to an impossibility. If there were only a finite number of primes, then we could write them as $p_1, p_2, p_3, \ldots, p_n$. The key step in the proof is to introduce a new number, P, which we get by multiplying all the primes together and then adding 1: $P = (p_1 \times p_2 \times \ldots p_n) + 1$, where p_1 is 2, p_2 is 3, p_3 is 5, and so on. We then turn our attention to whether P can be divided by anything other than itself. It will be clear that P must be an odd number ($p_1 \times p_2 \times \ldots p_n$ must be even since it is a multiple of 2, so when we add 1, the resulting number will be odd). Similarly, a little reflection will show that P cannot be divisible by 3, since $p_1 \times p_2 \times \ldots p_n$ is divisble by 3. More generally, since any

words something is established about infinity. But what is established is precisely not any kind of mastery over numbers, but something more like a proof of their unmasterability. We have discovered that we can never compile the complete list of the primes, never find the building blocks of all the numbers, never get a manageable set of numbers through which all the others can be understood. There is a kind of dominance of the numbers which Euclid's proof tells us we will never have.

Although I made reference to infinity in the previous paragraph, it would also have been possible to avoid using the word – one can describe Euclid's proof as merely showing that there is always another prime, so that there cannot be any such thing as a 'biggest' prime number. Infinity, one might say, is here just a *façon de parler*. In the second half of the nineteenth century, however, Georg Cantor engaged with the question of infinity more unequivocally.

Cantor worked with a notion of size – 'cardinality' – which could be used for infinite sets. Two sets are said to have the same cardinality if they can be paired up, put into 'one-to-one correspondence'. With finite collections this tallies obviously and uninterestingly with our ordinary conception of size: the collection of seven eggs can be paired up with the collection of seven breakfast eaters, because the two collections have the same size – there are seven in each. With infinite collections, the notion of one-to-one correspondence turns out to be more interesting. One can show that the set of natural numbers (1, 2, 3, etc) has the same cardinality as the set of all *even* natural numbers – you can remove an infinite number of numbers, in other words, and the set remains the same 'size'. And one can prove, in the other direction, that if one supplements the original set of natural numbers by throwing in all the fractions, the new set will have the same cardinality as the old.[10] What is surprising, at least initially, is that this is true in spite of the fact that between any two natural numbers (e.g. 1 and 2) there are infinitely many fractions.

Thus so far all the infinite sets have turned out to be the same 'size'. At this point the reader might find here nothing but a confirmation of the instinct that infinity is a murky concept, and anything you care to think of that is infinite will turn out to be the same size as anything else. But when we take what seems to be the obvious next step, which is to explore the 'real' numbers (which one might think of as a set including not only the fractions but also such things as π and the square root of 2, or, more simply, as all the numbers that can be written in decimal

---

of the primes in our list are divisors of $p_1 \times p_2 \times \ldots p_n$ none of them can be divisors of P – or to put it another way, if we divide any prime into P, the result will be the product of all the *other* primes, and a remainder of 1. So if $p_1, p_2, p_3, \ldots, p_n$ is the complete list of primes, we have found a number, bigger than all of them, which is not divisible by any of them, which means that this number (P) must itself be prime. This is in contradiction to our hypothesis that $p_1, p_2, p_3, \ldots, p_n$ is the complete list of primes, and we have arrived at a contradiction.

10. Expressed technically, the set of rational number (all those which can be represented as p/q, where p and q are both integers and q is not zero) has the same cardinality as the set of natural numbers, even though the latter is a proper subset of the former.

notation), it turns out that they cannot be put into one-to-one correspondence with the rationals. They are *uncountable* – one cannot count them, even if one could go on counting forever.[11] Indeed, it is not just the real numbers as a whole that are bigger than the rationals, but any portion of them. Thus, if one takes any two distinct rational numbers, no matter how close, between them one can find an infinite set of real numbers which is bigger than the *whole* of the set of rational numbers. So between .98 and .99, for instance, there are uncountably many real numbers.

Of course, philosophical reflection on infinity has a long history, well over two thousand years, and one could not say that what Cantor does (which includes not only what I have just described, but also the definition of a whole infinite series of infinities, each one infinitely bigger than its predecessor) resolves all philosophical issues about infinity, or puts an end to the range of debates and discomforts surrounding the idea. One *can* say, however, that Cantor introduces a radically new kind of clarity to some aspects, at least, of the debate: the philosophy cannot be the same after him as it was before. The key point for my purpose is that in introducing this clarity, Cantor does not in any way domesticate, tame or dissolve infinity: he does not bring it under control or reduce it to something which can be grasped and manipulated. Instead, I think, he intensifies the sense of the ungraspability, the incomprehensibility of infinity. What had previously been a hazy and unthinkable topic becomes something with which we can deal with precision and coherence, and yet it does not cease to be unthinkable, but becomes all the more so.

In suggesting that what goes on with infinity in mathematics is not that something is grasped and domesticated, but that its ungraspability is intensified – its mysteriousness deepened – I am clearly not simply stating mathematical truths, but attempting to characterize them in extra-mathematical language, and any such characterization is likely to be disputable. The opposing reactions to Cantor's work from Ludwig Wittgenstein and David Hilbert illustrate this. To Hilbert's famous comment that 'no one shall drive us from the paradise Cantor has created for us', Wittgenstein replied rather testily 'I would say "I wouldn't dream of trying to drive anyone from this paradise." I would do something quite different: I would try to show you that it is not a paradise – so you'll leave of your own accord'.[12] It is not by chance, however, that in this case the more positive view of Cantor's work is expressed by the working mathematician. Though the language I have used of ungraspability, of mystery, or indeed of domestication, might not be found on the lips of most pure mathematicians, at the very least I think it is safe to say that most mathematicians would have the sense of something wonderful and beautiful in Cantor's work, and would more likely see it as deepening than as dissolving a prior sense of infinity.

---

11. This is nothing but a less precise but more evocative way of saying that they cannot be put into one-to-one correspondence with the natural numbers.

12. From Wittgenstein's *Lectures on the Foundations of Mathematics* (Chicago: University of Chicago Press, 1975), Lecture XI, 103.

A final example to consider is Kurt Gödel's first incompleteness theorem. Gödel famously proved in 1931 that no finite and consistent set of axioms could be used to establish all the truths of arithmetic. Given any particular list of axioms, and assuming that they are not inconsistent with each other, there will always be some true arithmetical proposition which cannot be proven from these axioms. One can, then, never have a complete mathematical system. Gödel showed, in some sense, that there is an infinity to mathematics which escapes the grasp of any axiomatic systemization. And he showed this with a rigorous mathematical argument. The significance of Gödel's theorem may be contested, but the theorem itself is as well-established as anything else in classical mathematics. Gödel establishes, with clarity and precision, a truth which is precisely a truth about the limits of what we can construct and control, about what one might call the ultimately elusive nature of numbers.

In mathematics, then, we find points where our clarity about something and our awareness of its escaping us, its ungraspability, go hand in hand. As we get clearer, we become more aware of the way in which the thing exceeds us, exceeds our imagination and our comprehension. In mathematics we find points where clarity and certainty do not serve to fortify any system of reduction and control, but serve to finally and definitively undercut the possibility of a reductionist, controlling programme.

Mathematics can provide us, in other words, with an example of clarity and mystery varying in direct, rather than inverse, proportion. And this in turn allows a fundamental question to be raised about the place mystery occupies in theology. What I want to propose is that a significant question to put to any theologian, to any theological system or theological work, is how the *success* of the theology as an intellectual endeavour, and the *mystery* of its subject matter, are thought to be related. Do theology and mystery stand in a competitive relationship, so that the more successful theology is, the smaller the realm of mystery, or perhaps the more *penetrable* the mysterious is; or in a non-competitive relationship, so that the more successfully theology performs its task, the more radically the mysteriousness of its subject matter can be acknowledged?

Very often it is the first of these options which seems the obvious one. Of course God is mysterious, of course we can never *completely* know God, but surely we must suppose we can learn *something* about God from theological reflection, some dim glimmer, some beginnings of an understanding. Theology helps us, in a phrase of Matthew Levering, to squint into the infinite light,[13] and so presumably to see at least a *bit*. On such a view, God is mysterious, of course, but not in such a way that one can make no inroads. God's mysteriousness still leaves *some* room for making theological headway. Piety and theological modesty are preserved here by the language of size or degree: we do not of course know God wholly, but we at least know a little, maybe only a *very* little. Or alternatively, to use the language of degree, we don't dissolve God's mystery *wholly* so that we could get God *entirely*

---

13. Levering, *Scripture and Metaphysics*, 240.

in focus, but we do at least *dimly* make out something through our theological efforts. In all such formulations God's mystery and theological achievement are fundamentally conceived as in competition, even if it is a competition that the modest theologian acknowledges God *mostly* wins. God is mysterious, but not *so* mysterious that I cannot make some little progress. The key point here is that the *bit* of progress I make is represented in some way as a *diminishment* in the unknowness of God. Take, for instance, the doctrine of the Trinity. The ordinary Christian is often convinced that they are not clever enough to understand it, that it is simply a mystery to them. The theologian who takes the competitive view might acknowledge that of course the Trinity is always going to be a mystery, but will maintain that theological study, approached properly, patiently, perhaps piously, should allow one to grasp at least a *little* of its meaning.

Much of contemporary theological common sense seems to presuppose this essentially competitive conception of the relation of theology to mystery. The purpose of the mathematical tour, then, was to provide plausibility for a claim which, in such a climate, might otherwise sound like sheer paradox-mongering: perhaps mystery and the success of theology can go together, can be directly rather than inversely related, so that the more effectively the theologian does her job, the deeper the sense of mystery becomes.[14]

Rather than leave this at the level of bare possibility, it is helpful to consider examples. Once again, as in the case of the mathematical examples, I will touch on three: one pre-modern and two more recent.

A positive relationship between clarity and mystery can be found on various levels in the thought of Thomas Aquinas.[15] Denys Turner makes part of the case here very effectively by arguing that natural theology and negative theology work together in Thomas. Thomas thinks that 'God can be demonstrated to exist', says Turner, but 'what such inference to God succeeds in showing is precisely the unknowability of the God thus shown'.[16] Turner focuses primarily on the question of the proofs, but a similar point can be made in respect of Thomas' understanding

---

14. It is worth underlining that this is a limited invocation of mathematics, not a proposal that mathematical reasoning should in general become a model for theological reasoning. Mathematics is *unlike* theology in many ways: it makes a kind of progress and achieves a kind of certainty which theology manifestly does not. Even the clarity of mathematics has a different quality from any clarity for which the theologian can hope. In most ways theological reasoning is more naturally compared with literary, historical or philosophical modes of reasoning than with the mathematical. Mathematics is being used here, then, not to model a method but only to show that to relate clarity and mystery positively need not be simply sheer obfuscation or an irresponsible love of paradox.

15. Readings of Aquinas, notoriously, vary, and the claim I am making here is embedded in a particular way of reading him, a way broadly aligned with Victor Preller, David Burrell and those whom they have influenced.

16. Denys Turner, *Faith, Reason and the Existence of God* (Cambridge: Cambridge University Press, 2004), 254.

of theological language, of how our words gain purchase on God. Aquinas famously contrasts analogical predication with univocal predication on the one hand, and equivocation on the other. It is tempting, but in my opinion mistaken, to think of Thomas as simply taking a middle position, to read him as advocating the view that analogy lies roughly half way between the univocal (we can describe God very well) and the equivocal (we cannot describe God at all). The way Thomas actually sets out the notion of analogical predication it would be more illuminating to say that both extremes apply than that the truth lies somewhere in the middle. If one considers the *res significata*, Thomas tells us, what the words mean, a term such as 'good' not only does genuinely apply to God, but applies more properly to God than to anything or anyone else. But if one considers the *modus significandi*, the way the word signifies, what we understand by the word turns out to be in no way appropriate. Thomas thinks he can show, in other words, that we can know that certain words apply to God, and at the same time that we do not know what we *mean* when we say them of God.[17] Whether or not he succeeds, the point for our purposes is that he is attempting both to bring clarity to the question of what we can say about God, and at the same time to intensify, to deepen, our sense of God as unknown, as beyond what we can grasp. In Chapter 3 I argued that something similar can be said about Thomas's treatment of the Trinity – that Thomas sets out simultaneously to clarify the grammar of the Trinity, the way in which we must talk about it, and to confront us with the fact that we cannot understand it.

A rather different way of exemplifying the same pattern can be found in Kathryn Tanner's first book *God and Creation in Christian Theology*.[18] Tanner proposes that certain rules have governed otherwise diverse traditional forms of Christian talk about God and the world, rules in particular which ensure what she calls non-contrastive accounts of divine transcendence. One must never, for instance, speak about God and created agents in such a way that the more God does, the less the creature does, or vice versa. So, in particular, one must not talk of human freedom as though it is incompatible with divine causality, as if we can only be free if God draws back. Tanner argues that these rules, followed consistently by theologians through to the fifteenth century, have been systematically distorted in modern times, leading to persistent division and incoherence in Christian theology.

Suppose, for the sake of argument, that Tanner's analysis is correct. What does it do? On the one hand, it brings tremendous clarity: it gives a very simple account of common underlying patterns in otherwise very different theological works, a

---

17. Thomas Aquinas, *Summa Theologiae* 1a.13.3, in Laurence Shapcote, O.P., trans., *Latin/English Edition of the Works of St. Thomas Aquinas* Vol. 13 (Lander: The Aquinas Institute for the Study of Sacred Doctrine, 2012), 126.

18. Kathryn Tanner, *God and Creation in Christian Theology: Tyranny or Empowerment?* (Minneapolis: Fortress Press, 1988). This theme is most extensively developed here, but Tanner continues to unfold its significance across a number of subsequent books, including for instance *The Economy of Grace* (Minneapolis: Fortress Press, 2005), and *Jesus, Humanity and the Trinity*.

simple set of rules for speaking in a coherently Christian way about God and the world, and a simple diagnosis of why so much Christian theology in more recent times runs into difficulties. At the same time, however, Tanner's approach gives us no help whatsoever in getting a handle on God, or how God works in the world. Any attempt actually to make intelligible God's agency in the world will be an attempt to place it – God is acting here but not there, at one point rather than some others. Perhaps God gets things going at the beginning and sets up the laws but then does not subsequently intervene. Perhaps God invisibly influences things at the quantum mechanical level without violating any physical laws. Perhaps God offers grace if we ask but does not interfere with our decision to accept it or not. All such proposals would give us some way of concretely integrating a vision of God's activity with our general understanding of how things – and indeed we ourselves – work, but all of them, in saying that God acts here whereas over there it is only a created being who acts, violate the non-contrastive principle Tanner articulates. Tanner brings clarity to the issue of how to relate God and creation, divine and human agency, while at the same time moving it right beyond any chance of our grasping it. To say that divine and created agency cannot be contrasted is not to offer an explanation of how they go together, but a rule which defeats all possible explanations.

Different again is the way we find this pattern in the thought of Karl Rahner, who makes the notion of mystery a matter for sustained reflection in his 1959 essay 'The Concept of Mystery in Catholic Theology'. Rahner develops at some length an understanding of mystery in contrast with the one he takes to be prevalent in the Roman Catholic thought of the period. The view he rejects is that mystery is a property of certain propositions. These are truths which we accept because they are revealed, but which we cannot yet understand: they are for the moment obscure and impenetrable to us, but it is assumed that at some future point they will become clear. Mystery was thus understood fundamentally negatively, as a lack in our ability to comprehend certain truths, a lack which is in principle overcome-able. And it was assumed that there are a multiplicity of mysteries, an array of such not-yet-understood truths that we accept in faith.

By contrast, Rahner proposes an understanding of mystery which is, first, not provisional – mystery is not a temporary lack of perspicuity, but a fundamental incomprehensibility; secondly, not plural – there are not many mysteries, but ultimately only one which confronts us; thirdly, positive rather than negative – incomprehensibility will also characterize the beatific vision, and we must not think of this incomprehensibility 'as a sort of regrettably permanent limitation of our blessed comprehension of God' but 'as the very substance of our vision and the very object of our blissful love';[19] and finally, mystery is not merely a property of propositions but a fundamental aspect of our *experience*.

---

19. Karl Rahner, 'The Concept of Mystery in Catholic Theology', *Theological Investigations 4* (New York: Crossroad, 1973), 41.

The conception Rahner develops of the 'holy' or the 'absolute' mystery ties in closely with his theological anthropology, with his insistence that to be human is to be always open to, always already related to, God. Rahner thinks that we always encounter God on the level of what he calls transcendental experience, on a level that is both distinguished from and the condition of the possibility for our experience of objects. He also thinks that we *never* experience God as an object – God can never be caught on the level of categorical experience. The description of God as the holy, or absolute, or abiding mystery, in other words, is very closely connected to the idea that God is something toward which, on the transcendental level, we move, while never being able to grasp in our categorical experience. To some extent, then, to speak of God as holy mystery is to express rather more poetically something which can equally be said in Rahner's technical vocabulary.

Rahner also, in an intense passage which is something of a theological *tour de force*, uses the notion of mystery to bring together the doctrines of the Trinity, the incarnation and grace into a single conception of God's self-communication, God's giving of God's self. He is aiming to develop an understanding according to which the body of Christian doctrine is not a complex collection of information, of truths to believe (some of which, it just so happens, one cannot understand) but rather is something which all points to a single mystery, a mystery which will never cease to be a mystery, and a mystery to which we are all already and profoundly related.

Once again my interest here is not whether Rahner is right – whether he is right to tie all of Christian doctrine so closely in with his anthropology, whether his notion of divine self-communication is adequate, whether the concept of transcendental experience is coherent. The interest rather is in the structure of what he is doing, in the *kind* of project he is engaged in. For what Rahner is aiming to do is not to clear up mysteries that are around in Catholic theology, to make them go away or be in some way diminished, but to *intensify* the sense of the mysterious. He is not trying to explain God a little bit more than others have managed to do, but to make it more clear that God is essentially inexplicable. His theology, if it is successful, does not reduce the realm of mystery, push back the bounds of what is unknown – not even a little bit – but makes us aware of mystery as a deeper, and a more inescapable, phenomenon. Rahner is thus simultaneously trying to simplify and clarify Christian theology, to bring it all into focus around a single center, and to make it clear that in fact theology has no subject but the unknowable, nothing to do except to gesture towards mystery.

So in Aquinas, Tanner and Rahner we have three examples of a non-competitive relation between theology and mystery. I have stressed that they are *different* examples – I am not proposing that the three thinkers ultimately say the same thing, nor even conceive of God's unknowability in the same way. Indeed, I am myself using the word mystery more broadly and loosely than Rahner does – in a way that is, one might say, systematically vague. The object is not to develop a single account of God as mystery, but to point to a common pattern, a common instinct, across a variety of positions which may otherwise be very different.

Although the language in this essay of mystery and of knowing and not knowing has of necessity a certain vagueness, then, the *distinction* between two conceptions of theology which it enables us to draw is I think quite a sharp one. Its importance may become clearer if we consider it in relation to some live issues in theology.

One arena in which this distinction is helpful is the doctrine of the Trinity. As I have touched on in the first essay in this volume, while the social trinitarians are typically convinced they are the inheritors of Cappadocian theology, the continuity is not really so very strong. One way to see this is by asking, how is theology thought to be related to mystery? If one asks this question, it turns out that the Cappadocians and the contemporary social Trinitarians who appeal to them are pointing in distinctly different directions. The Cappadocians were, as discussed in the third essay of this volume, profoundly apophatic thinkers, who stressed the unknowability of God even in their debates with neo-Arians. Contemporary social theorists of the Trinity, on the other hand, frequently present themselves as knowing, through the doctrine of the Trinity, quite a bit about God and God's inner life. They think of the doctrine of the Trinity as giving Christians a *fuller* picture of God than we would otherwise possess. For them, a proper interpretation of the doctrine of the Trinity *diminishes* the unknowness of God; for the Cappadocians, it preserves this.

For another live issue in contemporary theology, and to revisit in slightly different language the themes of Chapters 6 and 7, consider the question of evil. Evil is typically thought to be, either in itself or in the fact of its coexistence with a good and powerful God, to some degree or other mysterious. It is not, evidently, mysterious in the same way God is, nor in an equal and opposite way to God, but nevertheless, in some manner or other, it is a mystery. How then is the role of theology conceived in relation to this mystery? If theology is successful, is the mystery of evil and its relation to God diminished? One can quite neatly divide discussions of evil into two camps according to their response to this question, and one can interpret a number of recent attacks on the very project of theodicy as an indication that those which aim to diminish the mystery of evil turn out to be deeply problematic, not just intellectually but also in some sense morally.

Consider, to take another example, the debate around the divine attributes. It is common, among a range of theologians and philosophers of religion, to raise questions about what one might call the traditional metaphysical attributes of God – God's simplicity, for example, or God's aseity and impassibility. These are frequently thought to be philosophically derived distortions of the Biblical picture of God, the product of Christianity's encounter with Greek philosophy rather than any response to revelation. The God of the attributes is criticized also as a fundamentally static, non-relational, and ultimately unloving God – how can you love if you cannot suffer?

Defenders of the tradition rarely respond, 'but yes, of course God *is* basically static, non-relational and unloving'. Instead they suggest that in one way or another the critics have misunderstood the import of the traditional attributes. Here too, it seems, we can construe the difference between the two camps as in great part a difference in their understanding of the relation of our language about God to God's mystery. The critics of aseity or simplicity reject aseity and simplicity because they think these words do not adequately *describe* God, because the picture of God they evoke is an unattractive or unconvincing one. Defenders of this aspect of the tradition, on the other hand, see such attributions not as depicting, defining or describing God, but as setting out the limits of our speech, showing that language of change and composition, for instance, cannot be used of God. The debate should not ultimately be interpreted as a clash between two pictures of God, but as a clash between different assumptions about whether theology ought to be providing a picture of God at all.

In mathematics theology can find, then, neither a particular content nor a particular method, but a model for a way in which clarity and mystery, clarity and incomprehensibility, can be related. Common sense seems to tell us that too much talk in theology of mystery, of incomprehension, of unknowing, amounts to the abandonment of rationality and responsibility, the abandonment of serious effort to be clear and to make good arguments. But mathematics, a discipline with as little cause to be worried about its rationality and responsibility in making arguments as any, can allow us to lay to rest this worry, and perhaps to reshape this common-sensical reaction.

How to conceive its own task in relation to the mysteriousness of its subject matter, furthermore, is something which deeply effects *all* of theology, not just those bits of it which explicitly address questions of, say, the darkness of God: many debates which seem to be about something else ultimately revolve around this. And, finally, to recall the first part of this essay, where we find ourselves in relation to this issue – a competitive or a non-competitive understanding of theology in relation to mystery – may ultimately be determined by an aesthetic judgement, a judgment about the beauty of theology.

BIBLIOGRAPHY

Abbot, Christopher. *Julian of Norwich: Autobiography and Theology*. Cambridge: D.S. Brewer, 1999.

Adams, Marilyn McCord. *Horrendous Evils and the Goodness of God*. Ithaca and London: Cornell University Press, 1999.

Adams, Marilyn McCord and Adams, Robert Merihew, eds. *The Problem of Evil*. Oxford: Oxford University Press, 1990.

Anselm. *Proslogion*. In *Anselm of Canterbury: The Major Works*. Oxford: Oxford University Press, 1998.

Aquinas, Thomas. *Summa Theolologiae*. In *Latin English Edition of the Works of St. Thomas Aquinas*, Vol. 16. Edited by John Motensen and Enrique Alarcón. Translated by Laurence Shapcote, O.P. Lander: The Aquinas Institute for the Study of Sacred Doctrine, 2012.

Augustine. *De ordine*. In *Corpus Christianorum Series Latina*, XXIX. Tournhout: Typographi Brepolis, 1970.

Augustine. *Letters*. The Works of Saint Augustine: A Translation for the 21st Century, Part 2, Vol. 4. Translated by Roland Teske, S.J. New York: New York City Press, 2005.

Augustine. *The City of God against the Pagans*. Edited and translated by R.W. Dyson. Cambridge: Cambridge University Press, 1998.

Augustine. 'The Gift of Perseverance'. In *Answer to the Pelagians, IV*. Edited by John Rotelle. Translated by Roland J. Teske. New York: New York City Press, 1999.

Augustine. *The Trinity*. Translated by Edmund Hill, O.P. New York: New York City Press, 1991.

Badiou, Alain. *Being and Event*. Translated by Oliver Feltham. London and New York: Continuum, 2005. Originally published as *L'être et l'évenement*. Editions du Seuil, 1988.

Barnes, Michel René. 'Rereading Augustine on the Trinity'. In *The Trinity*, edited by Stephen T. Davis, 145–76. Oxford: Oxford University Press, 1999.

Barnes, Michel René. 'The Use of Augustine in Contemporary Trinitarian Theology'. *Theological Studies* 56 (1995): 237–50.

Barth, Karl. *Church Dogmatics* III. Translated by G. W. Bromiley et al. Edinburgh: T&T Clark, 2010.

Basil of Caesarea. *The Father of the Church, Volume 13: St Basil's Letters*. Washington, DC: Catholic University of America, 1951.

Behr, John. *The Mystery of Christ: Life in Death*. Crestwood: St Vladimir's Seminary Press, 2006.

Behr, John. *The Nicene Faith*. Crestwood: St Vladimir University Press, 2004.

Bielik-Robson, Agata. 'Nihilism through the Looking Glass: Nietzsche, Rosenzweig, and Scholem on the Condition of Modern Disenchantment'. *Revero. Revista de Estudas da Religiao* (Spring 2008): 39–67.

Bielik-Robson, Agata. 'Troubles with Divine Aesthetics: A. J. Heschel's Tarrying with the Sublime'. In *Abraham Joshua Heschel: Philosophy, Theology and Interreligious Dialogue*, edited by Adam Lipszyc et al., 67–88. Wiesbaden: Harrasowitz Verlag, 2009.

Burrell, David. *Aquinas: God and Action*. London: Routledge and Kegan Paul, 1979.
Coakley, Sarah. *God, Sexuality and the Self*. Cambridge: Cambridge University Press, 2013.
Crammer, Corrine. 'One Sex or Two? Balthasar's Theology of the Sexes'. In the *Cambridge Companion to Hans Urs von Balthasar*, edited by Edward T. Oakes, S. J. and David Moss, 93-112. Cambridge: Cambridge University Press, 2004.
de Lubac, Henri. *Surnaturel*. Paris: Aubeir-Montaigne, 1945.
Edwards, Denis. *The God of Evolution: A Trinitarian Theology*. New York: Paulist Press, 1999.
Emery, Gilles. *Trinity in Aquinas*. Ypsilanti: Sapientia Press, 2003.
Gagey, Henri-Jérôme. *La vérité s'accomplit*. Paris: Bayard, 2009.
Gregory of Nazianzus. 'The Second Theological Oration'. In *Nicene and Post-Nicene Fathers of the Christian Church, Vol. VII*, edited by P. Schaff and H. Wace. New York: The Christian Literature Company, 1894.
Gregory of Nazianzus. 'Third Theological Oration'. In *Library of Christian Classics, Volume III: Christology of the Later Fathers*, 160-76. London: SCM, 1954.
Gunton, Collin. *The One, The Three and the Many*. Cambridge: Cambridge University Press, 1993.
Gunton, Collin. 'Trinity, Ontology and Anthropology'. In *Persons: Divine and Human*, edited by Christoph Schwöbel and Colin E. Gunton, 47-61. Edinburgh: T&T Clark, 1991.
Healy, Nicholas J. 'The Christian Mystery of Nature and Grace'. In *The T&T Clark Companion to Henri de Lubac*, edited by J. Hillebert, 181-204. London: Bloomsbury, 2017.
Healy, Nicholas M. *Church, World and the Christian Life: Practical Prophetic Ecclesiology*. Cambridge: Cambridge University Press, 2000.
Healy, Nicholas M. *Thomas Aquinas: Theologian of the Christian Life*. Aldershot: Ashgate, 2003.
Holmes, Stephen R. *The Holy Trinity: Understanding God's Life*. Milton Keynes: Paternoster, 2012.
Insole, Chris and Harris, Harriett, eds. *Faith and Philosophical Analysis: The Impact of Analytic Philosophy on the Philosophy of Religion*. Farnborough: Ashgate, 2005.
Joint Declaration on the Doctrine of Justification. 1999. Available at http://www.vatican.va/roman_curia/pontifical_councils/chrstuni/documents/rc_pc_chrstuni_doc_31101999_cath-luth-joint-declaration_en.html.
Julian of Norwich. *A Revelation of Love* (Middle English Text). In *The Writings of Julian of Norwich*, edited by Nicholas Watson and Jacqueline Jenkins, 121-382. University Park: Pennsylvania State Press, 2006.
Julian of Norwich. *Revelations of Divine Love*. Translated by Elizabeth Spearing. London: Penguin Books, 1998.
Jung, Carl. *Collected Works of C.G. Jung*, Volume 11.
Juster, Norton. *The Phantom Tollbooth*. New York: Epstein and Carroll, 1961.
Kerr, Fergus. *After Aquinas: Versions of Thomism*. Oxford: Blackwell, 2002.
Kerr, Fergus. *Twentieth Century Catholic Theologians*. Oxford: Wiley-Blackwell, 2006.
Kilby, Karen. *Balthasar: A (Very) Critical Introduction*. Grand Rapids: Eerdmans, 2012.
Kilby, Karen. 'Balthasar and Karl Rahner'. In *The Cambridge Companion to Hans Urs von Balthasar*, edited by Edward T. Oaks, S.J. and David Moss, 256-68. Cambridge: Cambridge University Press, 2004.

Kilby, Karen. 'Eschatology, Suffering and the Limits of Theology'. In *Game Over? Reconsidering Eschatology*, edited by Christophe Chalamet et al., 279–92. Berlin: De Gruyter, 2017.

Kilby, Karen. 'Hans Urs von Balthasar on the Trinity'. In *The Cambridge Companion to the Trinity*, edited by Peter C. Phan, 208–22. Cambridge: Cambridge University Press, 2011.

Kilby, Karen. 'Seeking Clarity'. In *The Routledge Companion to the Practice of Christian Theology*, edited by Mike Higton and Jim Fodor, 61–71. London: Routledge, 2015.

Kilby, Karen. 'The Seductions of Kenosis'. In *Suffering and the Christian Life*, edited by Karen Kilby and Rachel Davies, 163–74. London: Bloomsbury T&T Clark, 2019.

Kilby, Karen. 'Trinity, Tradition and Politics'. In *Recent Developments in Trinitarian Theology: An International Symposium*, edited by Christoph Chalamet and Mark Vial, 73–86. Minneapolis: Fortress Press, 2014.

Kilby, Karen E. 'Negative Theology and Meaningless Suffering'. *Modern Theology*, 36, no. 1 (2020): 92–104.

Lash, Nicholas. *Believing Three Ways in One God*. London: SCM, 1992.

Levering, Matthew. *Scripture and Metaphysics: Aquinas and the Renewal of Trinitarian Theology*. Oxford: Blackwell, 2004.

Lindbeck, George. *The Nature of Doctrine*. Philadelphia: Westminster, 1984.

Marshall, Bruce. 'Quod Scit Una Uetula: Auinas on the Nature of Theology'. In *The Theology of Thomas Aquinas*, edited by Rik van Nieuwenhove and Joseph Wawrykow, 1–35. Notre Dame: University of Notre Dame Press, 2005.

McCabe, Herbert. 'Aquinas on the Trinity'. In *Silence and the Word: Negative Theology and Incarnation*, edited by Oliver Davies and Denys Turner, 76–93. Cambridge: Cambridge University Press, 2002.

McCabe, Herbert. *God Matters*. London: Continuum, 1987.

McFadyen, Alistair. *Bound to Sin: Abuse, Holocaust, and the Christian Doctrine of Sin*. Cambridge: Cambridge University Press, 2000.

McFarland, Ian et al., eds. *The Cambridge Dictionary of Christian Theology*. Cambridge: Cambridge University Press, 2011.

Metz, J. B. 'Facing the Jews: Christian Theology after Auschwitz'. In *The Holocaust as Interruption*, edited by Elisabeth Schüssler Fiorenza and David Tracy, 26–33. Edinburgh: T&T Clark, 1984.

Moltmann, Jürgen. *History and the Triune God*. London: SCM, 1991.

Moltmann, Jürgen. *The Trinity and the Kingdom of God*. New York: Harper and Row, 1981.

Murray, Paul. 'Discerning the Dynamics of Doctrinal Development'. In *Faithful Reading: New Essays in Theology in Honour of Fergus Kerr*, edited by Simon Oliver, Karen Kilby and Tom O'Loughlin, 193–220. London: Continuum, 2012.

Ochs, Peter. *Another Reformation: Postliberal Christianity and the Jews*. Grand Rapids: Baker Academic, 2011.

O'Hanlon, Gerard. *The Immutability of God in the Theology of Hans Urs von Balthasar*. Cambridge: Cambridge University Press, 1990.

Oliver, Simon. 'Review of Analytic Theology: New Essays in the Philosophy of Theology'. *The International Journal of Systematic Theology* 12, no. 4 (2010): 464–75.

Percy, Emma. *Mothering as a Metaphor for Ministry*. Farnham: Ashgate, 2014.

Percy, Emma. *What Clergy Do: Especially When It Looks like Nothing.* London: SPCK, 2014.

Plantinga, Cornelius. 'Social Trinity and Tritheism'. In *Trinity, Incarnation and Atonement*, edited by Ronald J. Feenstra and Cornelius Plantinga, Jr. Notre Dame, 21–47: University of Notre Dame Press, 1989.

Preller, Victor. *Divine Science and the Science of God: A Reformulation of Thomas Aquinas.* Princeton: Princeton University Press, 1967.

Quash, Ben. *Theology and the Drama of History.* Cambridge: Cambridge University Press, 2005.

Quinn, Frank. 'A Revolution in Mathematics? What Really Happened a Century Ago and Why it Matters Today'. *Notices of the American Mathematical Society*, 59 (2012): 31–7.

Rahner, Karl. *Encounters with Silence*, 45–52. South Bend: St. Augustine Press, 1999.

Rahner, Karl. *Foundations of Christian Faith: An Introduction to the Idea of Christianity.* New York: Crossroad, 1989.

Rahner, Karl. *Encounters with Silence.* South Bend: St Augustine's Press, 1999.

Rahner, Karl. 'The Concept of Mystery in Catholic Theology'. In *Theological Investigations* 4, 36–73. New York: Crossroad, 1973.

Rahner, Karl. *The Trinity.* Translated by Joseph Donceel. New York: Crossroad, 1997.

Ray, Stephen G. *Do No Harm: Social Sin and Christian Responsibility.* Minneapolis: Augsberg Fortress, 2003.

Rober, Daniel. *Recognising the Gift: Towards a Renewed Theology of Nature and Grace.* Minneapolis: Fortress Press, 2016.

Rosenzweig, Franz. *The Star of Redemption.* Translated by Barbara E. Galli. Madison: University of Wisconsin Press, 2005.

Rowe, William L. 'The Problem of Evil and Some Varieties of Atheism'. In *Philosophy of Religion: The Big Questions*, edited by Eleanor Stump and Michael J. Murray, 157–63. Oxford: Blackwell, 1999.

Samuelson, M. *An Introduction to Modern Jewish Philosophy.* Albany: State University of New York Press, 1989.

Sarot, Marcel. 'Auschwitz, Morality and the Suffering of God'. *Modern Theology* 7 (1991): 135–52.

Smith, Timothy. *Thomas Aquinas' Trinitarian Theology: A Study in Theological Method.* Washington, DC: Catholic University of America Press, 2003.

Sobrino, Jon. 'Spirituality and the Following of Jesus'. In *Mysterium Liberationis: Fundamental Concepts of Liberation Theology*, edited by Ignacio Ellacuria and Jon Sobrino, 677–701. Maryknoll: Orbis, 1993.

Soulen, R. Kendall. *The God of Israel and Christian Theology.* Minneapolis: Augusburg Fortress, 1996.

Surin, Kenneth. *Theology and the Problem of Evil.* Oxford: Basil Blackwell, 1986.

Tanner, Kathryn. *Christ the Key.* Cambridge: Cambridge University Press, 2010.

Tanner, Kathryn. *Christianity and the New Spirit of Capitalism.* New Haven and London: Yale University Press, 2019.

Tanner, Kathryn. *God and Creation in Christian Theology: Tyranny or Empowerment?* Minneapolis: Fortress Press, 1988.

Tanner, Kathryn. 'Human Freedom, Human Sin, and God the Creator'. In *The God Who Acts: Philosophical and Theological Explorations*, edited by Thomas F. Tracy, 111–36. University Park: Pennsylvania State University Press, 1994.

Tanner, Kathryn. *The Economy of Grace*. Minneapolis: Fortress Press, 2005.
Tanner, Kathryn. *The Politics of God*. Minneapolis: Augsburg Fortress Press, 1992.
Tanner, Kathryn. 'Trinity'. In *The Wiley Blackwell Companion to Political Theology*, 2nd ed., edited by William T. Cavanaugh and Peter Manley Scott, 165–80. Oxford: Wiley Blackwell, 2019.
Tatarkiewicz, Wladyslaw. 'The Great Theory of Beauty and Its Decline'. *The Journal of Aesthetics and Art Criticism* 31, no. 2 (1972): 165–80.
The Congregation for the Doctrine of Faith. *Libertatis Nuntius*. 'Instruction on Certain Aspects of the "Theology of Liberation"'. Available at http://www.vatican.va/roman_curia/congregations/cfaith/documents/rc_con_cfaith_doc_19840806_theology-liberation_en.html.
Ticciati, Susannah. *A New Apophaticism: Augustine and the Redemption of Signs*. Leiden: Brill, 2013.
Tilley, Terrence. *The Evils of Theodicy*. Washington, DC: Georgetown University Press, 1991.
Torrell, Jean-Pierre. *Saint Thomas Aquinas: Volume 2 Spiritual Master*. Washington, DC: Catholic University of America Press, 2003.
Turcescu, Lucian. '"Person" versus "Individual", and other Modern Misreadings of Gregory of Nyssa'. In *Rethinking Gregory of Nyssa*, edited by Sarah Coakley, 96–110. Oxford: Blackwell, 2003.
Turner, Denys. *Faith, Reason and the Existence of God*. Cambridge: Cambridge University Press, 2004.
Turner, Denys. *Julian of Norwich, Theologian*. New Haven: Yale, 2011.
Turner, Denys and Davies, Oliver. *Silence and the Word*. Cambridge: Cambridge University Press, 2002.
Volf, Miraslov. '"The Trinity is Our Social Program": The Doctrine of the Trinity and the Shape of Social Engagement'. *Modern Theology* 14, no. 3 (1998): 403–23.
Von Balthasar, Hans Urs. *Dare We Hope 'That All Men Shall be Saved'? with A Short Discourse on Hell*. San Francisco: Ignatius Press, 1988.
Von Balthasar, Hans Urs. *Elucidations*. San Francisco: Ignatius Press, 1998.
Von Balthasar, Hans Urs. *Explorations in Theology II: Spouse of the Word*. San Francisco: Ignatius Press, 1991.
Von Balthasar, Hans Urs. *My Work: In Retrospect*. San Francisco: Ignatius Press, 1993.
Von Balthasar, Hans Urs. *The Grain of Wheat: Aphorisms*. San Francisco: Ignatius Press, 1995.
Von Balthasar, Hans Urs. *Theo-Drama: Theological Dramatic Theory Volume IV: The Action*. San Francisco: Ignatius Press, 1994.
Von Balthasar, Hans Urs. 'Theology and Sanctity'. In *Explorations in Theology Volume I: The Word Made Flesh*. San Francisco: Ignatius Press, 1989.
Von Balthasar, Hans Urs. *Truth Is Symphonic: Aspects of Christian Pluralism*. San Francisco: Ignatius Press, 1987.
Weinandy, Thomas. *Does God Suffer?* Edinburgh: T&T Clark, 2000.
Williams, A. N. *The Ground of Union: Deification in Aquinas and Palamas*. Oxford: Oxford University Press, 1999.
Williams, Rowan. 'What Does Love Know? St. Thomas on the Trinity'. *New Blackfriars* 82 (2001): 260–72.
Wilson-Kastner, Patricia. *Faith, Feminism and the Christ*. Philadelphia: Fortress Press, 1983.

Wittgenstein, Ludwig. *Lectures on the Foundations of Mathematics*. Chicago: University of Chicago Press, 1975.

Wolterstorff, Nicholas. 'The Migration of the Theistic Arguments: From Natural Theology to Evidentialist Apologetics'. In *Rationality, Religious Belief & Moral Commitment*, edited by R. Audi and W. J. Wainwright, 38–81. Ithaca: Cornell University Press, 1986.

Zizioulas, John D. *Being as Communion*. New York: St. Vladimir's Seminary Press, 1985.

INDEX

Adams, Marilyn McCord   69 n.2, 71, 72
analogical language   85, 123, 124, 130, 150
analytic theology   46 n.2, 85
Andrew   23–4
Anselm of Bec   14, 87, 142–4
anti-liberalism   32, 115–16
apologetics   42
Aquinas, Thomas
   abstract theism   70
   beauty   142–4
   divine transcendence   74
   evil   82–3, 129, 133
   grace   89 n.10
   mystery   149–50, 152
   sin   92
   Trinity   17–30, 40
Arendt, Hannah   111
Athanasian creed   26
Athanasius   32 n.4, 62
Augustine
   apophaticism   1
   beauty   40
   evil and sin   69, 82, 87–92
   grace   88–90
   Trinity   7–8, 18, 19, 21, 23, 26, 40–1
Augustinian tradition   87–94, 98, 129–30, 133
Ayres, Lewis   6 n.4, 46 n.3

Badiou, Alain   39 n.1
Balthasar, Hans Urs von
   danger of paganism   117–19
   nuptial theology   63, 118–19
   relation to Rahner   116–17, 119
   remythologization   117–19
   suffering   121–38
   Trinity   31, 143
Barnes, Michel René   6 n.4, 11 n.21, 46 n.3
Barth, Karl
   beauty   143, 144
   evil   82 n.26
   Trinity   7, 32 n.3, 54

beauty   140–4, 154
Behr, John   34 n.9, 41 n.18
Bielik-Robson, Agata   2, 3, 113, 115 n.10
Bloch, Ernst   111
Boff, Lenoardo   7 n.5
Book of Common Prayer   101
boredom   65
Buber, Martin   111

Cantor, Georg   139, 146–7
capitalism   95, 100, 107–9
Coakley, Sarah   53 n.22, 62 n.3
communion   7, 50, 62–4
contemplation, *see* Trinity, contemplation and

Davies, Brian   86 n.5, 91
De Lubac, Henri   102–3
deism   31, 42
Denys the Areopagite   1, 144
disenchantment   114–15, 116
divinization   102

ecclesiology   9, 10, 50, 61–5, 118–19, 127
Eckhardt, Meister   1, 144
Edwards, Denis   13 n.26
Emery, Gilles   19
enlightenment
   deism   31, 34, 42
   and Jewish thought   112, 119, 120
   and theodicy   67, 69, 70, 78–81
essence, divine   17, 20, 24–5, 27–8, 40
eucharist   61, 63, 64
Euclid   141, 145–8

Fedorov, Nicholas   45–7
Forsyth, P. T.   76
free-will defense   68, 71–4, 84, 91, 130

Gagey, Henri-Jérôme   65 n.16
gender   9, 118–19, 123
Gödel, Kurt   148

grace
  and Holy Spirit 29, 58–60
  nature and 99–100, 102–7
  sin and 58, 99–102, 108–9
Gregory of Nazianzus 23, 31, 38–40, 62 n.3
Gunton, Colin 7 n.5, 6, 10–11, 31 n.2

hell 118, 122
Heschel, Abraham Joshua 111, 114 n.8
Hick, John 69
Hilbert, David 147
Hirsch, Samuel 112
Holmes, Stephen R. 6 n.4, 46 n.3, 62 n.4
Holy Saturday 117–18, 122 n.4
Hume, David 69

ideology 55, 56
idolatry 32, 43, 53, 55, 63–5, 115
immutability 18, 124
impassibility 18, 124, 153
incarnation 80, 106, 113, 114, 127, 152
infinity 83, 103, 139–40, 145–8
innocence 96 n.23

joy 8, 126–8, 132–3
Julian of Norwich 92–3, 98, 121–3, 125–33
Juster, Norton 26 n.22

Kant, Immanuel 117, 119
kenosis 132

LaCugna, Catherine Mowry 19
Leo XIII, Pope 139
Levering, Matthew 19–20, 26 n.20, 28, 102 n.6, 148
Levinas, Emmanuel 111
liberalism 32, 34, 42, 115–16, 119, 120
liberation theology 57 n.27, 59 n.28, 94–5, 97
Lindbeck, George 16 n.28
love
  sacrificial 134
  and suffering 121–37, 153

McCabe, Herbert 27, 74, 26 n.5, 91
McFadyen, Alistair 96
MacKinnon, Donald 61, 132
Marcion 80

Marshall, Bruce 29 n.27
mathematics
  and abstraction 34–6
  and beauty 140–2
  and mystery 144–8
Metz, J.-B. 78 n.22
ministry 61, 134
modernity 113–17, 119–20
Moltmann, Jürgen
  engagement with modern Jewish thought 111
  suffering of God 76, 78
  teacher of Volf 45, 50
  Trinity 5–10, 13, 18–19
Murray, Paul 59 n.23

nuptial theology 63, 118, 123

Ochs, Peter 111
Oliver, Simon 15 n.27, 53 n.22

paganism 112–20
paradox 51, 87, 99–109, 134, 149
Pelagianism 88, 89 n.11
Percy, Emma 134 n.37
perichoresis 7, 8, 10–11, 14, 32–8, 48–52, 54
Peters, Ted 47
philosophy of religion 31, 67–73, 79, 85–7, 98
Plantinga, Alvin 69, 73
Plantinga, Cornelius 8
Preller, Victor 27, 149 n.15
privation of the good 82, 83 n.28, 87–8, 129–30, 133, 136
process theology 82
progress 36, 41, 45, 70, 107, 149
projection 12–15
Protestantism 99–109

Quine, Willard van Ormand 53–4
Quinn, Frank 144 n.4

Rahner, Karl
  beauty 143
  Encounters with silence 103–4, 65 n.5
  grace 89, 107 n.28
  mystery 151–2
  relationship to Balthasar 116–17, 119, 132

Trinity 5, 7, 18–19, 54
  and Zizioulas 61, 65 n.5
Ratzinger, Joseph 94 n.21
Ray, Stephen G. 95 n.23
relations, *see* Trinity, relations in
relationship 9, 11–14, 24, 51, 71, 119
Rober, Daniel 102 n.6
Robert 23–4
Romero, Oscar 135 n.39, 136
Rosenzweig, Franz 111 n.1, 113–15
Rowe, William 86, 92

salvation history 18, 28, 80
sanctification 101, 107
Sarot, Marcel 78 n.22
Schleiermacher, Friedrich 32 n.3, 34, 116, 143
set theory 139 n.1
simplicity, divine 18, 20, 23, 24, 133
sin
  and freedom 75
  and grace 58, 99–102, 108–9
  and intelligibility 82, 85–98
  as privation 129–33
  structural 94–7
  and suffering 91–2, 126, 127, 131
Smith, Timothy 25 n.19
Sobrino, Jon 56, 57 n.27
Sölle, Dorothee 76
Soulen, Kendall 111, 112 n.4
Speyr, Adrienne von 122, 124
suffering 56–60, 71, 73, 76, 80–1, 85–6,
    see also sin, suffering and
  of God 131, 68, 76–8
  and love 121–37
supernatural, natural desire for the 102, 106
Surin, Kenneth 67–8, 70–81
Swinburne, Richard 69

Tanner, Kathryn
  capitalism 107–9
  divine and created agency 73, 89, 150–1
  gift 134 n.36
  grace 100, 104–9
  politics 12, 55 n.24
  sin 88 n.8
  Trinity 50, 51, 55 n.25

Tatarkiewicz, Wladyslaw 140 n.2
theodicy 68–78, 81, 91, 153
Ticciati, Susana 90 n.14, 91–2
Tilley, Terrence 67, 68, 70–3, 75–6
Torrell, Jean-Pierre 19, 20 n.10
Trinity
  begetting in 39, 48
  and contemplation 20–1, 28–9, 37–8, 52
  immanent 15 n.27, 20–1, 36, 37, 48–9
  persons in 6–14, 23–5, 27–8, 48, 54, 118
  processions in 17, 21–3, 27–8, 33, 40, 54
  relations 33, 36
    in Aquinas 20–5
    in Balthasar 118
    in Moltmann 10
    in Tanner 55 n.25
    in Volf 50, 52, 55
  relevance 5, 7, 14–16, 18, 46, 53
  social theories of 5–16, 23, 39, 45–8, 50–3, 59, 153
Turner, Denys
  evil 81 n.5
  on Julian of Norwich 92 n.17, 93, 122 n.1, 129–30, 131 nn.32, 33
  on Thomas Aquinas 149

universal salvation 123

Vatican Council, Second 122
vestigia trinitatis 10
Volf, Miroslav 45–53
vulnerability 131 n.33, 132

Weber, Max 107–8
Weinandy, Thomas 77 n.13
Williams, A. N. 19, 20 n.11, 12
Williams, Rowan 19, 22 n.15, 102 n.6
Wilson-Kastner, Patricia 8–9, 12–13
Wittgenstein, Ludwig 147
Wolterstorff, Nicholas 70 n.4
Wyschogrod, Michael 112 n.4

zero 83, 101, 146 n.10
Zizioulas, John 7 n.5, 61–5

www.ingramcontent.com/pod-product-compliance
Lightning Source LLC
Chambersburg PA
CBHW052049300426
44117CB00012B/2047